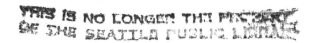
The New Information Professional

Your Guide to Careers in the Digital Age

Judy Lawson, Joanna Kroll, and Kelly Kowatch

Neal-Schuman Publishers, Inc.

New York   London

Published by Neal-Schuman Publishers, Inc.
100 William St., Suite 2004
New York, NY 10038

Printed and bound in the United States of America.

The paper used in this publication meets the minimum requirements of American National Standard for Information Sciences—Permanence of Paper for Printed Library Materials, ANSI Z39.48-1992.

Library of Congress Cataloging-in-Publication Data

Lawson, Judy.
    The new information professional : your guide to careers in the digital age / Judy Lawson, Joanna Kroll, and Kelly Kowatch.
      p. cm.
    Includes bibliographical references and index.
    ISBN 978-1-55570-698-2 (alk. paper)
    1. Information science—Vocational guidance. 2. Library science—Vocational guidance. 3. Information services industry—Vocational guidance. I. Kroll, Joanna. II. Kowatch, Kelly. III. Title.

Z682.35.V62L39 2010
020.23—dc22

                                  2010009306

Table of Contents

List of Career Planning Diagrams

Preface

What should you major in? Which career is right for you? These are challenging questions facing many, if not most, college students today. The place to start addressing these questions is not "out there" but rather by taking a look inward. What interests you, what motivates you, what problems would you like to help solve, and what impact do you want to have? Yet you can't choose what you don't know about, and it's hard to choose something you aren't sure (or your parents aren't sure) is a viable choice. If you're considering graduate school and/or seeking a career change, it may be time to revisit these questions or to explore them for the first time.

The New Information Professional: Your Guide to Careers in the Digital Age is designed to introduce some of the most cutting edge career and educational opportunities available. It's about opportunities that are directly emerging from the rise of the Information Age, which has created the need for leaders who can connect people, information, and technology in effective and innovative ways in order to address the critical and complex issues and problems facing our fast-paced, global, and increasingly digital society. It's about people who want to make a positive difference in the world, who want to develop or use information and technology in ways that help to make the world a better place for individuals, groups, schools, businesses, governments, and society as a whole.

It's about the field of information. What's that, you say? It's the rising profession of our time, with roots in fields that have collided, including library and information science, information technology, archival science, business, public policy, and computer science. Just as business, public policy, public health, and social work evolved into recognized disciplines and professional career fields with professional schools offering educational preparation, the newest evolving professional field is information. It includes library science and archives management, but it also encompasses intertwining specialties such as information policy, human–computer

interaction, social computing, information analysis and retrieval, community informatics, and more.

The "opportunity space" is just beginning, and the future for those who move
with or ahead of this curve in their career trajectory is very bright. Turns out, Albert Einstein was on to something when he said, "Know where to find the information and how to use it—that's the secret of success" (ThinkExist.com, accessed
2009). The Information Age has already had a major effect on our society and has
spurred the development of a wide range of new jobs and career fields. Before the
year 2000, job titles such as information architect, usability specialist, Web services
librarian, digital curator, and search engineer didn't exist or were in their infancy.
Technology is no longer the purview of only computer scientists and engineers—
today it is the effective design, implementation, and use of information and technology that is driving career opportunities as much as the development of technology itself.

According to Martha Pollack, Dean of the School of Information at the University of Michigan,

> We're in the midst of a revolution—an information revolution. It's having ef-
> fects that are every bit as significant as the industrial revolution. Everything
> we do has changed—our economic systems, our political systems, the way we
> educate ourselves, the way we educate our children, the way we entertain our-
> selves. . . . There is a great need to address the challenges and opportunities
> that arise from the information revolution. (University of Michigan, 2008)

At the dawn of the industrial age, we saw the rise of business careers and the master
of business administration (MBA) degree. "The MBA appeared in the United
States at the start of the 20th century, developing from the accounting and book-
keeping courses introduced as the country lost its frontier image and began to in-
dustrialise" (Economist.com, 2003). The MBA quickly became an expected cre-
dential for business leaders across the nation and world. In the late 1990s the
Information Age was emerging, and society responded with changes in jobs and
careers as well as in academic courses and programs. Over the past decade, we have
seen the momentum building—an increasing number of employers are aware of
and are seeking the skill set of graduates who have received cutting edge preparation to serve as leaders and innovators in addressing issues related to people, information, and technology.

The rapid and continuing development of the "iSchools" caucus (www.ischools
.org), a set of 24 schools offering undergraduate and graduate degrees for the information professions at top tier institutions nationwide, signifies a natural step in the

progression of information as a profession. According to The iSchools Caucus Web site:

> The iSchools are interested in the relationship between information, people and technology. This is characterized by a commitment to learning and understanding the role of information in human endeavors. The iSchools take it as given that expertise in all forms of information is required for progress in science, business, education, and culture. This expertise must include an understanding of the uses and users of information as well as information technologies and their applications. (The iSchools Caucus, 2009)

A number of iSchools grew out of library and information science programs or are the result of merging programs or departments including computer science, library and information science, communication, and even education. Many American Library Association accredited programs have broadened their curriculum in response to the digital age, including some that are iSchools and some that retain a focus on library and information services. Other programs continue to have a specific focus such as human–computer interaction or information systems management. Over time we are likely to see the academic curricula for information coalesce not unlike other professional fields that have multiple specialties and subfields. See the Appendix for a listing of iSchools and links to additional program listings that are providing preparation for information careers.

As a leading institution in the rise of the professional information degree, the University of Michigan's School of Information (SI) has been at the forefront of the emergence of information as a discipline and as a professional career field. Moreover, SI has played a leading role in its development, through research and curricular offerings but also through our efforts in career services. SI has invested in providing professional career development services to our students, and in the past ten years our career development staff has gained a strong awareness of the opportunities and the need for information professionals in the workforce today and certainly the workforce of tomorrow. It is with this context and background that the authors, who run the Career Development Office at the University of Michigan School of Information, have undertaken writing *The New Information Professional: Your Guide to Careers in the Digital Age* as a service to both the field of information and the field of career development and to anyone who may find their career path in the pages of this publication.

The growing prominence of information careers is highlighted in the *U.S. News and World Report*'s list of 31 "Best Careers for 2009," which profiles car "strong outlooks and high job satisfaction" (Nemko, 2008) and includes librarian as well as usability/user experience specialist and systems analyst. The report also lists "ahead of the curve" careers, which "are relatively new but already viable and promising future growth"; includes additional information careers: health informatics specialist, data miner, and simulation developer; and indicates the "increasingly digitized world" as one of six megatrends driving emerging career opportunities.

Who's hiring graduates in information careers? Employers include the major software firms such as Microsoft, Apple, and IBM; eBusiness firms such as Google, Amazon, and EBay; social media companies including Facebook and LinkedIn; companies and corporations from small to large in a wide range of industries including health care, entertainment, consumer goods, education, consulting, and banking/finance; nonprofit organizations and government agencies; public, academic, research, school, and corporate libraries; national libraries such as the Library of Congress and the National Library of Medicine; private and public archives including the National Archives and Records Administration; and museums and cultural institutions. Or one could join a start-up company or create a business of one's own. The opportunities are diverse, and the skill set and career opportunities afford flexibility through the changing economic scene and job market.

In *The New Information Professional: Your Guide to Careers in the Digital Age*, you'll learn about an exciting array of newly established, newly evolved, and just-emerging information careers. These are careers that require bright minds, can-do attitudes, innovative approaches, flexibility, entrepreneurial spirit, and progressive thinking. You can browse segments of interest for ideas and to brainstorm possibilities or read in depth to gain a solid understanding of one or more information fields and to see the interconnections of one area to the next. There are eight career information chapters:

    Chapter 1: Archives and Preservation of Information
    Chapter 2: Records Management
    Chapter 3: Library and Information Services
    Chapter 4: Human–Computer Interaction
    Chapter 5: Social Computing
    Chapter 6: Information Systems Management
    Chapter 7: Information Policy
    Chapter 8: Information Analysis and Retrieval

Each of the eight career information chapters starts with a forward-looking intro-duction to provide context and build awareness and understanding of issues, op-portunities, and future trends. The introduction is followed by all the information you'd expect from a career guide—types of jobs and career paths, skills and quali-ties needed for success, salary information, and employment outlook. Yet you'll also find definitions of field-specific jargon and descriptions of common jobs to help you compare and contrast professional roles and responsibilities. Profiles from new professionals who describe their path from undergraduate major to ca-reer give you a real-world, realistic view of how others have successfully pursued information career paths. Given the amazing diversity of content and interest areas that can be connected with careers in information, examples of real jobs in exciting tracks such as health, media/entertainment, social justice, and global are featured in the "at a glance" sections of each career information chapter.

Even though *The New Information Professional* is designed more as a career ex-ploration book than a job search manual, lists of professional associations and job listing sources are included for each information field, since these sources provide additional information and insight on career opportunities. For those who choose to pursue an information career, these lists will soon become a valuable resource for professional development as well as for internship and job searching. The edu-cation and training segment in each chapter provides a concise overview of how you can prepare to enter various information fields through undergraduate or graduate level degrees, and it describes opportunities for training as an alternative or to augment formal studies. For those who prefer to absorb information visually, each career information chapter includes a career planning diagram to provide a snapshot of career options and pathways and to help you map your own path to a career in information.

In the career planning chapter (Chapter 9), you can explore how to best ap-proach making a decision about whether information is a good career choice for you, and if so, which pathway might be a good fit. In fact, this is one book in which reading the last chapter first may make sense for those who wish to follow a reflec-tive career planning strategy as they read the guide. The career planning chapter will lead you through a self-assessment process where you will learn how to re-search and evaluate career options through the most effective and current re-sources available. You can then put your assessment and evaluation into action by following a detailed approach to creating your own career objective, followed by an individualized career action plan to accomplishing your objective successfully. Gathering information on the numerous possibilities, being self-reflective, making career decisions, and putting a plan into action are exciting yet challenging endeavors. Following a step-by-step process and gaining the perspective of the authors' combined 40+ years of career development and career counseling experience can help you define your career goals and determine a path to realizing career success—as you define it.

Imagine the possibility of having one of the following job titles: e-community manager, user experience designer, business intelligence analyst, youth outreach librarian, information policy specialist, digital art curator, information architect, social networks engineer, online auction manager, health informatics specialist, emerging technologies librarian, cultural resource manager, e-marketing associate, moving image archivist, or information security consultant. Now imagine having a few of these titles over the course of your career, or rising to a leadership position in your chosen specialty. It really is possible. Undergraduate degrees in informatics and information science are available at a number of colleges, and students with any major can pursue an advanced degree in information to access this exciting set of careers. It begins with you, and your interest in joining the rising profession of our time—information!

References

Economist.com. 2003. "The MBA—Some History." Available: www.economist.com/ globalExecutive/education/mba/displayStory.cfm?story_id=2135907 (accessed October 14, 2008).

The iSchools Caucus. 2009. *iSchools*. Available: www.ischools.org (accessed November 18, 2009).

Nemko, Marty. 2008. "Best Careers 2009: Librarian." *U.S. News & World Report*, December 11. Available: www.usnews.com/articles/business/best-careers/2008/12/ 11/best-careers-2009-librarian.html (accessed August 14, 2009).

ThinkExist.com. "Albert Einstein quotes." Available: http://thinkexist.com/ quotation/know-where-to-find-the-information-and-how-to-use/347851.html (accessed November 10, 2009).

University of Michigan. 2008. "School of Information Multimedia View Book: Introduction." Available: www.si.umich.edu/viewbook/index.htm?nav=intro (accessed November 2, 2008).

Acknowledgments

There are many individuals who deserve our thanks and recognition. We are greatly appreciative of the support we received from our Dean, Martha Pollack, and our Associate Dean for Academic Affairs, Jeff MacKie-Mason, as we undertook and completed this project. We sincerely thank everyone at Neal-Schuman, especially our editor Sandy Wood as well as Charles Harmon, Paul Seeman, Amy Knauer, and Kathryn Suarez for their patience with us as first-time authors. We sincerely thank our wonderful coworkers who encouraged us every step of the way. We are grateful to our families for their understanding and support during this long project. Finally, we thank the wonderful School of Information students we have worked with over the years who inspired us to write this book.

CHAPTER 1

Archives and Preservation of Information

Introduction

Archivists and Preservation Specialists are managers of memory—individual memories and the collective memory of societies and cultures. They are the keepers of the historical record, which, documented in original notes, memos, letters, photographs, videos, and films, is a testament to the truth of what has happened and which provides context that helps us understand and remember why events unfolded as they did.

With the vast stores of past information combined with the speed and volume at which new information is created and shared day to day, creating ongoing access to historical and newly produced information is indeed a mind-boggling problem. Archives and records are all around us, but what meaning do they have if we can't access what we need when we need it, or if the volume of material is mishandled or damaged and important information or objects are lost forever?

The Society of American Archivists attests to the important role of archivists and preservation managers in our society:

> Archivists help to secure society's cultural heritage. . . . Without a careful selection of records, our social, cultural, institutional, and individual heritages will be lost. Without the preservation of legal documents, individual and institutional rights cannot be preserved and protected. (Society of American Archivists, 2002)

Increasingly, it is important to gain knowledge and expertise in both archives and preservation management, yet there is ample room to specialize in one or the other.

1

From our family photo collections to documents of national and international importance, information and materials determined to have enduring value (archives) represent a significant component of our lives and our society as a whole. Thus the archivist and the preservation manager play important professional roles, roles that, like the records they save and protect, have particularly enduring value. What is retained today can truly make a difference tomorrow, and far into the future. Yet, unless what is saved is given proper care, the access to cultural and historical information for future generations is at risk.

With the majority of new records and data now being generated in electronic form, and the increasing effort to digitize and scan nonelectronic records and data from the past, information technology is now a critical aspect of the archives and preservation fields. Even with digital access, finding meaningful information among scads of archived documents and databases can be elusive. As with other information professions, it is critical that systems used for archives be designed with a user-centered focus to create intuitive and efficient access.

Archives are often used by multiple people for multiple purposes, and these people and purposes change over time. Only through wise judgment of professionals can meaningful items of potential future value be saved and preserved. With time comes the risk of materials and documents deteriorating, becoming technically inaccessible, or being lost or damaged through improper care or through disasters.

For example, following Hurricane Katrina, while the safety of humans had to be the foremost concern, it quickly became apparent that there was also a crisis of potential loss of archival collections of all sorts. The *Christian Science Monitor* reported in September 2005 that "at the New Orleans courthouse, crews spent a day and a half pumping out thousands of gallons of water. Snakes slithered across the muddy floor. After removing 60,000 books, they stored dry volumes in trucks in the parking lot. They loaded wet books into two freezer trucks, to be transported to a restoration firm near Chicago" (Gardner, 2005). Louisiana has a particularly high number of historic documents, so this was just the beginning of a huge and costly effort to save truckload after truckload of records, photographs, and other items important to the region's cultural heritage.

While disaster response is an important aspect of archives and preservation work, ideally the emphasis is on preparedness, planning, and prevention to reduce the chances and number of situations where restoration and renewal are required. As more materials are archived and preserved electronically, another challenge emerges: the speed at which technologies become outdated. Archivists and preservation managers must proactively ensure ongoing and reliable access to critical information and data over time as technologies develop and change.

Thus the growth area for archivists and preservation managers is connected to our increasingly digitized world, and in fact these professionals are helping to make old documents and materials accessible online, creating a digital treasure trove of information once difficult or impossible for the average person to locate. The National Archives and Records Administration (NARA) reports that the holdings of our nation's archives stand at "more than 10 billion pages of unique documents, many handwritten, including maps, charts, photos, motion pictures, and sound and video recordings" (National Archives and Records Administration, 2008). In May 2008, NARA published their strategy to digitize an extensive amount of archival materials for public access (National Archives and Records Administration, 2008). Soon, for example, there will be online public access to the Founding Fathers' complete papers.

Digital archiving and digital preservation is a major challenge and presents ongoing, exciting opportunities for future directions in these ever-evolving fields. According to Dr. Francine Berman, director of the San Diego Supercomputer Center at the University of California, San Diego:

> Digital preservation is critical for research and education in the information age. Data is the natural resource of the information age; it is fragile and needs to be stewarded in the "cyberworld" just like we need to take care of rain forests and the environment in the physical world. (Library of Congress, 2008)

When you stop and think about it, the vast amount and endless kinds of information worth saving is overwhelming now and will only grow in the future. So many content areas, interest areas, and issue areas are documented and preserved through archives. Often the archivist and preservation manager can specialize in an area that has particular meaning or significance to them. In addition to larger domains such as research, government, education, and business, there are countless content areas that require attention and expertise. The Academy of Motion Pictures and Film Archive, the *Sports Illustrated* Archive, the American Political Archive, the African American History Archive, and the Archive of American Television are a few of the many collections that provide a cumulative history of our society and culture and for which specialized content knowledge or experience in addition to training in archives and preservation is valued.

Is archival and preservation work exciting and glamorous? You might think so to watch the popular movie *National Treasure* starring Nicholas Cage. In the film

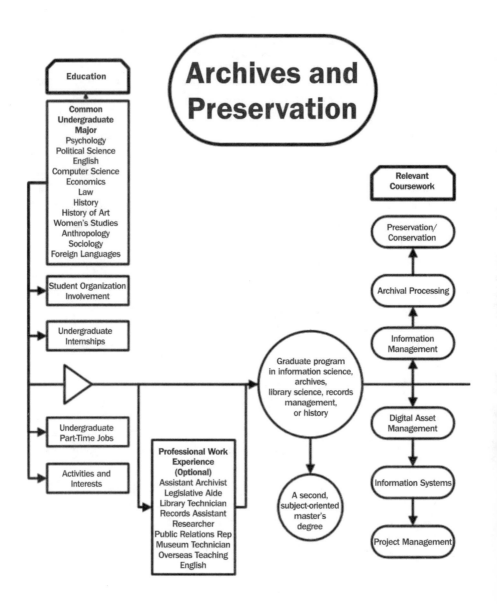

Figure 1. Archives and Preservation Career Map
This diagram demonstrates several of the potential paths associated with a career in the field of archives and preservation.

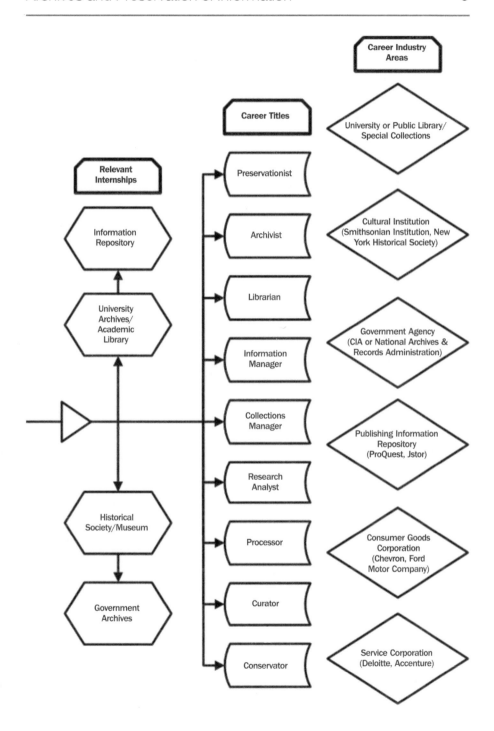

Cage's costar Diane Krieger plays the character of Abigail Chase, an archivist at the National Archives who gets pulled into an unexpected and dangerous treasure hunt led by Benjamin Gates, played by Cage. An exciting chase scene through the Library of Congress ensues, and the characters use new technologies to find and interpret clues from historical documents and artifacts—in particular the Declaration of Independence—to solve the mystery and locate a massive treasure.

While *National Treasure* is a far-fetched action film, many authors and filmmakers have relied on archives for historical accuracy and authenticity, but none more so than renowned documentary filmmaker Ken Burns. Burns created the *Civil War* documentary in the 1990s and produced the 2007 PBS documentary *The War*, which provides a captivating and horrific view of the realities of World War II as told by veterans themselves and gives a simultaneous depiction of the experience of those at war and those on the home front. Burns is a major advocate for the importance of archives. He is a member of the Board of the Foundation for the National Archive and is featured in the NARA and Discovery Channel video *Democracy Starts Here*, which explains the purpose and value of archives and preservation (National Archives and Records Administration, 2006a,b).

In reality, the day-to-day work of the archivist and preservation manager is interesting and stimulating more than exciting and glamorous. Yet there are plenty of instances where the items that archivists and preservation managers keep and protect lead to truth, justice, and even treasure. When Miriam Kleiman was doing research on a class action lawsuit on behalf of holocaust survivors and heirs, she came across documents with Jewish names and Swiss bank accounts. The document turned out to be "golden" in that it uncovered a Nazi gold scandal and helped recover Jewish assets lost in World War II. According to Kleiman, the document was sitting in an archive for "over 50 years, just waiting for someone to discover it" (National Archives and Records Administration, 2006b). The find helped hundreds of individuals and families recover what was rightfully theirs.

Information professionals who focus on a career path in archives and preservation management will find a field with a rich history, strong professional ethics, and close ties to other information fields, especially library and information services. Those who value sustainability will find a connection to this field that eschews a "throwaway" mentality. Archivists and preservation managers understand that their work has multiple benefits and implications, including educational, political, and legal. They value technology as a tool that, when used well, creates levels of access and protection previously unattainable. If these values and benefits resonate for you, you may find that a career in archives and preservation management provides significant career fulfillment—which is a treasure, in its own right.

Skills and Abilities

One of the most exciting prospects of the field of archives and preservation is the wide array of growing career opportunities in almost every industry. As with any professional career field, there are required skills and abilities that are important for success. If you hope to pursue a career in archives and preservation, many of the skills required for both fields are similar, including skills and abilities that will help you land that dream job and that are critical for advancement.

While positions in archives and preservation vary as far as skill level, experience, and education required, there are key skills, abilities, and characteristics that are highly sought for most any professional archives and preservation position in any industry. Outlined in the following sections are both the soft skills and abilities (behavioral/personality traits and characteristics) and hard skills and abilities (technical and career-specific knowledge) that are important for success in the field of archives and preservation. Note that these are the most common skills and abilities; this is certainly not an exhaustive list of all of the valuable skills and abilities that are beneficial for this career field.

Soft Skills

- Ability to communicate (both written and verbal)
- Analytical/problem solving skills
- Detail-oriented work practices
- Ability to work in collaboration/ be a team player
- Leadership capability
- Flexibility/adaptability

> ☑ QUICK FACT!
> Soft skills are just as important and critical to success in the field as hard/technical skills and abilities.

Cataloging skills are in high demand for the digital revolution!

Hard Skills

- Archival processing: Arrange and describe the papers of an individual or family or the records of an organization.
- Cataloguing: Organize a descriptive, detailed list of items arranged systematically.
- Collections management: Ensure effective documentation, preservation, and access to objects in a museum or library collection.

- Reference/user services: Provide resources and information to information seekers.
- Outreach/public services: Provide information of services and resources to the community and external constituents.
- Information retrieval: Search for documents, for information within documents, and for metadata about documents in databases and on the Internet.
- Technical skills: Administer databases and have some Web skills.
- Archival technical skills: Know MARC Standards and Encoded Archival Description (EAD).

KEY WORDS TO KNOW

Here are a few basic archives and preservation terms you will see throughout this chapter. If you are interested in pursuing this career field, it's a good idea to know what they mean:

- **metadata**: Data about data, of any sort in any media.
- **finding aids**: A document containing detailed information about a specific collection of papers or records within an archive.
- **digitization**: To convert an image or signal into digital code by scanning, tracing on a graphics tablet, or using an analog to digital conversion device.
- **conservation**: Attempts to preserve records in their original format.
- **accessibility**: Ability to locate relevant information through the use of catalogs, indexes, finding aids, or other tools.
- **compliance**: Conforming to a specification or policy, standard, or law that has been clearly defined.
- **Web archiving**: Process of collecting portions of the World Wide Web and ensuring that the collection is preserved in an archive for future researchers, historians, and the public.
- **digital assets**: Any form of content and/or media that has been formatted into a binary source, which includes the right to use it.
- **taxonomy**: The practice and science of classification.
- **MARC (machine readable cataloging) Standards**: Data communications form that specifies a data structure for bibliographic description, authority, classification, community information, and holdings data.
- **EAD**: Standard used to encode finding aids that reflects the hierarchical nature of archival collections and that provides a structure for describing the whole of a collection as well as its components.

Employers hiring archives or preservation specialists often value soft skills and hard skills equally. While certain hard skills and specific knowledge areas will always be required for a career in this field, soft skills such as strong communication and leadership skills are equally important, and they are viewed by some employers as being even more critical for long-term success in the field.

As many archives and preservation professional journals and research indicate, we are in the midst of a digital revolution. According to a report by Paul Ayris, librarian at University College, London, libraries are experiencing a boom of digitization, a boom that is only starting and that has no end in sight. Ayris confirms there is still a lot of growth potential for digitization since only a small percentage of libraries worldwide have been digitized (Joint Information Systems Committee, 2007).

This focus on digitization in the archives and preservation fields means technical skills are becoming increasingly important. While it's not expected that archives and preservation professionals are required to have technical skills at the level of a computer scientist, what is expected is a solid level of understanding, comfort, and ability to work with digital technology. Knowledge of file formats, ability to evaluate recordkeeping systems, and the ability to conduct research through various databases are becoming highly sought after—and sometimes required—skills for many archives and preservation professional positions today.

Professional Roles

Because the field of preservation includes a strong focus on archival practice, yet also has become increasingly specialized as a specific career path, it might help to understand the role of an archivist versus a preservationist. In addition, it may also help to compare and contrast the nature of archives work with the work of other closely related professions:

- **Archivist versus Preservationist**
  Similarities: Both work to ensure permanent accessibility and longevity of information records.
  Differences: While not exactly a difference, preservation is an archival function. Preservationists work to prevent deterioration of archived historical records as a whole.

- **Archivist versus Librarian**
  Similarities: Collect, preserve, and make accessible materials for research.

Differences: The ways in which these materials are arranged, described, and used.

- **Archivist versus Museum Curator**
  Similarities: Study, interpret, and classify objects.
  Differences: Museum curator collects, studies, and interprets mostly three-dimensional objects, while the archivist works with paper, film, and electronic records.

- **Archivist versus Historian**
  Similarities: Preservation and conservation.
  Differences: The archivist identifies, preserves, and makes the records accessible for use, while the historian uses the archival records for research.

- **Archivist versus Records Manager**
  Similarities: Both collect, organize, manage, and make accessible materials for research.
  Differences: While the records managers control huge quantities of institutional records, most of which will be eventually destroyed, the archivist is concerned with relatively small quantities of records deemed important enough to be retained for an extended period.

- **Preservationist versus Conservator**
  Similarities: Sustainability of library materials or records as long as they are needed in their original form.
  Differences: Preservation is more reactive, while conservation involves proactive treatment of materials. (Society of American Archivists, 2008)

Occupational Outlook

According to the U.S. Bureau of Labor Statistics *Occupational Outlook Handbook*, 2008–2009 Edition, "faster than average employment growth is expected in the field of Archives through the year 2016." Keen competition is expected for most jobs as archivists and curators as qualified applicants generally outnumber job openings. Those with highly specialized training, such as a master's degree in library science, with a concentration in archives and records management, practical experience, and extensive technical skills will have stronger employment prospects (U.S. Department of Labor, Bureau of Labor Statistics, 2009).

Jobs are expected to grow as public and private organizations emphasize establishing archives and organizing records and information and as public interest in science, art, history, and technology increases. Although the rate of turnover among archivists, preservationists, and curators is relatively low, the need to re-place workers who leave the occupation or retire will create some additional job openings (U.S. Department of Labor, Bureau of Labor Statistics, 2009).

As more information-rich corporations try to keep up with the demand to digi-tize information and records, the need for archivists who specialize in electronic records and records management will grow more rapidly than for archivists who specialize in older media formats. Digital asset management is expected to be a multibillion dollar industry as corporations and individuals shift from traditional graphic, broadcast, and print assets to the digital format. Companies including Apple, Oracle, Microsoft, Getty Images, and others are aggressively expanding their enterprises to provide third-party digital asset management via Web-based repositories. This trend will continue as businesses and consumers shift from analog to digital materials (Powers et al., 2008).

There are many industry areas that offer opportunities for careers in archives and preservation at all levels: local, state, and federal government; museums, his-torical sites, and cultural institutions; and state and private educational institu-tions, mainly college and university libraries.

Most federal archivists work for the National Archives and Records Administra-tion; others may take positions managing military archives in the U.S. Department of Defense. The majority of federal government curators work at the Smithsonian Institution, in military museums of the Department of Defense, or in archaeologi-cal and other museums and historic sites managed by the U.S Department of the Interior. All state governments have archival or historical-record sections employ-ing archivists. State and local governments also have numerous historical muse-ums, parks, libraries, and zoos employing curators (Society of American Archivists, 2008).

A growing number of large corporations have archives or records centers and employ archivists to manage the growing volume of records created or maintained as required by law or necessary for the firm's operations. Other corporations con-tract with archive and data management firms to provide archives management services.

Take a look at just some of the exciting job titles and high-profile, diverse orga-nizations that hire archives and preservation professionals:

- Archivist, National Archives & Records Administration (government ar-chive)
- Assistant Archivist, Yale University Libraries (university library/archive)
- Preservation Officer, National Parks Services (government)

- Digital Preservation Specialist, Generation Networks (Internet/Web)
- Film and Video Archivist, NBC Universal (entertainment/media)
- Digital Asset Manager, Internet Archive (nonprofit/technical archive)
- Database Librarian, Entertainment Weekly (entertainment/media/publishing)
- Historian, New York Historical Society (historical/cultural institution)
- Electronic Records Manager/Archivist, Duke University Libraries (university library/archive)
- Metadata Specialist, Fidelity Investments (financial services)

Salary Information

Salaries, benefits, and working conditions vary greatly in the field of archives and preservation. Salaries vary depending on the size and nature of the employing institution, the geographic location, and the education and position level. Over the past few years, salaries in this field have continued to increase at a fairly steady rate. According to the Bureau of Labor Statistics, the median annual salary of archivists is $50,730. The middle 50 percent earned between $30,610 and $53,990. This range is typically associated with a relevant master's degree. The lowest 10 percent earned less than $23,890, which is typically associated with a relevant bachelor's degree, associate's degree, and little work experience. The highest earned more than $73,060, which is typically associated with a master's degree or PhD with significant work experience (U.S. Department of Labor, Bureau of Labor Statistics, 2009).

Higher salaries are typically found in federal government and corporate positions. In 2007, the average annual salary for archivists in the federal government was $79,199; for museum curators, $80,780; for museum specialists and technicians, $58,855; and for archives technicians, $44,547 (U.S. Department of Labor, Bureau of Labor Statistics, 2009). Average starting salaries in corporate settings for new professionals with a master's degree range from $50,000–$70,000. These positions are also quickly growing in demand as there are not enough qualified applicants with the technical skills required for the number of positions available.

Lower salaries in the archives field are typically associated with bachelor-level positions or smaller organizations. Bachelor-level positions are seen as entry-level such as an Archives Technician, Archives Assistant, Preservation Assistant, or Museum Assistant. A master's degree and relevant work experience are encouraged if you want to advance in the field and land a higher paying salary.

Many archives and preservation professionals decide to enter the field because of a keen interest, enthusiasm, and commitment to the field, weighing these as more important than salary. Although management level positions and longevity in the field will yield a higher salary, there are other benefits and perks that certainly lead to both professional and personal satisfaction. These include a good work/life balance, schedule flexibility, professional development support, and continuing educational opportunities. These additional benefits/rewards are often highly valued and, almost universally, archivists express a high degree of professional and personal satisfaction with their work.

Profiles—Perspectives of New Professionals

Jennifer Sharp, Manuscript Librarian
Special Collections
John D. Rockefeller Jr. Library
Colonial Williamsburg Foundation
Williamsburg, Virginia

I have found that the practical experiences in my life have only furthered the ability to do what I love, which is being the Manuscript Librarian at the John D. Rockefeller Jr. Library Special Collections at Colonial Williamsburg Foundation in Williamsburg, Virginia. After attaining a bachelor of arts in history and Russian studies at Colgate University, I knew that I did not want to end up at a big corporation. But I did just that after sampling what I thought would be the ideal work environment.

After graduation, I spent time working as a docent at the Nantucket Historical Society where I learned that I wasn't as interested in working in the museum field as I thought. Instead of spending time presenting someone else's research, I learned that I wanted to do my own research and develop my own perspective based on what I discovered. I left Nantucket and took a job in information technology at a large insurance company and stayed there for seven years. The job paid well and I gained experience in problem solving and providing support, what I now refer to as excellent reference training, to clients in need of assistance.

While working first as a technician, then as a developer, I took courses at Trinity College in American Studies. It was the experience of taking a class on Hartford architecture that provided me with my first interaction with an archivist. I thought it sounded like a cool job and decided that it might be an ideal career path for my interests. Already, I knew that I didn't want to pursue a master of arts in history or a graduate degree in computer science, which would require calculus. Through research, I learned about information schools (iSchools) and found that this type of program's interdisciplinary nature was a perfect fit for my technology background and the other facets of my interests.

I identified the University of Michigan School of Information (SI) as an ideal fit for my personality and interests. While in graduate school, I had several practical experiences that I feel directly contributed to my being where I am now. I worked at the Bentley Historical Library as both a reference assistant and a processor and also at the University of Michigan Special Collections Library as a processor. These experiences helped me attain a coveted summer internship at the Seeley G. Mudd Manuscript Library at Princeton University. Although I do attest that the coursework that I participated in was a great and knowledgeable experience, the practical, hands-on experience that I gained was what made me attractive to employers at graduation time. Having experience in processing, reference, creating finding aids, and other relevant tasks gave me a certain level of experience that made me a more ideal candidate.

At the Colonial Williamsburg Foundation, I have had a wide range of daily tasks and special projects, mainly focused on manuscripts, rare books, and some archeological and architectural records. I was hired to integrate several cataloging systems into one. I also complete finding aids regularly, and since many of the "collections" contain only one item, this involves the creation of detailed MARC records. Every day, I also provide reference services to staff of the foundation and Colonial Williamsburg, researchers and fellows, and the general public. I also have collection development responsibilities for the archeology collection, which sometimes includes field trips for research to the Williamsburg Archeology Lab.

A variety of skills are essential for this position. Being comfortable with technology is a must. Because the shift in the archives field is to digitization, being knowledgeable and comfortable with computers and the wide range of associated applications is necessary. Being an adept information searcher is important also, and the ability to process and create finding aids is also vital. Being diplomatic due to the wide range of clientele that uses the collection is also an important skill to possess and will make the everyday work of providing access straightforward.

The best part of my job includes the lack of stress that comes with my responsibilities. It's a nine-to-five job and there aren't evenings or weekends where I have to work. It's a very relaxed environment, and another perk is that the information that I work with is very interesting for me to learn about and read. However, I work among a very small staff, which was a big shift, coming from the Bentley Historical Library, which has a staff of almost 50. Also, my position is a temporarily funded position, which is common in the field and lends a certain degree of uncertainty in where I'll be a year from now. Working one's way up into permanently funded positions takes some time in the area of museum work.

The earnings of museum archivists basically cover rent and food. People don't work in this field for the short or long-term earning potential; they do it because they love the work and find it interesting. I admit, I make less money now than I did ten years ago while working in corporate America, but it's worth it.

This is an ideal career choice for those who love this field of work and value providing this sort of service more than a high salary. I suggest trying out processing and reference at local cultural institutions and libraries for anyone who is intrigued by this field. Building experience at different types of institutions is also important.

Museums and similar cultural institutions face financial difficulties often and even more so during economic downturns. However, the need for positions such as mine is static, and I don't see the industry disappearing anytime soon. A typical archivist's role is rapidly changing every day due to advances in technology, and I foresee that the job description for an archivist will be radically different in five and ten years. Moreover, the range of function associated with being a librarian/archivist is great; a career path in this field could involve a wide range of responsibilities and skills, thus it can be a job in which one is trying new things and applying new solutions constantly. Digitization is the up and coming area for archives in most cultural institutions (where funding allows).

Overall, my position and the function of the organization have a strong impact on the world. Through providing reference service and accessibility to the collections, I'm able to aid in the teaching of history in the United States. The lasting impact of archivists and their work is significant and can help to educate generations for years to come. (Sharp, 2008)

Since the interview, Jennifer has taken a position as the Project Archivist at Connecticut Historical Society in Hartford, Connecticut.

Mary Ann Williams, Digital Archivist
Animation Research Library for Disney Animation Studios at the
Walt Disney Company
Los Angeles, California

I am a person who has many interests. Not just a few, but a lot. I'm always on the go, salsa dancing, or baking cookies, or process-mapping information flows. This is why my multifaceted role as Digital Archivist is perfect for my high-energy personality. At an internship with the Federal Bureau of Investigation, I reconsidered my previous career goals and I learned that I could use an art degree and have a career with the FBI Photo and Video Forensic lab. So, I went back to Michigan State

University and completed a bachelor (BA) of studio arts degree with a focus on photography (in addition to the BA in criminal justice) while working as the Lead Michigan Promise Fellow with AmeriCorps.

By the time I had completed my art degree, funding for federal jobs had disappeared, and I had to consider other career options. I decided to attend the University of Michigan School of Information (SI) Master of Science in Information program. I made this choice because I realized that something I had been doing as a part-time job for many years—being the seasonal Music Librarian at the Greater Lansing Symphony Orchestra—was quite related to something I might want to do for a career.

Beyond the educational experience at SI, the practical experience I gained was the best thing that I did to help myself land my current position. Building on my wide range of interests and experiences, I took advantage of courses that offered client-based projects, part-time work, and internships. I also took advantage of part-time jobs that required me to learn technology and teach others what I learned, furthering my own instructional and communication abilities in addition to my technology prowess.

One key advantage that I had as an edge over other candidates is my comfort with technology. But I didn't start out that way—I used my time at SI to strengthen an area that had previously been weak in my skill set. I took programming courses, which later helped me to communicate with the engineers that I work with and also proved to be useful when I had to self- build the database and applications I use every day. Learning as much about the building blocks of technology as possible is a skill that helps me understand what is realistic in information management, search, and retrieval.

My role at Walt Disney is multifaceted. I provide digital solution support to the staff of the Animation Research Library. This encompasses information architecture, process redesign, taxonomy, and metadata scheme development. I oversee the design and usability of the database being used to build the digital catalog, and I educate users on what services I can provide and how they can use the accessible information. I also often assess and reassess how information flows through the department and analyze these flows through process mapping. For example, I recently mapped the daily production process of how research requests are filled from start to finish. This was used for legacy documentation as well as to improve efficiency in service.

In addition to working with rare and expensive original art, I love my job because I get to work in a museum-like setting with all of the perks of working in corporate America. My projects are highly visible and I enjoy the recognition that comes with the success of what I do. The opportunity to network and meet highly influential people is always a plus; having lunch with archivists at Pixar is never a bad thing. My favorite aspect of my job is getting to work with the artists who make the films—I never get tired of helping them retrieve archived art as they create the next movie. I get to see the movies grow from start to finish.

I also enjoy being in the position where I'm not the engineer, but I'm also not the everyday technology user. But it's not all perfect. I work a lot and I'm always busy and thinking hard. And for exciting as my role is, there's no precedent for a lot of what I do, so it can be a lonely road of discovery. Because most of my peer institutions are money-strapped cultural institutions, working in the corporate realm means that I am required to develop the systems and applications and let them trickle down through the field.

I use my communication abilities to educate and help my users make use of my information. I also find the ability to collaborate a necessary skill, and I have found that my past experience working in groups to be helpful in my role. Networking is a skill that is necessary to learn and to hone in order to be successful. Being a successful networker and being a hub of connections increases the value of yourself and thus the organization that employs you. Because many projects I work on fall into a realm of corporate confidentiality, learning how to prudently discuss information regarding projects is essential. Traditional skills are also essential: cataloging, research, and reference abilities are used every day and help me do my other functions even better.

Documentation is an important part of digital archiving and also a step that's often neglected. I'm also always trying to determine better ways to apply metadata to what's being saved that makes it accessible. It's pointless to digitize something if you don't know you even have it. Within the entertainment field, copyright and digital rights management are important areas. Because of contracts with celebrities and other organizations, a minor misuse of information or an image can be of considerable cost.

This field is growing, and the earning potential is only positive. After graduate school, my starting salary with Disney was in line with annual salary averages ($60,000) for the area, and within a year I received a raise. With the function of digitization increasing exponentially, careers in digital archiving are only going to also increase. Corporations are in the position to fund such activities, so there will be more jobs in this industry sector than in that of nonprofits and cultural institutions. However, to guarantee future employment, individuals in this field must constantly be willing to explain their function and educate-up to further promote their own value to the company.

Of course, working at Disney comes with perks, such as free admission to the theme parks, discounts on food and merchandise, connections to events and lectures such as art openings, and many free promotional items such as DVDs, movie screenings, etc. Working at a corporation also provides access to a full package of benefits.

For those who are interested in this career role, an interest in technology is essential. If a person isn't interested in technology, this doesn't mean that one can't do this role, but they must be willing to learn the skills nonetheless. While in school, taking coursework on how to research is critical. Research is beyond using Google to look things up; in fact, most people do not even know how to use Google correctly for retrieving the information that they seek. Also, staying current on technology and digital issues is valuable; reading magazines such as *Wired* and the online magazine *Slate* or TechCrunchBlog is helpful to keep up on what's going on. Obviously, I'm going to push the value of networking. Most people undersell themselves because they can't identify and sell their skills. To be successful, I believe one needs to be able to articulate his or her value.

I'm having a great time in my job and I'm able to see a big impact that results both from what I do and from what Disney is doing. Because of my unique skill set, I'm able to provide a specialized service to my users to help them make their jobs easier or better. Also, because of the flexibility and funding that corporations have for digitization, they can lead the way in new technology that can later assist nonprofits and cultural institutions with digital access. (Williams, 2008)

Thomas Teper, Associate University Librarian for Collections
University of Illinois at Urbana–Champaign
Urbana, Illinois

I was exposed to the world of libraries and archives as an undergraduate at the College of Wooster in Wooster, Ohio. As an archives and special collections assistant/researcher, I gained fundamental archival experience processing and appraising collections and developing databases and finding aids. I also had the unique experience of processing special collections that included rare domestic and foreign propaganda materials. It was at the College of Wooster that I was exposed to the field of preservation; my responsibilities included rehousing, encapsulation, cleaning, and environmental monitoring.

After graduation, I moved to Washington, DC, and took a position first as a museum technician, then as a library technician at the United States Holocaust Memorial Museum. As a library technician I focused on acquisitions and copy-cataloging services oriented toward foreign language, out-of-print, and rare books. I also participated in the implementation of the acquisitions and cataloging modules of the library's integrated online system and circulation module.

While at the Holocaust Museum, I realized that if I wanted to advance in the field, a professional degree would be necessary. After a year and a half at the museum, I enrolled in the Master of Library and Information Science program at the University of Pittsburgh, in Pittsburgh, Pennsylvania, where I focused on preservation administration. I supplemented my educational experience with several graduate assistantships and practical experiences. As a graduate assistant I learned the fundamentals of book repair and preservation techniques.

I also worked as a special project assistant at the Carnegie Library of Pittsburgh and as a consultant at Preservation Technologies, LP. I deviated from what I thought would be my area of interest—traditional library services and archives—after I had interactions with Sally Buchanan, a professor at the University of Pittsburgh whose area of expertise was the preservation of library and archival materials, especially books, manuscripts, and photographs. Her primary area of expertise was preservation management for research collections and recovery from disasters. I determined that from my experience working at the Holocaust Museum, my interests laid in working with materials on this level.

After graduation, I took a position at the University of Kentucky as a preservation reformatting librarian. The position involved the management of the Reprographics Department and the in-house microfilm unit. I was soon recruited by the University of Illinois at Urbana–Champaign (UIUC). I took the role of the first full-time preservation librarian (formal title: Head of Preservation and Assistant Professor of Library Administration) at UIUC. I remembered that while in graduate school, I had the thought that all of the major institutions would already have established preservation programs, thus eliminating the opportunity to be part of the development of such a program, but I was wrong, and it worked out well for my career plans.

Surprisingly, UIUC did not have an established library preservation program. Staff at UIUC held preservation-oriented roles, but the work was done more on an ad hoc basis than as part of an established program. Prior to my move to UIUC, new leadership had come to the libraries and this new dean recognized the need for such a role. When I came to UIUC, much attention was given to the preservation of special collections, but overall the library's general collections weren't cared for properly. At the time, UIUC had nine and a half million volumes that needed some attention. I developed book binding operations and brittle book programs among a variety of other activities that led to the increased quality of preservation at the library. My days were spent developing preservation policy, managing a staff of over ten full-time employees, and participating in development and activities and funding initiatives.

I'm now the Associate University Librarian for Collections and Associate Dean of Libraries at UIUC, after six years in the role of Head of Preservation. My days are filled with meetings with a variety of different constituents and stakeholders. I focus on building buy-in for my department's services and abilities with faculty and library staff.

I participate in a lot of decision making; decisions range from what to do with a gift of ten thousand books from a donor to everyday decisions on acquisitions. However, I still love the feeling that I get when we improve the library's care for its collections. Sometimes these are highly visible changes such as improving the level of general preservation for a collection; other more monumental changes are less visible. For example, we are currently working to replace the heating, ventilating, and air-conditioning system in the Rare Books and Manuscript Library. This step will be realized by few but will make a huge difference in the quality of preservation provided for those materials.

A less favorable part of my job is saying no. I would like to say yes to every proposal, idea, or suggested collection that comes to me if I could, but resources never allow all to be accepted. The main restriction is budgetary; some materials are very expensive, and preservation procedures can be costly.

On a day-to-day basis, my most utilized skills are those acquired as an administrator at a research-one institution. The most valuable is patience. I often can see the direction in which an agenda item needs to move, but getting all of the stakeholders on board can take weeks or months. Being able to exercise patience and focus on the result is essential. This skill comes from experience, not so much from a graduate degree. The other skill that I find necessary for success is the ability to say, "I don't know." The ability to know everything is impossible, but in a high-level administrative role, it's often expected. Being able to professionally table a matter until more information can be gained is crucial to being able to successfully lead a program.

I feel that the profession is in a degree of transition. I see similarities to when I graduated from graduate school. Although technical skills were desired at that time, the need for technical abilities has greatly increased and will only continue to do so. In the future, the people who work in preservation or in collection development are going to be in roles that are less than static. Every day and every year will be something different; the days of the same job for 30 years are long past. Subject specialists will still need to be experts in their field; however, technical competence will be as important, if not more so. In the long term, the field is changing to be more technical, and related positions will experience growth. As librarians retire, they will be replaced with roles that are more technically oriented, but also by individuals who are more focused on extending the library's outreach and liaison roles.

For people who want to learn more, I suggest trying the profession on. Any interested person will be well served by volunteering or getting a part-time job in a library. Try out different types of libraries—public, school, and academic—because each is so different in function and have such varying missions. Also, take time between the undergraduate educational experience and graduate school to gain further practical experience. When I'm looking to hire a new staff member, I consider the experience that a person would bring to my staff beyond that of what he or she may have learned in iSchool. By taking time to work before going to graduate school, a person develops a broader perspective. This not only develops a better student but also allows him or her to experience the program in different ways, thus bringing to the work place a more comprehensive set of skills. (Teper, 2008)

Careers in Archives and Preservation: At a Glance

Your career in archives and preservation can take many directions as you connect your interests and values to the type of functional area and type of organization that you pursue. Here are a few examples of real jobs representing some exciting "tracks" you can follow.

Corporate Track
Digital Asset Librarian
Enfatico
New York, New York

Process, access, and manage digital files (images and photographs) and paper records using digital asset and collection management systems; perform traditional archives activities such as developing finding aids, collection processing, assessment, accessions, storage, and handling; apply metadata techniques for digital arts and photography, working with taxonomies, controlled vocabularies, and current metadata schemas; work closely with staff to create digital workflows, organizational methods, and records management policies; incorporate Web 2.0 technologies in organizations to foster productivity and creativity; assist employees in gaining control of information overload and connecting to the information they need. (Enfatico Human Resources, accessed 2008)

Social Justice Track
Archivist or "Keeper O'Stuff"
Ben & Jerry's Ice Cream
Burlington, Vermont

Keeping track of the design elements for Ben & Jerry's fun, distinctive packaging and graphic design is part of what the Ben & Jerry's archivist—or "Keeper o' Stuff"—does. When the marketing department wants to know what was in a particular ad, when the design staff remembers using an element that was particularly interesting, but can't think of exactly where it was used, they go to the archivist. Ben & Jerry's socially conscious business model is an attractive component for those who want to work in an organization that supports their own values. (Ben & Jerry's Ice Cream, accessed 2008)

Green Track
Environmental Archivist
People for Puget Sound
Seattle, Washington

Sort, categorize, systematize, and store the important records of our advocacy efforts, protecting and preserving the waters of Puget Sound, including policy statements, maps, media clips, comment letters, brochures, research reports, news releases, meeting minutes, photographs, and letters to the editor; make a substantial and positive impact on our Policy Team and, indeed, the organization at large; work in collaboration with our historian and policy guru, bringing order to the chaos of our documents. (People for Puget Sound Human Resources, accessed 2008)

Media/Entertainment Track
Sports Network Archivist
Turner Sports
Atlanta, Georgia

Process requests for information and footage from users from Turner Sports, CNN Sports, other Turner Properties, broadcast partners, and out-of-house clients; maintain the library catalog and thesaurus for Turner Sports Archive; take part in collection development; schedule broadcast records and set up video feeds; maintain sports library Web site; handle and distribute Turner Sports tape stock inventory; and maintain workspace and monitor all equipment within library and viewing/clipping area. Read and monitor sports publications/Web sites to be aware of NBA, NASCAR, Golf, Football, etc. news/ events. (Turner Human Resources, accessed 2008)

Resources for Further Information/Exploration

The following resources can help guide you in your career exploration within the field of archives and preservation. Note that this is not a comprehensive list; there are numerous resources available related to the nuances of the field that are not included. The purpose of identifying key job posting sites and professional organizations is to make you aware of some of the main resources available and also to provide you with gateways to resources that will inform you of the types of careers available in the field.

Professional Organizations Relevant to Archives and Preservation

- SAA—Society of American Archivists
  www.archivists.org
- NARA—National Archives and Records Administration
  www.archives.gov
- AMIA—Association of Moving Images Archivists
  www.amianet.org
- AHA—American Historical Association
  www.historians.org
- ALA—American Library Association
  www.ala.org
- AAM—American Association of Museums
  www.aam-us.org/index.cfm
- IS&T—Society for Imaging Science and Technology
  www.imaging.org
- Digital Preservation Coalition
  www.dpconline.org

Career Sites Relevant to Archives and Preservation

- Society of American Archivists Online Employment Bulletin
  www.archivists.org/employment
- National Association of Government Archives and Records Administrators Job Bank
  www.nagara.org/classified.cfm
- National Archives and Records Administration Jobs, Internships, and Volunteering Opportunities
  www.archives.gov/careers

- American Library Association Job List
  www.ala.org/al/Aeducation/empopps/employment.htm
- Global Museum Careers
  www.globalmuseum.org
- PreserveNet Job Board
  www.preservenet.cornell.edu/employ/index.cfm

Education and Training

To pursue a professional career in archives management or preservation of information, graduate education is essential. While some may be able to obtain professional archives and preservation positions with a bachelor's degree, for career advancement to higher positions, an advanced degree is expected. However, experience is also greatly valued by employers in this field, and as such one can benefit from gaining paraprofessional level experience after obtaining a bachelor's degree and before continuing one's education. A common undergraduate major is history, though any major combined with internship experience could lead to a relevant position. Those interested in working with images such as photographs or films might major in photography or film and video studies, and those interested in working with materials from a particular country or region of the world might major in a foreign language. Yet it is at the graduate level where essential knowledge and skills are gained for professional practice in archives and preservation.

The Society of American Archivists maintains an online directory of archival education (see www.archivists.org/prof-education) and has published guidelines and standards for degree programs. While there are a few master's programs that focus exclusively on archival studies (mostly in Canada), it is more common to find archival courses as part of an information or library and information science degree. Some programs have more robust offerings in archives and preservation than others, so it is important to evaluate the courses, faculty research, and internship or practicum opportunities when considering different programs.

In some colleges and universities, archival science and preservation coursework is offered as part of a master's in history degree. Museum studies is another educational option to consider and may be offered either as a degree or as a certificate program.

Workshops and institutes are offered by the Society for American Archivists as well, and combined with substantial experience and an undergraduate degree may be sufficient to land professional positions. Educational workshops are also offered specifically in the field of preservation by organizations such as the Northeast Document Conservation Center.

Certification is available for professional archivists through the Academy of Certified Archivists (ACA). Though it isn't always essential when one has formal education in the field, some employers view it as an additional sign of credibility and commitment to the profession. Specific criteria must be met to sit for the certification exam, and if the exam is passed, certification is awarded. Additional details are available at www.certifiedarchivists.org.

References

Ben & Jerry's Ice Cream. "Job Opportunities." Available: www.benjerry.com/company/jobs/ (accessed May 1, 2008).

Enfatico Human Resources. "Enfatico Careers." Available: http://tbe.taleo.net/NA1/ats/careers/jobSearch.jsp?org=ENFATICO&cws=1 (accessed May 1, 2008).

Gardner, Marilyn. 2005. "Saving History from a Hurricane." *Christian Science Monitor*, September 28. Available: www.csmonitor.com/2005/0928/pl2s01-lihc.htm (accessed October 3, 2009).

Joint Information Systems Commitee. 2007. "Podcast: Why Is Google Showing Us the Way Forward in Digitisation? Asks Senior UK Librarian." Available: www.jisc.ac.uk/Home/news/stories/2007/12/podcast21paulayris.aspx (accessed October 2008).

Library of Congress. 2008. "Digital Preservation Pioneer: Fran Berman." *Digital Preservation Newsletter* (July). Available: www.digitalpreservation.gov (accessed October 10, 2008).

National Archives and Records Administration. 2006a. "An 'American conversation' with Ken Burns and Allen Weinstein." National Archives and Records Administration press release, January 6. Available: www.archives.gov/press/press-releases/2006/nr06-50.html (accessed October 12, 2008).

National Archives and Records Administration. 2006b. *Democracy Starts Here.* Available: http://videocast.nih.gov/sla/NARA/dsh/index.html (accessed October 2008).

National Archives and Records Administration. 2008. "Strategy for Digitizing Archival Materials for Public Access, 2007–2016. Available: www.archives.gov/digitization/strategy.html (accessed October 10, 2009).

People for Puget Sound Human Resources. "Employment Opportunities." Available: www.pugetsound.org/connect/employment (accessed May 1, 2008).

Powers, S., K. McNabb, S. Catino, and D. Levitt. 2008. "Managing the Production and Distribution of Rich Media." Forrester Research, April 14. Available: www.forrester.com/Research/Document/Excerpt/0,7211,44525,00.html (accessed September 2009).

Sharp, Jennifer. 2008. Interview by Kelly Kowatch. May 30.

Society of American Archivists. 2002. "Guidelines for a Graduate Program in Archival Studies." Available: www.archivists.org/prof-education/ed_guidelines.asp (accessed May 13, 2009).

Society of American Archivists. 2008. "So You Want to Be an Archivist: An Overview of the Archival Profession." Available: www.archivists.org/profession/overview .asp (accessed October 2008).

Turner Human Resources. Careers. Available: www.turner.com/careers/index.html (accessed May 1, 2008).

Teper, Thomas. 2008. Interview by Kelly Kowatch. October 6.

U.S. Department of Labor, Bureau of Labor Statistics. 2009. "Archivists, Curators, and Museum Technicians." *Occupational Outlook Handbook*, 2008–2009 ed. Available: www.bls.gov/oco/ocos065.htm (accessed October 2008).

Williams, Mary Ann. 2008. Interview by Kelly Kowatch. October 1.

Additional Source

Wikipedia. "Search Results: Archives and Preservation." Available: http://en .wikipedia .org/wiki/Special:Search?search=archives+and+preservation&go= Go (accessed September 2008).

Chapter 2

Records Management

Introduction

Records managers are the guardians of documents and data that evidence the activity our lives—from personal, educational, medical, legal, commercial, and governmental domains. They are entrusted to safeguard the record of critical incidents that result from communications and documentation of actions, decisions, and results. Yet with so many records in so many different hands, how can we ensure privacy and security and balance these with our growing expectations for information at our fingertips?

From our medical records we hope are handled confidentially to vast sets of data in financial institutions that if compromised pose a major threat for identity theft, we all have a stake in the field of records management. Some of us, however, will lead the way in this time of unprecedented growth in records creation and unparalleled speed in technological advancement that affords both greater access and greater risk.

Records—documents and data in print or digital form—are being created at an explosive rate as the Information Age unfolds. And the information explosion is no illusion. The growth rate of information is accelerating at "mind-boggling" levels, according to the April 2007 issue of *Law Technology Today*, on online industry magazine, which describes the Internet as driving the exponential growth of information creation. The article refers to a 2006 International Data Corporation study (IDC is a global provider of market intelligence for the information technology, telecommunications, and consumer technology markets):

> [IDC] estimated that the world created 161 exabytes of information in 2006. That reflects a 32 fold increase over 2002 . . . [which] equates to an 800% annual growth rate. . . . By way of analogy, if you could print 161 exabytes, you

would end up with 12 stacks of paper extending from the earth to the sun. . . .
It would be enough paper to wrap the Earth four times over. The [IDC] authors [expect] that the trend will continue, with the amount of data being created in 2010 growing to 988 exabytes. That represents another 6 fold increase.
This time the resulting stack of paper could go from the sun to Pluto and
back. (Tredennick, 2007)

Why is this growth a concern for readers of *Law Technology Today*? Referring to
another IDC report that 20 percent of new data generated is subject to various
compliance rules and regulations calling for the attention of the legal community,
the author states "corporate legal has a substantial amount of data to worry about
whether for litigation holds or just implementing a records retention program"
(Tredennick, 2007).

Indeed, law and policy issues are a key aspect of the records management profession. The Sarbanes-Oxley Act of 2002 brought forth new regulations for corporations and financial institutions, and the Health Insurance Portability and
Accountability Act of 1996 provides national standards for health and medical records privacy. These along with other governmental regulations are important for
records managers to understand and follow as they guide their organizations to implement records retention schedules, manage access to information for employees
and the public, and implement technology in ways that balances access with security and privacy.

It is no small feat to move an organization toward best practices with records
management—each person in the organization has a role and a responsibility in
the process and each person's actions or inactions could result in significant problems for the organization. This is especially true given recent amendments to the
Federal Rules of Civil Procedures (FRCP), which govern access to electronic data
for legal proceedings, known as "e-discovery." A June 2007 online article in *CNET
News* indicates that the new rules require the e-discovery process to begin at the
outset of a lawsuit and "broadens the definition of electronic items that may be subject to discovery . . . to include all electronically stored information. . . . [T]he other
side now can demand everything from standard Word documents and e-mails to
voice mail messages, instant messages, blogs, backup tapes, and database files"
(Sinrod, 2007). Organizations are increasing their focus on e-discovery readiness
to help reduce the time and expense of recovering information relevant to a lawsuit
should one arise. Records managers are central to this process, working alongside
legal counsel and IT (information technology) professionals.

The same *CNET News* article reported survey results produced by:

LiveOffice, a provider of on-demand messaging security, archiving and compliance solutions . . . that show many companies are not prepared to comply with the foregoing FRCP amendments. Indeed, of the 400 IT managers and consumers polled on a nationwide basis . . . 63% already have been required to produce email as part of litigation, 53% admit they are not in a position to meet all of the requirements of the FRCP amendments, and 52% do not have an "e-discovery" plan. . . . Indeed, 28.9 percent . . . were not even aware of their FRCP obligations. (Sinrod, 2007)

It is not surprising, then, that the 2008 Socha-Gelbmann 6th annual Electronic Discovery Survey estimates continued growth for this Information Age industry, suggesting that "based on consumer and provider expectations . . . we project that the (electronic discovery) market growth will continue to be strong with increases of approximately 21% from 2007 to 2008, another 20% from 2008 to 2009, and 15% from 2009 to 2010" (Socha Consulting, 2008).

Even in the federal government, home of the regulations with which businesses are scrambling to comply, the challenge and opportunity of the records management field is clear. A September 2008 *New York Times* article reported:

Countless federal records are being lost to posterity because federal employees, grappling with a staggering growth in electronic records, do not regularly preserve the documents they create on government computers, send by e-mail, and post on the Web. . . . "All of us have stored personal memories or favorite music on eight-track tapes, floppy disks or 8-millimeter film," said Allen Weinstein, the archivist of the United States. "In many cases, these technologies are now relics, and we have no way to access the stored information. Imagine this problem multiplied millions and millions of times. That's what the federal government is facing." (Pear, 2008)

While the challenge of records management in the digital age is indisputable, the records management profession continues to advance organizational practices and regulatory compliance, guided by the field's primary professional association, ARMA International, which develops professional standards, offers training and certification, and publishes reports on market trends and legislative issues. The National Archives and Records Administration (NARA) also plays a pivotal leadership role for the records management profession, managing and safeguarding the immense set of records produced by federal agencies nationwide.

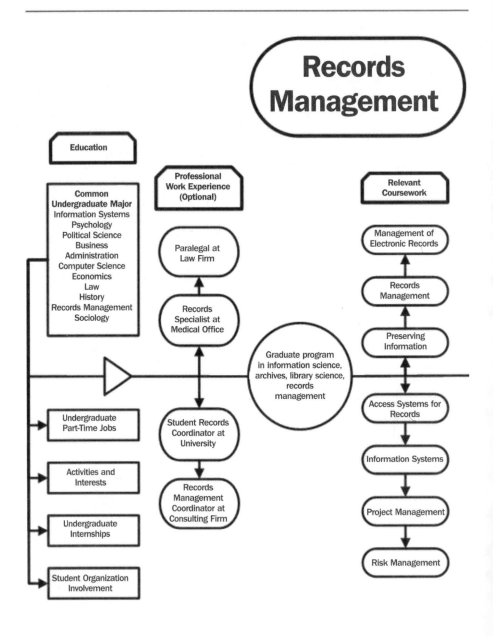

Figure 2. Records Management Career Map
This diagram demonstrates several of the potential paths associated with a career in the field of records management.

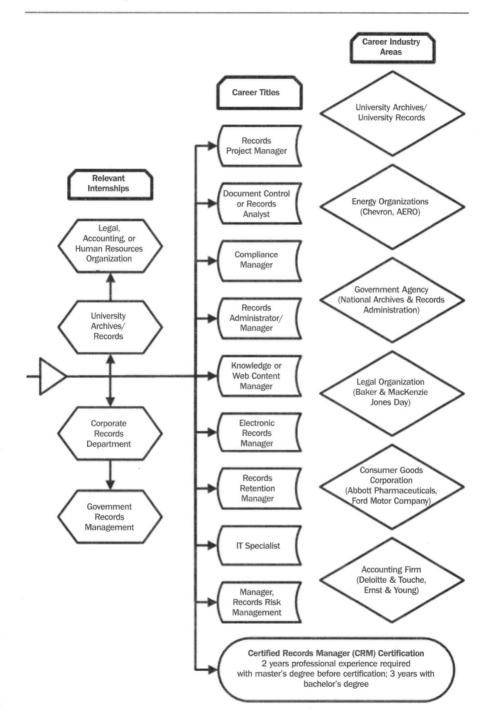

Career Industry Areas

University Archives/
University Records

Career Titles

Records
Project Manager

Relevant Internships

Document Control
or Records
Analyst

Energy Organizations
(Chevron, AERO)

Legal,
Accounting, or
Human Resources
Organization

Compliance
Manager

Government Agency
(National Archives & Records
Administration)

University
Archives/
Records

Records
Administrator/
Manager

Knowledge or
Web Content
Manager

Legal Organization
(Baker & MacKenzie
Jones Day)

Corporate
Records
Department

Electronic
Records
Manager

Consumer Goods
Corporation
(Abbott Pharmaceuticals,
Ford Motor Company)

Records
Retention
Manager

Government
Records
Management

IT Specialist

Accounting Firm
(Deloitte & Touche,
Ernst & Young)

Manager,
Records Risk
Management

Certified Records Manager (CRM) Certification
2 years professional experience required
with master's degree before certification; 3 years with
bachelor's degree

In their daily professional practice, records managers develop records retention schedules; conduct records inventories; ensure adherence to standards and legal regulations; guide development of technology systems to support records management goals and requirements; train employees to handle records correctly; develop strategies for digitization of paper records; create systems for records storage, retrieval, access, and circulation; and coordinate with archivists to transfer records selected for permanent retention. The materials records managers may supervise extends from paper and digital documents to imaged documents, e-mail, instant messages, analog and digital audio and video, and materials on or converted to CDs or DVDs. Moreover, records managers must ensure sustainability and security by maintaining access to records despite technological change while protecting against loss or damage. They must safeguard records from theft and improper access or release (ARMA International, 2008).

The work of records managers is increasing in importance, and career opportunities are growing. From the Enron scandal of the 1990s to the increasing stories of records security breaches in financial institutions and health care settings, the risks of the digital age require the steady hand of trained records management professionals. In fact, the frequency of compromised records is alarming. An April 2008 *Washington Post* article reported:

> At least 8.3 million personal and financial records of consumers were potentially compromised by data spills or breaches at businesses, universities and government agencies in the first quarter of 2008. . . . A review of the data (from the San Diego based Identity Theft Resource Center) . . . suggests that only about 13 percent of the breaches were the result of an outside hacker. . . . Most of the data (leaks) appear to have resulted from lost or stolen laptops, hard drives or thumb drives. Insider access and the inadvertent posting of sensitive data to a Web site or through e-mail also were cited frequently throughout the report. (Krebs, 2008)

While lawyers and IT professionals are involved in addressing records management issues, the records management professional has a central focus on the integrity and importance of records and provides the leadership, advocacy, and know-how to create and guide organizational systems and procedures that meet organizational needs, follow federal regulations, and respect individual privacy concerns.

In addition to increasing needs across diverse industries in the United States, records management is a key concern for overseas and global organizations as well. According to ARMA International, "Organizations in the European Union are experiencing increased regulatory compliance, and information accessibility and privacy challenges. They also are realizing that records and information managers hold the key to ensuring business continuity within their organizations" (ARMA International, 2006).

For those who care to invest their career in safeguarding privacy without sacrificing access to information and who wish to create organizational efficiency and effectiveness amid the exabytes of information that surround us, records management offers extensive opportunities for professional fulfillment.

Skills and Abilities

One of the most exciting prospects of the field of records management is the wide array of growing career opportunities in almost every industry. For any professional career field, there are required skills and abilities that are important for success. If you have a particular type of position and work setting in mind, perhaps at an organization in which you have a special interest, in records management there are skills and abilities that will make you so marketable that you'll have a good chance to land that dream job.

While most positions in records management are quite varied as far as skill level and education required, there are some common skills and abilities that are required and highly sought after for any type of professional records management position in any industry. Outlined in the following sections are both the soft skills and abilities (behavioral/personality traits and characteristics) and hard skills (technical and career-specific knowledge) and abilities that are important for success in the field of records management. Note that these skills are identified as the most common skills and abilities; this is certainly not an exhaustive list of all of the valuable skills and abilities that are beneficial for this career field.

Soft Skills

- Ability to work in collaboration/be a team player
- Ability to communicate (both written and verbal), achieving:
  - Persuasion
  - Negotiation
  - Presentation
- Leadership capability
- Motivated/enthusiastic approach to work
- Flexibility/adaptability
- Analytical/problem-solving/strategy skills

☑ QUICK FACT!
Strong team skills are essential. Records management work is dependent on collaboration with diverse groups of people.

Hard Skills

- General business management: Advise about and respond to the business needs of an organization. It is important to understand the strategic vision and mission of an organization.

- Risk management: Identify, assess, communicate, and manage the risks facing an organization to ensure that the organization meets business objectives.

- Archival processing standards and procedures: Arrange and describe the records of an organization.

- RIM Practices: Have expert knowledge of records information management (RIM) standards and policies.

- Technical skills: Administer databases, have some Web skills, and know MARC standards and XML.

- Web content management: Manage and control a large, dynamic collection of Web material (HTML and associated images) through Web application systems.

☑ QUICK FACT!
Business knowledge and technical skills are important.

As many records management professional journals indicate, we are in the midst of a digital revolution. All types of businesses from corporate to nonprofit to academia, both large and small, are all facing the same challenge of trying to keep up with the demand to digitize information and records. Not only are records managers faced with this task, they are responsible for creating policies and procedures to ensure compliance with laws and regulations surrounding information and records. Thus technical skills proficiency, archives knowledge and practice, and business management knowledge is increasingly important. While it's not expected that records managers have a strong technical skill set at the level of an IT professional, what is expected from employers is a certain level of understanding, a comfort level and ability to work with digital technology, and a familiarity with emerging technology trends.

Employers hiring records managers often value soft skills and hard skills equally. While certain hard skills and specific knowledge areas will always be required for a career in this field, soft skills/characteristics are equally important and are sometimes viewed by employers as even more critical to career advancement and long-term success in the field. Strong collaboration and team skills are important because effective records management work is often dependent on collaboration with IT professionals, archivists, records creators, and records users. Equally important are communication skills (both written and verbal) since records managers must be able to effectively communicate with diverse groups of people to explain complex records management, archival, and IT issues. Records managers must often promote "buy in" for their ideas, goals, policies, and overall mission within an organization, making persuasive communication skills an important asset.

Strong analytical skills are just as important. Records managers must be able to create a planned approach for achieving the objectives of the organization and develop policies in accordance with the organizational mission and vision. This connects with the need for general business management skills. Records managers often advise about and respond to the business needs of an organization. Therefore, they must understand the strategic vision and mission of an organization in order to gain credibility and convince others to follow through on their advice.

KEY WORDS TO KNOW

Here are a few basic records management key terms you will see throughout this chapter. If you are interested in pursuing this career field, it's a good idea to be familiar with their meaning:

- **record**: Recorded information, regardless of medium or characteristics, made or received by an organization in the pursuance of legal obligations or in the transaction of a business.
- **electronic records management**: The application of records management principles to electronic records.
- **archiving**: Conducting all activities related to caring for records of continuing value.
- **e-discovery**: Discovery in civil litigation that deals with information in electronic format.
- **metadata**: Data about data, of any sort in any media.
- **taxonomy**: The practice and science of classification.
- **digitization**: To convert an image or signal into digital code by scanning, tracing on a graphics tablet, or using an analog to digital conversion device.
- **accessibility**: Ability to locate relevant information through the use of catalogs, indexes, finding aids, or other tools.
- **compliance**: Conforming to a specification or policy, standard, or law that has been clearly defined.

Professional Roles

To better understand the role of a records manager and how they approach their work, it may help to compare and contrast the nature of records management work with the work of closely related professions:

- **Archivist versus Records Manager**
  Similarities: Collect, organize, manage, preserve, and make accessible materials for research.
  Differences: Records managers control vast quantities of institutional and organizational records, most of which will be eventually destroyed, while the archivist is concerned with relatively small quantities of records deemed important enough to be retained for an extended period.
- **Electronic Records Manager versus Records Manager**
  Similarities: Overall approach to their work.
  Differences: Electronic records managers work with records in electronic format, whereas records managers work with records in all forms, specifically physical records.
- **Records Manager versus IT Specialist**
  Similarities: Maintain and provide access to information and records.
  Differences: IT Specialists develop and maintain the networks and systems that store electronic records—they are the technical expert of the organization. Records managers are charged with controlling the life cycle of the records in all forms, however they are stored.
- **Business Manager versus Records Manager**
  Similarities: Mission and goal is to manage in accordance with the overall business plan, goals, vision, and mission of the organization.
  Differences: A business manager manages the work of others in order to run a business efficiently. A records manager manages records in order to run a business or any organization efficiently.

Occupational Outlook

> ☑ QUICK FACT!
> More than 90 percent of information in business today is created electronically (ARMA International, 2009).

Information is any organization's most important asset. All organizations need experts in records management and information management policies and practices. In response to this demand, we should see records management jobs continue to grow as organizational leaders increase their dependence on electronic records to make strategic decisions that have an impact on shareholders or constituents.

Additionally, as most offices, departments, and organizations are adapting to the concept of a paperless office, electronic records have accelerated and will continue to do so as organizations strategically strive to advance with technology (ARMA International, 2009). In fact, it is estimated that 93 percent of all the information that a business generated in 2006 was produced in electronic format—e-mail, word processing documents, information on databases—and this percentage will only continue to increase (Redgrave, 2007).

In accordance with this trend, it is not surprising that a faster than average employment growth is expected in records management through 2016, with stronger growth for those who specialize in electronic records (U.S. Department of Labor, Bureau of Labor Statistics, 2009). Those with highly specialized training, such as a master's degree in records management or related degree such as library or information science (with a concentration in records management), along with some practical experience and technical skills, will prove to be the most competitive in this field. Those holding a bachelor's degree in records management, information science, business administration, or related degree, in addition to holding a records management certification and with some practical experience and technical skills, will also have strong employment prospects.

A significant growth area for records managers is in the legal industry. As e-discovery continues to be a critical component in all types of litigation suits, and as law firms continue to integrate archival and records management systems to manage their information/research centers, the legal industry will have an increased need for records management professionals. The medical/health care field is another key growth area. There is a great need to bring in professionals who understand and can implement effective practices of electronic records management to handle not only the digitization of medical records but to manage records "born digital" and to ensure compliance with electronic records management standards, policies, and laws.

There are many industry areas that offer opportunities for careers in records management at all levels: universities and academic libraries, corporate information centers, corporate archives, law

> ☑ QUICK FACT!
> Industries to watch: health care and law

and research firms, health care and pharmaceutical companies, software firms, and even nonprofits. Pursuing a career in records management opens the door for a range of interesting, diverse, and substantial positions. The services and expertise records managers bring into any organization are increasingly invaluable.

Whether you have an interest in working with more traditional forms of records versus electronic/digital records, or you would like to combine your interest in archives and records management or business and records management, you can bet there will be many interesting jobs available to you in most any industry. Take a look at just some of the job titles and organizations that hire records management professionals.

The following job titles are typically associated with jobs requiring a bachelor's degree in records management or related degree:

- Records Management Coordinator, Accenture (consulting)
- Records Assistant, Pfizer Research and Development (pharmaceutical/ health care)
- Technical Records Assistant, Fidelity Investments (financial services)
- Records Management Officer, International Atomic Energy Agency (energy)
- Medical Records Specialist, University of Michigan Hospital (health care)
- Records Specialist, Ropes & Gray (law)

The following job titles are typically associated with jobs requiring a bachelor's degree in records management or related degree and a certification in records management or a master's degree in records management or related degree.

- Records and Information Analyst, Abbott Labs (pharmaceutical/health care)
- Records Administrator, County of Los Angeles (government/nonprofit)
- Records Manager, Yale University (university library)
- Records Specialist, Deloitte Consulting (consulting)
- Digital Archivist, Disney Research Library (entertainment/media)
- Web Content Manager, Entertainment Weekly (media/publishing)
- Electronic Records Manager, Environmental Protection Agency (environmental/nonprofit)
- Corporate Records Manager, Microsoft Corporation (IT corporation)
- Information Management Manager, Ford Foundation (nonprofit)
- Digital Asset Manager, Internet Archive (nonprofit)
- Electronic Records Archivist, Ohio Historical Society (museum/cultural institution)

Salary Information

Records management salaries vary depending on the size and nature of the employing organization as well as the level of position and education. The U.S. Bureau of Labor Statistics does not classify records management salaries as separate from archives salaries (which tend to be lower than records management salaries); therefore, the overall range $30,610–$50,730 could be considered a low range or more in line with entry-level records management positions not requiring a master's degree or RM certification. The Bureau of Labor Statistics (U.S. Department of Labor, Bureau of Labor Statistics, 2009), does indicate that median annual earnings of records managers as $50,730. There are a few online resources with salary information specific to the records management field.

According to Indeed.com (a metasearch engine for professional job postings), across all industries, the average salary range for records managers is $44,000–$80,000. This range is typically reported by new professionals entering the field with a master's degree in records management, library or information science or a bachelor's degree in records management, library or information science and holding a records management certification (CRM). Corporate records managers' earnings tend to be on the higher end of the salary range. Records managers' earnings in nonprofits or cultural institutions tend to be on the lower end of the range, but may provide added value in terms of work satisfaction, vacation time, work hours, and schedule. Thus, those with particular lifestyle goals can find these opportunities highly attractive.

Profiles—Perspectives of New Professionals

Brett Wise, Boston Records Supervisor
Wilmer Cutler Pickering Hale & Dorr LLP
Boston, Massachusetts

As the Boston Records Supervisor at the law firm Wilmer Cutler Pickering Hale & Dorr LLP, every day I am responsible for administrative oversight of the Boston Records Management Department. I also provide administrative support for the firm's records management system. Additionally, I work with the firm's director of records and the other firm records supervisors on strategic planning.

My background includes a bachelor of science degree in political science with a minor in general business from Missouri Western State College and a master of public administration degree from Southern Illinois University at Carbondale. In addition to those degrees, I have been or am in the process of being certified for two certifications in the records management profession: the Certified Records

Manager (CRM) certification and the Enterprise Content Management Practitioner certification. I am also a member of ARMA International, Association for Information and Image Management (AIIM), and the Project Management Institute (PMI). After graduate school, I worked in two different managerial roles in municipal government and the movie theatre industry. In 2005, I took a position with a law firm in Kansas City, Missouri, as a records supervisor, which eventually led to my current position.

I got my start in the profession due to my work history in management, especially personnel management. My undergraduate and graduate coursework helped me meet prerequisites for the position. My education in management, budgeting, and writing has also helped out immensely with the demands of the job.

The crucial skills necessary for my records and information management (RIM) positions have included personnel management, which is often overlooked in RIM literature but essential to success as a records manager, information technology, budgeting, project management, and strong analytical abilities. Also important is the ability to effectively communicate with others (especially in business settings), a strong work ethic, and, of course, knowledge of RIM principles and best practices.

I love the challenges of my job. In the several years I have worked in the field, I have faced many challenges familiar to the profession. First, and foremost, the importance of RIM within a business is not always fully understood (even by those who rely on our services daily). My staff and I have to focus daily on educating our customers while providing a quality end product. Also, the need to help prepare my employers for the emergence of digital records requires continual training for our staff on the technology skills necessary to deal with digital records and provide related RIM best practices. Additionally, there are always substantial projects that require careful planning and oversight to successfully complete.

Other challenges include personnel management and the marketing of the RIM program. Proper management of RIM staff requires that a records manager demand from her or his staff a strong work ethic, dedication to quality, and application of best practices. It is challenging to attract candidates who can successfully meet all of these demands, so emphasis on training, mentoring, and coaching is important. Also, records management has a tendency to get lost in the organizational structure of a business, so earning and maintaining the respect of one's peers and key decision makers is crucial. All of these challenges are demanding, yet rewarding, aspects of records management.

The enjoyment of my job is the greatest perk I could receive. I have worked with and learned from wonderful staffs, tackled administrative challenges with dedicated peers, met incredibly talented people throughout records management, and been mentored by two of the most knowledgeable and devoted records managers in the profession.

For readers who are considering a career in records management, the medical records industry and consulting/project management positions are areas where there is currently high demand, but it is hard to determine where high demand may lie in the future. I anticipate that consulting and project management work will continue to be in demand because many companies will not be willing to maintain large staffs as technology makes records management more efficient. For more information, check out the ARMA Web site and talk to current professionals in the field. Most industry professionals are more than willing to give advice and help mentor you. It also doesn't hurt to make as many connections as possible in the industry.

In the current market place, a bachelor and/or graduate degree is quite often required for consideration for mid- to high-level records management positions, and the requirement of a degree will likely become an absolute necessity over the next ten years. When looking toward higher education to help prepare you for the records management profession, seek degrees in library and information science or information technology. It is still rare to find dedicated programs in records management, but many reputable library and information sciences programs offer core classes in our profession, including some degrees with concentrations. Information technology/management degrees are also a sure way to go as digital technologies will permeate much of records management within the next decade. Business degrees are also a good foundation, but I recommend a minor in information systems/technology if pursuing a business degree.

Salary is highly dependent on your geographic area, and the industry you are in is a determiner. That being said, with my education, experience, and the field in which I work, I would currently expect a salary range of $45,000 to $65,000. In another five to ten years, my salary expectations would approach or exceed $80,000 to $100,000. This would entail a high-level records management position, possibly as a records manager, director, or consultant.

Hopefully, the opportunities in our profession will continue to grow. However, employment opportunities in the RIM field will be predicated on experience in information technology management as well as knowledge of records management principles and best practices. In addition to working toward my CRM certification, I am pursuing a second master's degree in project and program management. With my experience and current/future education, I feel secure that there will be many opportunities for me. However, proficiency in information technology manage-

ment will be a must in our profession as we move forward in the "digital age."
(Wise, 2008)

Nancy Deromedi, Associate Archivist
University Archives and Records Program
University of Michigan Bentley Historical Library
Ann Arbor, Michigan

I am Associate Archivist in the University Archives and Records Program (UARP)
at the University of Michigan's Bentley Historical Library (BHL). After receiving a
bachelor of science degree in business administration from Ferris State University,
I returned to school and received a bachelor of arts degree in history and a master
of science degree in information, both from the University of Michigan.

The university archives are the records of the university and related materials
that are selected, preserved, and made accessible for their enduring historical and
administrative value. One of the main responsibilities of the UARP staff is to ap-
praise records in consultation with offices and individuals across campus. These
records may be paper-based, on audiovisual media, or digital in origin; they are ap-
praised for their content. Once the records are transferred to the BHL, the records
are preserved within climate-controlled conditions. Key responsibilities include
the functions of appraisal, description, and preservation of records. My position
also provides a range of consultative services helping to address questions concern-
ing proper management of active records, the appraisal and transfer of inactive
records, and access to specific records for administrative and historical research.

The variety of the position is one of the job's characteristics that keeps me coming back to work each day. My day might include being involved in a visit to a faculty member's home to talk about records to be transferred to the library, research
of documents for a university unit asking about a past decision-making or
fact-checking issue, and working on processing and describing a record group. I
am also part of a team that maintains the library's Web site and part of a team that
researches and designs online exhibits such as the online timeline for the History of
Computing at the University of Michigan. Every day I use a variety of skills in order
to accomplish my responsibilities. Communication, analysis of information, and
an understanding of the organization and history of the institution are essential in
my position, which involves a lot of meetings and interactions with people who expect me to be a knowledgeable expert on a broad range of subjects.

My position allows for participation in major professional conferences and
meetings such as the annual meeting of the Society of American Archivists, the
American Association of Records Managers International Conference, and the
AIIM International Conference and Expo. Beyond professional conferences, I also

have been afforded the opportunity to travel globally. I have traveled to China, Vienna, and Paris as part of my job. The trip to China is part of an ongoing professional exchange the library has with the State Archives of China. My trips to Vienna and Paris were to present papers mainly on records in digital form.

There is a transition in records management right now. Records are largely being created in digital form. With this transition, all organizations, businesses, and other institutions will need persons in this field to make sure that records with informational, evidential, and historical value will be managed properly over time. The roles that will be growing the most in the coming years will involve working with record-keeping systems, policy and guideline development, and aspects of digital preservation. Persons going into this field will most likely be part of a team to design/implement record compliant systems and/or monitor, maintain, and preserve record collections in digital form.

There are two main experiences that helped open the door to my current position. One was the experience of taking a history seminar that required a research paper on an aspect of Michigan in the Progressive Era. The paper required the use of primary sources, which led me to use the archives at the BHL. There, I realized my fascination with the use of original material that allowed me to draw my own conclusions based on the material reviewed.

The other experience was my pursuit of my master's degree at the University of Michigan's School of Information. Many courses were valuable, but "Management of Electronic Records" provided me with an excellent foundation for understanding digital records issues. The association with the course's professor also led me to a part-time job in my last semester at the School of Information to "process" a new digital collection that the Bentley Library received. This experience really exposed me to the challenges of working with digital materials.

For those who are considering this role, I offer the following advice: One of the best ways to learn about a profession is to get some experience in the field. I suggest getting involved in an organization on a part-time or volunteer basis. While the work will be "entry-level," it will expose you to the overall operation of the organization and tools that are used in the management of records. There are many types of organizations that have records and need assistance in record keeping issues. While many people might just think of government offices like city and county offices, there are lots of organizations that could provide experience, such as churches, nonprofit organizations, and small businesses.

The earning potential for entry-level records manager or archival professionals working with records varies depending on the type of environment that one works in. For example, archivists and records managers work in government, business/private corporations, and universities, and the salaries are a reflection of the industry. I have been in my position for ten years and I make a competitive salary for university standards. (Deromedi, 2008)

Mimi Dionne, Records Manager
Technip, USA
Houston, Texas

I knew at age 12 that I wanted to work with records. Later, on the first day of college, I toured the library and saw a sign that read "University Archives" with an arrow leading up to the second floor. Following the arrow, I applied for and was employed by the university as a student worker in the Archives, which changed the course of my career aspirations completely.

As I finished my senior thesis at Louisiana Scholars' College, I looked for a graduate program that would teach me archival repository management. I began my studies at the University of Texas (UT) at Austin School of Library and Information Science in the archival enterprise certificate track but soon found records and information management, which seemed more encompassing in regard to the life cycle of the record and offered more corporate opportunities. The university encouraged real-world experience to augment studies, so as I completed my classes, I found local opportunities to improve my skills in a real-world setting.

I am now a records manager at Technip, USA. I have had a pure records management (RM) career since I graduated and accepted a role with the State of Michigan as a Department Analyst in the Records Management Application Pilot Project. I have progressed through RM-oriented roles at the University of Texas Health Science Center at Houston, the law firm Vinson & Elkins, LLP, Administaff Inc. as an Auditing Manger, and with Cheniere Energy Inc. Now, my daily role is a mix of broad responsibilities and extremely specific tasks. The overall goal is to create a records culture, augment justifications for future projects, manage business process re-engineering regarding data collection, and make strategic decisions in regard to knowledge management implementations. Specifically, I oversee policy and procedure development, employee departure notifications, retention schedule updates, taxonomy and metadata rework, developing records and information management (RIM) training, and creating records flow into off-site and electronic storage. Among all of this, I must also market and promote the RIM program, partner with departments to enhance the treatment of their records, establish auditing techniques, all in addition to various other administrative responsibilities related to RIM.

I think success in RIM is 60 percent soft skills, 40 percent hard—regardless of culture, although some are more aggressive than others, of course. It's been my experience that one can be a terrifically skilled records and information manager, but if no one wants to work with you, your program will not succeed. So, the pressure to be smart, funny, generous, know exactly what to say at the right moment, and to take advantage of the opportunities given to you can be pretty daunting as a younger professional. Furthermore, I place special emphasis on the technology component of this profession as traditional records and information management career opportunities are transitioning into unrecognizable enterprise content management positions. I also espouse the concept of patience. Colleagues always think they can manage their records better than you, the records and information manager. However, they never get around to managing them properly; it's always the job that's pushed to the end of the day, the end of that week, then the end of next week, and the next thing they know, months have passed. My advice is to not get frustrated and use that time wisely on other projects until they gain the understanding of the necessity of your role.

What I enjoy most about my career is the opportunity to talk with colleagues about RIM. Every so often I interact with opponents of RIM who profess that IT is IT and records is boxes and I'm to stay out of their department. This kind of conversation requires a sensitive, but firm, rebuttal to the contrary: IT owns the system and records has custody of the data within. Again, this is when patience is essential.

I would like the opportunity to verify my current RIM program against ISO 15489, the RM standard set by the International Organization for Standardization. However, the challenge is to communicate successfully with colleagues that putting records and information management best practices into effect does not mean that business comes to a screeching halt. That's the main goal and future trend of RM in my environment. Beyond this, I'm highly focused on compliance with records and information management best practices, which include keeping the right amount of information for the right length of time, meeting all legal requirements, controlling costs, demonstrating good faith through consistent implementation, protecting vital/historic records, producing information quickly and efficiently, integrating policies and procedures organization-wide, establishing ownership and accountability, ongoing organization-wide training, and compliance controls (auditing against ISO 15489).

For those considering the field of records management, this discipline is the most fundamental set of issues an organization faces today. It's the toughest, too. But this makes the payoff that much more rewarding. Salary will be in alignment with the level of commitment to the field and to professional development opportunities. Overall, I don't have a clear answer to what the future of RIM career roles looks like, but I think that records and information managers are at a true crossroads. If we don't pin down the IT ideology soon, we will be reduced to box management only. However, if RM professionals continue to pursue the digital and technological knowledge that I am incorporating into my everyday roles, the future looks bright. (Dionne, 2008)

Since the interview, Mimi has taken the position of Lead Records Management Consultant with Qwest Communications in Denver, Colorado, and has launched a consulting business, Mimi Dionne Consulting. She is also the incoming Regent of Exam Administration with the Institute of Certified Records Managers for 2009.

Careers in Records Management: At a Glance

Your career in records management can take many directions as you connect your interests and values to the type of functional area and type of organization that you pursue. Here are a few examples of real jobs representing some exciting "tracks" you can follow.

Medical/Health Track
Compliance Operations Manager
Amgen Inc.
Thousand Oaks, California

Serve as records and information management (RIM) expert for guidance on managing records and information across all media types; implement liaison-level training programs and supporting network of embedded records management liaisons globally; manage updates, revisions, and review of the Corporate Records Retention Schedule and associated processes and procedures; establish and maintain a "library" of project management tools and templates for records management area. (MBAfocus.com, 2008)

Corporate Track
Enterprise Records Management Program (ERMP) Manager
Exelon Corporation
Chicago, Illinois

Point of contact for vendors and services related to ERMP solutions and for communication and oversight of ERMP functions performed across the corporation; the point of contact to Legal, Information Technology, and other business functions to ensure effective governance, oversight, and management of the ERMP across the corporation; administer and maintain records retention schedules and participate in the resolution of records retention related issues; supervise staff related to daily operations and implementation of the ERMP. (MBAfocus.com, 2008)

Legal Track
Legal Records Manager
Forrest Solutions
New York, New York

Develop and implement records management and RIM policy and practices; monitor compliance; work with legal teams to facilitate litigation holds and discovery requests; administer and coordinate the destruction review process, including purge of on-site records; sponsor and support records management projects including existing and future records requirements; ensure the effective management of, and adherence to, the Records Management Program. (Yahoo! Hotjobs, 2008)

Consulting Track
Records Supervisor
Deloitte Services
Washington, DC

Track and safeguard all administrative and client working paper files and records utilizing the Deloitte Records Management System (DRMS); service the filing needs of the clients of Central Files; monitors compliance with established Central Files business processes for this office, using management reports and metrics; ensures that client working papers are securely stored, client confidentiality is maintained, and that Central files is routinely utilized for storage of all client working papers. (Deloitte, 2008)

Government Track
Records Specialist
United States Department of the Interior
Bureau of Land Management (BLM)
Phoenix, Arizona

Develop and implement statewide records management processes and procedures for BLM; assist in setting up records systems that include creating, maintaining, retrieving, and disposing of records in compliance with established life cycle management policies; evaluate existing records management procedures and guide improvement; work with various offices to determine suitable storage methods for records; coordinate with the National Archives and Records Administration

(NARA) and Federal Records Center (FRC) assuring that proper procedures are in place and adhered to for archival of records. (USAJOBS, 2008)

Nonprofit Track
Manager, Information Management
Ford Foundation
New York, New York

Manage the collection, organization, preservation of, and access to the foundation's records and intellectual assets; provide leadership in the application of information management and retrieval techniques; collaborate with staff to support research, discovery, and analysis needs of the foundation; implement appropriate practices, procedures, and technology to maintain and enrich the information resources; consult with the IT department in the application of information management practices to software development initiatives; ensures compliance standards are met. (Ford Foundation, 2008)

Resources for Further Information/Exploration

The following resources can help guide you in your career exploration within the field of records management. Note that this is not a comprehensive list; there are numerous resources available related to the nuances of the field that are not included. The purpose of identifying key job posting sites and professional organizations is to make you aware of some of the main resources available and to also provide you with gateways to resources that will inform you of the types of careers available in the field.

Professional Organizations Relevant to Records Management

- ALA—American Library Association
  www.ala.org
- ARMA International—The Authority on Records Information Management
  www.arma.org
- AIIM—Enterprise Content Management Association/Association for Information and Image Management
  www.aiim.org
- COSHRC—Council of State Historical Records Coordinators
  www.statearchivists.org

- IASSIST—International Association for Social Science Information Service and Technology
  www.iassistdata.org
- NAGARA—National Association of Government Archives and Records Administrators
  www.nagara.org
- NARA—National Archives and Records Administration
  www.archives.gov
- SAA—Society of American Archivists
  www.archivists.org
- PRISM International—Professional Records & Information Services Management
  www.prismintl.org
- Nuclear Information & Records Management Association
  www.nirma.org

Career Sites Relevant to Records Management

- American Library Association Job List
  www.ala.org/al/Aeducation/empopps/employment.htm
- AIIM Job Posts
  http://jobs.aiim.org/job_index.cfm?CFID=1378994&CFTOKEN= 95031802
- ARMA International's CareerLink
  www.arma.org/careers/jobseekers.cfm
- Association of Research Libraries Career Resources Online Service
  http://db.arl.org/careers/index.html
- Chronicle of Higher Education Chronicle Careers
  http://chronicle.com/jobs
- International Association for Social Science Information Service and Technology Job Postings
  www.iassistdata.org
- National Association of Government Archives and Records Administrators Job Bank
  www.nagara.org/classified.cfm
- National Archives and Records Administration Jobs, Internships, and Volunteering Opportunities
  www.archives.gov/careers

- Society of American Archivists Online Employment Bulletin
  www.archivists.org/employment

Education and Training

Those interested in records management have a number of educational options to consider. At the bachelor's degree level, one could major in any field, while taking some coursework in information technology and business and seeking relevant work experience through part-time jobs and internships. As for specific undergraduate majors, students might consider informatics, information science, management information systems, computer science, or business administration. Some universities offer an undergraduate major in medical records administration, typically as part of a college of allied health.

However, for future advancement and career growth, it can be important to seek postbaccalaureate studies either through certification programs and/or a master's degree. Few universities offer a program in records management alone, but there are a number of graduate programs in archives and records management, and students can focus their studies on the records management side of the curriculum through course selections, internships, and professional activities. To explore graduate level programs, see the Society of American Archivists educational directory at www.archivists.org/prof-education/edd-index.asp. Additional graduate degrees to consider include business, law, or public policy. At some universities, the archives and records management program offers dual or joint degrees with these programs.

Those with a bachelor's or a master's degree may benefit from online classes, seminars, and professional certification offered through ARMA International, the primary professional association for the records management field, and/or through the National Archives and Records Administration (NARA). The Institute of Certified Records Managers offers certification to practicing records managers based on substantial requirements for education and experience and successful completion of an exam. Records managers must complete ongoing professional development to maintain CRM certification status. For details, visit www.arma.org/careers/certification.cfm. NARA offers federal employees a certification program comprised of training and examinations in five knowledge areas. According to NARA's Web site, "Those who successfully pass all five examinations will receive NARA's Certificate of Federal Records Management Training, signed by the Archivist of the United States" (National Archives and Records Administration, 2008).

References

ARMA International. 2006. "EU, U.S. Experts Discuss Effect of Information Security, Protection, Preservation on Business Continuity During Brussels Seminar." Available: www.arma.org/international/brussels2006seminar.cfm (accessed November 12, 2009).

ARMA International. 2008. [Homepage.] Available: www.arma.org (accessed November 3, 2008).

ARMA International. 2009. "Records and Information Management Basics." Available: www.arma.org/rim/101/index.cfm (accessed August 2009).

Deloitte. 2008. "Who's Behind Some of the World's Biggest Companies? Maybe You." Available: http://careers.deloitte.com/glo/Bexperienced-professionals/opportunities.aspx?JobReqCode=E09MINSASCAN042-OPL4&LOR=&COR=&AOR (accessed October 21, 2009).

Deromedi, Nancy. 2008. Interview by Kelly Kowatch. November 6.

Dionne, Mimi. 2008. Interview by Kelly Kowatch. November 8.

Ford Foundation. 2008. [Homepage.] Available: www.fordfound.org/employment/jobs/203 (accessed November 10, 2008).

Krebs, Brian. 2008. "8.3 Million Records Spilled in Data Breaches This Year." *Washington Post*, April 2. Available: http://blog.washingtonpost.com/securityfix/2008/04/83_million_records_spilled_in.html (accessed November 12, 2008).

MBAfocus. 2008. "Job Listings." Available: www3.mbafocus.com/candidates/cand_jobview.asp?jobid=26448 (accessed November 6, 2008).

National Archives and Records Administration. 2008. "Federal Records Management Certification." Available: www.archives.gov/records-mgmt/training/certification.html (accessed November 8, 2008).

Pear, Robert. 2008. "In Digital Age, Federal Files Blip into Oblivion." *New York Times*, September 12. Available: www.nytimes.com/2008/09/13/us/13records.html?scp=1&sq=Federal+Records+Blip&st=nyt (accessed October 3, 2008).

Redgrave, J.M. 2007. "The Sedona Principles: Second Edition Best Practices, Recommendations and Principles for Addressing Electronic Document Production." A Project of the Sedona Conference. Available: www.thesedonaconference.org/content/miscFiles/TSC_PRINCP_2nd_ed_607.pdf (accessed October 2009).

Sinrod, Eric J. 2007. "Perspective: The New e-Discovery Burden." *CNET News*, October 17. Available: http://news.cnet.com/The-new-e-discovery-burden/2010-1030_3-6213845.html (accessed November 3, 2008).

Socha Consulting. 2008. "2008 Socha-Gelbmann 6th Annual Electronic Discovery Survey." Available: www.sochaconsulting.com/2008surveyresults.php (accessed November 8, 2008).

Tredennick, John. 2007. "There Is a Lot More Data Out There." *Law Technology Today*, April. Available: www.abanet.org/lpm/ltt/articles/vol1/is2/firewire/There_Is_a_Lot_More_Data_Out_There.shtml#bio (accessed November 8, 2008).

U.S. Department of Labor, Bureau of Labor Statistics. 2009. "Archivists, Curators, and Museum Technicians." *Occupational Outlook Handbook*, 2008–2009 ed. Available: http://stats.bls.gov/oco/ocos065.htm (accessed October 2009).

USAJOBS. 2008. "Records Specialist." Available: http://jobsearch.usajobs.gov/getjob
    .asp?JobID=77095297&brd=3876&AVSDM=2008-11-03+14%3A47%3A58&sort=
    rv&vw=d&q=records+manager&Logo=0&ss=0&customapplicant=15513%2C155
    14%2C15515%2C15669%2C15523%2C15512%2C15516%2C45575&TabNum1&rc
    =3 (accessed November 10, 2008).
Wise, Brett. 2008. Interview by Kelly Kowatch. October 8.
Yahoo! Hotjobs. 2008. "Legal Records Manager." Available: http://hotjobs.yahoo
    .com/job-JKI9SUF99NQ;_ylc=X3oDMTEwdjRiNTVqBF9TazM5NjUxMDMzNQ
    RjYXQDTEVHBHBjb2RlAzUwNTg0?source=partner&scode=50584   (accessed
    November 6, 2008).

Additional Sources
Wikipedia, s.v. "Records Management," Available: http://en.wikipedia.org/wiki/
    Records_management (accessed October 2008).
Wikipedia, "Search Results: Records Management." Available: http://en.wikipedia
    .org/w/index.php?title=Special%3ASearch&redirs=0&search=records+management
    &fulltext=Search&ns0=1 (accessed October 2008).

Chapter 3

Library and Information Services

Introduction

Librarians are navigators on the expanding sea of information and search czars for the digital world—a human form of Google, only better. The digital age is transforming the field of library and information science and is redefining the profession of librarianship, creating a new generation of librarians who are embracing a new world of career opportunities in our information-rich society. And the world is starting to notice this new breed of librarian. According to a 2007 *New York Times* article, "A Hipper Crowd of Shushers," with the digital age "a new type of librarian is emerging . . . with so much of the job involving technology and with a focus now on finding and sharing information beyond just what is available in books" (Jesella, 2007). Young professionals and career changers alike are discovering that the library profession is highly diverse in its opportunities and not only has room for—but truly needs—individuals from myriad backgrounds to join the profession.

Librarians have a long history, of some 3,000 years, yet in recent times the field of librarianship has expanded and collided with information technology, and the complexity of the digital age has created the need for information professionals who choose the path of librarianship to understand information needs and problems from multiple perspectives. In response, the professional training of librarians has changed and continues to evolve as well.

Many programs or schools in library and information science have broadened their curricula to incorporate perspectives from multiple fields including business, public policy, psychology, computer science, linguistics, economics, and more. Several programs have chosen to broaden their name as well (e.g., to schools of information), which reflects the changing roles of librarians and the changing needs of the libraries and other organizations that employ them.

Those trained in library and information services could be considered the "general practitioners" of the information profession—capable of tackling a multitude of information problems in a wide range of settings. Yet also like the field of medicine, library and information services boasts a multitude of areas and ways in which to specialize. If you have a strong interest in a particular content area, you could become a subject specialist in areas such as art history, Middle East studies, or science. Or you could pursue a career in special libraries such as law, medicine, government, or business.

Other specialties include K–12 school media, news librarianship, or functional specialties such as metadata, technical services, or acquisitions. With the world of work shifting rapidly to a knowledge-based economy, the skill set of a librarian is also well suited to information management positions in areas such as competitive intelligence and market research.

While many are quick to categorize library and information services (LIS) careers as either traditional or nontraditional, this is a false dichotomy. Librarians today, even those in roles some call "traditional"—such as youth librarian or reference librarian—are re-creating the meaning of librarianship in the digital age while retaining the core purposes and values of the profession, such as service to individuals and to communities and promoting democracy through information access. Those trained in library and information services will find their skill set valuable in research organizations, government agencies, consulting firms, and large ecommerce based companies and may enjoy a diverse career path without ever working in an actual library.

Moreover, new paradigms for libraries are emerging as well. Public libraries are transforming into community centers and research libraries into massive digital data repositories. Librarians are transforming into information technology experts and trainers as they deploy new technologies to meet the information needs of the individuals, communities, and organizations they serve. From 24 hour online chat service to Twitter pages to digital libraries, it's increasingly clear that the changing landscape of librarianship is just beginning. Not only do librarians work in a variety of positions outside of libraries, libraries themselves sometimes exist only in digital rather than physical space. Yet by no means are brick and mortar libraries going away.

Thomas Frey, Senior Futurist at the DaVinci Institute has outlined a vision for the future of libraries. He writes "libraries are going through an age of rebirth. . . . From rather hidebound monuments to knowledge laboratories, libraries are now evolving into interactive research and leisure centers. Yet this change, as impressive as it is, is only the beginning" (Frey, 2009). From facilitating interactive information exchange and completely digital collections downloaded instantly to electronic readers to holographic and space imaging for data visualization and image exploration, Frey's vision positions the library as the "nerve center" of the community, providing "myriad informational experiences." Increased telecommuting, entrepreneurship, and blending of work and personal lives will lead libraries to exist as a new form of cultural center amid day care centers, fitness centers, and places of business (Frey, 2009).

One only has to look at some of our country's leading public libraries to see this change underway. You may have heard about "Cool Cities," but the Salt Lake City Public Library was named by MSN.com as one of America's 10 coolest public libraries:

> Built in 2003, Salt Lake City's library building is a stunning piece of contemporary architecture with a six-story curving, walkable wall; ground-level shops; a rooftop garden and four floors of spiraling fireplace that looks like a column of flame. The physical building reflects the exciting and inclusive spirit of the library. (Kavanaugh, accessed 2009)

Beyond public libraries, there are many other "cool" libraries that could be your future employer, such as the *Entertainment Weekly* Library, the American Museum of Natural History Library, the Library of Congress, the United Nations Library, or the still-in-development National Sports Museum and Library. If you have interest in an international career, build strength in a foreign language (or two) and you could be employed in a library—or other information-rich organization—across the globe.

Named one of the best careers for 2009 by *U.S. News & World Report*, which describes librarians as "among our society's most empowering people," librarianship offers an intellectually stimulating career that is focused on helping people and organizations with their information needs (Nemko, 2008). Moreover, it provides a stable career with the potential to work in a variety of employment sectors and industries. Librarians typically have reasonable work hours that can support the work–life balance many younger professionals are seeking. Part-time professional options are available as well. Having a job that is meaningful—while making a decent salary—leads librarians to enjoy high levels of job satisfaction. New and veteran librarians alike point to the variety of the work, the dynamic nature of the field, and the satisfaction of helping individuals and contributing to a stronger so-

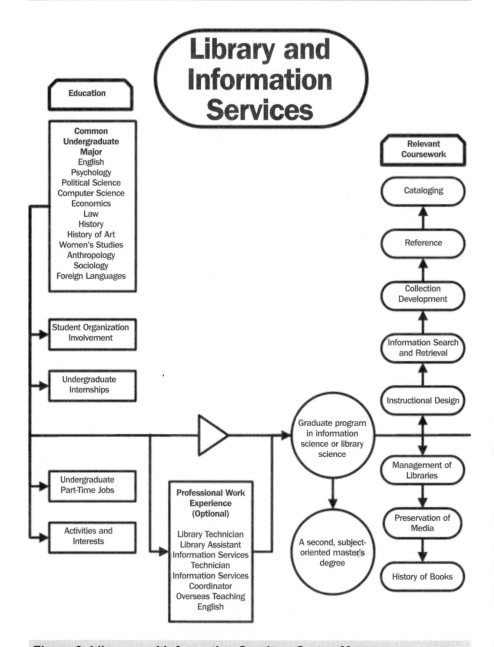

Figure 3. Library and Information Services Career Map
This diagram demonstrates several of the potential paths associated with a career in the field of library and information services.

ciety through literacy, education, and community building as offering, for them, the perfect career.

Indeed, librarianship enjoys both a long history and an exciting future as part of the array of information fields that now share the information career space. Library and information services offers a future of rewarding career opportunities in a field whose future will be shaped, in ways we can't fully predict, by those who choose to make this path their profession.

Skills and Abilities

One of the most exciting prospects of the field of library and information services is the wide array of potential employers. The positions within this field are diverse as well. Yet overall, there are common skills and abilities that are required and highly sought for most any library and information services position.

Outlined in the following sections are both the soft skills and abilities (behavioral/personality traits and characteristics) and hard skills and abilities (technical and career-specific knowledge) that are important for success in the field of library and information services. Note that these are the most common skills and abilities; this is certainly not an exhaustive list of all of the valuable skills and abilities that are beneficial for this career field.

> ☑ QUICK FACT!
> If you have a thirst for knowledge and a true passion for helping others, this may be the career for you.

Soft Skills

- Ability to communicate (both written and verbal)
- Flexibility/adaptability
- Problem-solving/analytical skills
- Customer service skills
- Ability to work in collaboration/be a team player
- Motivated/enthusiastic approach to work
- Ability to be innovative/creative
- Leadership capability

Hard Skills

- Reference: Provide resources and information to information seekers.
- Instruction/training: Provide instruction on both how to evaluate information resources and how to use library resources such as the library catalog or other bibliographic databases.

- Collection development: Plan and acquire a balanced collection of library materials of many formats, including books, periodicals, online resources, and other media.
- Outreach/public services: Provide information on services and resources to the community and external constituents.
- Database searching: Use a computer system to find subject-specific journal articles or other information.
- Network/systems administration/management: Plan, develop, implement, and administrate systems for the acquisition, storage, and retrieval of data.
- Web design: Create presentations of content that are delivered to end users through the Internet (i.e., HTML, xHTML, Dreamweaver, CSS).
- Research: Conduct diligent and thorough inquiry and investigation into a subject.
- Cataloging: Organize a descriptive detailed list of items arranged systematically.
- General business or human resources management: Understand the business needs of an organization, from strategic vision and mission, to supervision and budget management.

Don't believe the myth that as more resources and information are made available on the Internet that librarians will one day be obsolete. As technology advances, just the opposite is happening. The role of the librarian is evolving and expanding. Career pathways are opening up in industries and organizations where one might not have thought a "librarian" would be needed. Not only are industries opening up for this career field, job titles are changing—from Librarian to Information Architect, Web Master, Database Administrator, Information Scientist, and Content Manager— just to name a few. In addition to new job titles, the skills and characteristics of today's librarian have also changed considerably.

Historically, librarian job postings would not have listed traits such as creative, innovative, energetic, tech savvy, and forward-thinking as job qualifications. Today, these are essential traits for professionals entering the field. Moreover, this field seeks creative visionaries who are not afraid of and can embrace the emerging technology trends in the field. Today's librarian uses the latest information technology to perform research, classify materials, and help students, clients, and other users seek information. Expertise in electronic resources, database administration,

Web design, social networking, and technical services continue to be integrated into the professional services librarians offer.

It is expected that today's librarian has a strong knowledge of emerging technology trends such as social networking tools and resources and can apply new technologies to meet the needs of library users. Because every library or information center acquires specific database systems, skills in database management are often highly valued in the field as well. It is not expected that you be an expert user for all systems but rather are familiar with the most common databases and electronic resources in the field.

Equally important are strong communication, interpersonal, team, and collaboration skills, as LIS professionals will work closely with library users, clients, and other departments within their organization. For example, a technical services librarian in an academic library works very closely with those in the information technology (IT) department and faculty as well as with other libraries on campus to meet their goals and accomplish their mission. Some librarians may even act in a consulting role to other departments, making effective communication and collaboration skills essential. Furthermore, librarians must be able to effectively understand and analyze users' needs to not only determine what information is appropriate, but also to search for, acquire, and provide the information.

Research skills are also critical. Librarians and information services professionals in any industry must be able to perform extensive research to meet the needs of their customers or users. For example, in the health care field, the work of physicians, scientists, and other medical professionals relies heavily on research. The librarian or information professional is who they turn to in order to meet research goals.

Instruction and training often are a central component of a librarian's job; therefore, effective instructional skills will not only make you more marketable but will also lead to higher levels of success. Whether helping users navigate the Internet, teaching undergraduate students how to utilize electronic resources for research, or training staff on a new piece of software or content management system, effective instructional skills are critical.

There are exciting opportunities for growth into leadership positions in libraries and information centers. In order to advance to executive roles, such as director of a public library or associate dean of an academic library, human resources and budget management skills are important, but equally important are leadership skills and technical savvy.

KEY WORDS TO KNOW

Here are a few basic library and information services terms you will see throughout this chapter. If you are interested in pursuing this career field, it's a good idea to be familiar with their meaning:

- **information literacy**: The ability to recognize when information is needed and to be able to locate, evaluate, and use the information effectively.
- **intellectual freedom**: To resist all efforts to censor library and information resources.
- **access**: All information resources should be readily, equally, and equitably available to all library users.
- **outreach**: Provision of information or services to reach the needs of community groups.
- **Web 2.0**: Describes the changing trends in the use of the Internet and technology to enhance and improve ways of retrieving and sharing information. Some Web 2.0 technologies include social networking sites, wikis, blogs, and RSS feeds.
- **social responsibility**: To help inform and educate people on critical problems and encourage them to examine the many views on and the facts regarding each problem.
- **diversity**: To support and embrace multiculturalism. To provide a full spectrum of resources to reflect the diversity of library users.

Professional Roles

To better understand the role of a library and information services professional and how they approach their work, it may help to break down the most common responsibilities, critical issues, and populations served in these commonly followed career pathways:

- **Public Librarianship**
  Responsibilities: reference, instruction, cataloguing, collection development, acquisitions, public services.
  Services: library services for a diverse community of adults, children, and teens.
  Issues: intellectual freedom, community standards, information literacy, censorship, and legal and budgeting issues.
- **School Librarianship**
  Responsibilities: reference, instruction, collection development.

Services: library services for children in schools through grade 12. Local government may have stricter standards for the education and certification of school librarians than for other librarians, and the educational program will include those local standards.

Issues: intellectual freedom, pedagogy (instructional style or strategy), and how to build a cooperative curriculum with teaching staff.

- **Academic Librarianship**

  Responsibilities: reference, instruction, collection development, cataloguing, acquisitions.

  Services: library services for colleges and universities.

  Issues: copyright, technology, digital libraries, digital repositories, academic freedom, open access to scholarly works, specialized knowledge of subject areas important to the institution and the relevant reference works.

- **Special Librarianship**

  Responsibilities: research, competitive intelligence, collection development.

  Services: serves the needs of the industries they inhabit such as medical/hospital, corporations, news agency, entertainment, advertising, industry, publishing or other special collections.

  Issues: solo work, corporate financing, specialized collection development, extensive self-promotion to potential patrons.

Occupational Outlook

The *U.S. News & World Report* ranks library and information services as one of the "Best Careers for 2009" (Nemko, 2008). Despite being ranked as one of the best career choices, employment of librarians is expected to grow by 4 percent between 2006 and 2016, which is slower than the average for all occupations (U.S. Department of Labor, Bureau of Labor Statistics, 2007). Although expected new job growth is modest, there is still a solid job market due to turnover, retirements, and some new positions, not to mention the fact that an increasing number of LIS graduates are taking new kinds of roles in organizations outside of libraries.

While trends in the job market, by definition, will change over time, the Bureau of Labor Statistics projects the fastest job growth in the next decade will be in what is often termed "special" libraries, such as corporate, medical, law, and publishing libraries as well as nonprofits and consulting firms. Many organizations are realizing that librarians can manage vast amounts of information and analyze, evaluate, and organize it according to a company's specific needs. They are also looking for librarians and information professionals to organize information on the Internet;

to design, develop, and maintain company Web sites; or to develop and maintain a company intranet.

While job opportunities in public and academic libraries may not be growing at a faster than average rate, opportunities are still expected to be favorable. According to the Bureau of Labor Statistics, 2 out of 3 librarians are aged 45 or older, which is likely to result in many job openings over the next decade as many librarians retire. While recent increases in enrollment in library and information services graduate programs will prepare a sufficient number of new librarians to fill these positions, retirements will create a more steady state for the LIS job market. Opportunities for public school librarians, who are usually drawn from the ranks of teachers, should be particularly favorable.

Technical skills are increasingly important in this field and will no doubt open more job opportunities in all types of organizations, from a small city public library to a high profile software company. That said, don't rush out to learn all of the latest programming languages. It isn't expected that a library and information services professional have the technical skill set of a computer programmer. What is expected and highly sought after is a high level of understanding, comfort level and ability to work with technology, and familiarity with emerging technology trends. For example, being able to design a Web site or content management system that integrates Web 2.0 technology such as social networking capabilities, blogs, wikis, and RSS feeds to better meet the needs of users could make you more marketable, not only to libraries but to other types of organizations as well.

> ☑ QUICK FACT!
> Social networking is becoming a hot trend in the field.

While most professional library and information services jobs require a master's degree in library science, information science or related degree from an ALA (American Library Association) accredited institution, there are some opportunities for those with an associate's or bachelor's degree in any major. Take a look at some examples of jobs in library and information services.

The following job titles are typically associated with jobs requiring an associate's or bachelor's degree:

- Library Technician, City of Las Vegas (government)
- Library Assistant, University of Michigan Libraries (academic library)
- Information Services Technician, Abbott Labs (health care/pharmaceutical)
- Information Services Coordinator, OCLC Online Computer Library Center (nonprofit/research)

The following job titles are typically associated with jobs requiring a master's degree in library and information services or related degree from an ALA accredited program or school:

- Reference Librarian, Butzel Long Law Firm (corporate: legal)
- Senior Librarian, Federal Reserve Bank (corporate: financial services)
- Instruction Librarian, Texas A&M University Libraries (academic library)
- Media Specialist, Ann Arbor School District (K–12 school library)
- Science Librarian, Norris Medical Library (medical/research library)
- Information Scientist, Proctor & Gamble (corporate: health care)
- Children's Librarian, New York Public Library (public library)
- Systems/Technology Librarian, Yale University Libraries (academic library)
- Information Specialist, Sandia National Labs (government/defense)
- Information Architect, Travelocity (corporate: eCommerce)
- Research Analyst, Ernst & Young (corporate: consulting)
- Web Master, Clear Channel (entertainment/media)
- Usability Specialist, University of Michigan Digital Libraries (academic library)
- Branch Manager, Brooklyn Public Library (public library)

☑ QUICK FACT!
Master's level positions in some academic libraries are considered faculty and can be eligible for tenure.

The following job titles are typically associated with jobs requiring a PhD in library and information services, information, or related doctoral degree:

- Dean of Libraries, University of Maryland (university; academic library)
- Assistant /Associate Professor, University of Wisconsin (university; academic library)

Salary Information

Because the field of library and information services is strongly value-driven, salary is typically not the most critical factor for those pursuing this career field. That is not to say that there have not been impressive and well-deserved gains in salaries over the past ten years. These gains are due in large part to strong advocates in the field that have pushed for library salaries to reflect the level of professionalism,

> ☑ QUICK FACT!
> A career in library and information services could lead to a six-figure salary.

education, and service librarians provide to the community. As a matter of fact, those who accrue substantial experience in the field, have the appropriate educational credentials, and pursue high level management or faculty roles can expect six-figure salaries.

According to *U.S. News & World Report*, the median annual salary for the field of library and information services is $47,400 (Nemko, 2008). According to the Bureau of Labor Statistics, overall average salaries vary greatly in this field, ranging from $30,930–$74,760 or more (U.S. Department of Labor, Bureau of Labor Statistics, 2007). Most associate's or bachelor's degree level salaries will tend to fall on the lower end of this range, as will master's level salaries in small rural public libraries. Positions requiring a master's degree or PhD will typically yield salaries at the mid- to high-end of the range. Entry-level jobs at the master's level in academic and school libraries can expect salaries in the middle of this range. Because school librarian positions often require a teaching certificate and follow the structure of unionized school compensation plans, salaries tend to be slightly higher than the average.

Like any profession, there are variables that will have an impact on salary levels: geographic location, level of position, industry, type and size of organization, level of education, and skills required. Those with strong technical skills or with administrative duties and a master's degree from an ALA accredited school often have greater earnings. Higher salaries are reported in regions of the country where the cost of living tends to be higher, such as San Francisco (where average 2007 library salaries were reported at $64,400) compared with Philadelphia (with reported av-

---

AVERAGE SALARIES BY WORK SETTING/SECTOR
(U.S. DEPARTMENT OF LABOR, BUREAU OF LABOR STATISTICS, 2007)

- Federal government: $80,873
- Special library (corporate, medical, law, entertainment, publishing): $71,812
- Colleges, universities, and professional schools: $52,000
- Elementary and secondary schools: $50,710
- Local government: $44,960
- Public library: $41,334 (Davis and Grady, 2006) (Sosnowski, 2008)

erage salaries at $48,200), which has a lower cost of living index. Industries that yield higher salaries for librarians are in federal government and in the corporate sector. As you can see, there is quite a variance in salary levels in this field (Sosnowski, 2008; Davis and Grady, 2006).

There are many perks and benefits to working in this field that should be weighed equally, if not more than, salary. Involvement in professional associations is expected, and attending annual conferences is encouraged and supported in many libraries. The benefit of a good work/life balance can also be expected. While some evening and weekend hours may be required in some public and/or academic library settings, a 40 hour work week is typical. For those working in academic and school libraries, vacation days and breaks are plentiful. Telecommuting may be a possibility for those working in more research-related positions, which could include a position such as a research analyst for a consulting firm.

Given the great diversity of career options in library and information services, finding the right "fit" or "pathway" is possible for most anyone pursuing this field. Opportunities for advancement and/or for varied career pathways within or across libraries and other organizations provide career mobility for those who seek it, resulting in high levels of career satisfaction.

Profiles—Perspectives of New Professionals

Eric Frierson, Education and Political Science Librarian
University of Texas (Arlington)
Arlington, Texas

When I went to college at the University of Texas at Austin, I majored in computer science. However, three years in, despite getting great grades, I realized I liked computers because of how they could be used to help people—not because of the nuts and bolts inside of them. I ended up finishing the degree in computer science, but because I enjoyed writing and composition, I added a second major in English. I also became a certified teacher.

Upon graduation, I went to work at a school district in Dallas teaching students labeled "at risk." In this position, I learned how to engage and motivate students who traditionally struggled in school. All of this led to librarianship, a profession that is heavy in technology as it applies to information and learning, teaching, and a love of literature of all kinds.

As the Education and Political Science Librarian at the University of Texas at Arlington, I help staff our reference desk; I consult with students in my office, over e-mail, and in coffee shops; I work with faculty finding research relevant to their interests; I develop online learning tools; I teach library workshops to upper-undergraduate and graduate courses; I play with new technology; I evaluate information resources for purchase; and I share and "steal" new ideas from colleagues across the country.

At the University of Michigan (UM) School of Information, where I both worked and completed my master's degree, I was exposed to some of the greatest minds I have ever met—not just the instructors, but my classmates and coworkers at the UM Library.

The skills I deem most important to my position are teaching, active listening, assessment, understanding how computers "think," and understanding how humans learn. I love the teaching, the interactions with students learning to be lifelong learners, and the interactions with faculty investigating new ideas. I love being in a profession where people value creativity, drive, and progress. I love the connections I have with people all over the country who share a passion for the profession.

Yet, on the flip side, every job has its drawbacks. I am not a fan of statistics, and in an age where the value of libraries is increasingly in question, statistics are a necessary evil, even if they don't accurately reflect the impact a library has on a campus or a community. Other challenges exist, such as coping with a generation of college students who have grown up with Google—the computer savvy, but not information savvy generation—and redefining our role in the academy by developing expertise in technology, scholarly communication, publishing, and copyright.

For the student who is considering pursuing this path, I recommend focusing on improving communication skills. Be able to make sense of confusing things for others. Stay on top of the latest technologies. Enjoy helping others. Don't be too bookish—libraries aren't about books anymore; they're about knowing where to find information everywhere, including the hidden parts of the Internet that Google doesn't look through. And, the future librarian should be able to take abstract ideas and apply them to specific situations.

In the past, we were the organizers, collectors, and gatekeepers for information. Researchers relied on us to ensure they could find and access what they needed. We don't serve that role as much anymore—researchers can often find exactly what they need without stepping foot into a library. Libraries do very little original cataloging and less selection, thanks to widely available MARC records and vendor approval plans. Some roles we still have, such as helping people articulate an information need, helping them develop strategies to obtain what they need, and helping them understand how to use that information. We enable people to be lifelong learners. We're also developing new roles—those of technology experts, copyright and scholarly communication experts, usability testers, curriculum designers, and more. As new technology changes the information landscape, librarians will have to grapple with these changes and help users adapt.

Being at an institution of higher education has proven to provide job security, even during economic troubles. I started at a very competitive entry-level library salary at a major Tier 1 public institution when I started my professional career. In five or ten years, I hope to be running a department of my own, pulling in about $60k. (Frierson, 2008)

Jihae Hong, Coordinator of Library Training and Development
Brooklyn Public Library
New York, New York

Prior to receiving my MLS (master of library science degree), I worked at a gallery and an art museum and also as a freelance comic book translator. I realized I was really interested in public service, and since museums and galleries had a limited audience, I decided to become a public librarian. I started out as a librarian trainee while earning my MLS. As a trainee, I worked in branch libraries and on a large inventory project, and when I was done with the trainee program myself, I was asked to take over the program.

At the Brooklyn Public Library, we have about 350 librarians here, and I work to meet their training and learning needs, including some librarians who have subject matter expertise. I also take part in design and delivery of training. I organize a monthly Knowledge Seminar where we bring in internal or external experts to highlight topics that have relevance to urban public librarians such as immigration, homelessness, and consumer health. I also recruit entry-level librarians and coordinate rotations of our trainees and library-school interns.

As an undergraduate, I completed a double major in mathematics and English literature. I don't think much of what I learned as an undergraduate affects my work now, however. The important things that I learned in library school are the ethics and culture of the profession. Librarians are a peculiar bunch with pretty strong and particular ideas about democracy, intellectual freedom, equal access, and other related topics.

In regard to skills, I definitely need to have technical understanding of the systems we use and understand new databases and tools that we encourage our librarians to learn. For example, libraries are incorporating social networking tools to improve work processes. Through new tools like wikis, a new Web site, and sustained effort by the senior management, we have improved information sharing and communication with our 1,700+ staff and our public.

I also have to be a good presenter, an excellent communicator, and a nimble negotiator, and I need to be persuasive in an environment with limited resources. I think the most important part of my job is earning the trust of the librarians and trainees I work with and keeping that trust.

Our role in the community is not insignificant. We are tremendously important in Brooklyn. We are the connector of information and of cultures in a borough of 2.5 million working-class families, millionaires, celebrities, single moms, artists and writers, and immigrants from all over the world. Our libraries, on top of reflecting the diversity of life and experiences of our residents, provide access to worlds of information contained in books and other media.

Regarding the outlook for this particular career path, I don't think we will be replacing librarians at the rate they are retiring. Over the years, I think the profession will shed some services, and thus there will be more collaboration and less redundancy. In public libraries, I do think that we will be hiring librarians to manage programs and outreach but not at the rate that's being touted in magazine articles. I also think that trainee and internship programs are going to continue because there's a great emphasis on hands-on training nowadays.

Working or volunteering at your local branch can really help you understand if this is the right profession for you. Ask a librarian you know if you can speak with them—all of the librarians I know *love* giving out information and talking about what they do. (Hong, 2008)

Alisun DeKock, MLIS, Library Services Manager
John G. Shedd Aquarium
McCormick Foundation Library
Chicago, Illinois

While completing my undergraduate degree in English literature and French from Adrian College, I worked at the campus library. After college I worked for a law library outsourcing firm in Chicago for five years, four as a supervisor. Ready for a change, I had been volunteering at the Adler Planetarium for a couple of years and enjoyed it, so I applied to become their volunteer manager.

At Adler I discovered how much I appreciated the nonprofit world of museums and cultural institutions. I liked the people I worked with, the unique opportunities and perks, and the feeling that I contributed positively to society. I also realized that I missed the library field. I applied to University of Illinois at Urbana-Champaign's Graduate School of Library and Information Science distance learning program (LEEP), was accepted, and completed the program while working full time at the planetarium.

When I learned of the open position in the John G. Shedd Aquarium's McCormick Foundation Research Library, I jumped at it. Having worked independently in my first job and succeeded in a one-person department at the Planetarium, I knew I would thrive as a solo librarian at Shedd.

As a solo librarian, I need to know how to do every task any librarian does. My daily tasks include processing new periodicals, collection development, research projects, coordinating interlibrary loan, cataloging, maintaining the intranet page, and training the staff on using the library. In addition to daily tasks, I am in charge of creating and managing an archive to house the history of Shedd Aquarium. I am also in charge of my least favorite activity related to the library: budgeting and navigating necessary accounting regulations.

Having experience at another cultural institution gave me an important advantage in getting this job. The concerns of any cultural organization, whether it is a zoo, museum, historical home, or aquarium are similar. We worry about tourism, funding, education, and research just to name a few. My experience with those issues in a museum setting transferred easily to my position at the aquarium. I think the most important ability to have in this job and probably for any solo librarian is being willing to learn something new all the time, even if you have to teach yourself.

Working in a cultural institution offers a number of unique opportunities. We are the first to know about new exhibits and shows coming to the Chicago museum community. Employees and volunteers get free general admission to many other Chicago museums and sometimes even throughout the country. As a librarian, I get to read magazines and books for my job, which I think is a huge perk.

Cultural organizations are not immune to economic downturns; its effects trickle down to the library budget and the ability to renew subscriptions and purchase books. This is a small library; I cannot provide extensive electronic journal access like a university. Interlibrary loans can take time and our staff, especially in animal care, may not be able to wait. Short turnaround times on research requests are a priority.

My suggestion for those interested in a career like mine is to volunteer for a library in your area. Many libraries will have volunteer opportunities available, allowing you to not only get a glimpse into the field but also to give back to your community at the same time.

In nonprofit work, it's important to keep an open mind not only about what your tasks are but what other roles you could fill for your organization when needed. This not only provides new learning opportunities but can lead to pay increases as well.

I feel lucky to work for an organization that prioritizes conservation education and environmental stewardship. Part of our mission is to "inspire you to make a difference." Our staff takes that mission seriously, both outwardly toward our constituents and internally by staff actions and decisions made each day. I support our mission and goals through my work by providing meaningful and timely information to our staff. I hope that our message has an impact on our visitors, helping them connect to the living world in new and exciting ways. (DeKock, 2008)

Careers in Library and Information Services: At a Glance

Your career in library and information services can take many directions as you connect your interests and values to the type of functional area and type of organization that you pursue. Here are a few examples of real jobs from recent position announcements representing some exciting "tracks" you can follow.

Corporate Track
Business Information Searcher
Procter & Gamble (P&G)
Cincinnati, Ohio

Serve as a member of a global team of information professionals who support P&G business/commercial personnel around the world in their business, financial, and marketing information research needs; provide comprehensive and complex business research and analysis using online, intranet, and Internet databases; analyze and synthesize research results, prepare value-added reports, and provide actionable recommendations; track competitor and industry trends for clients in P&G global business units. (Procter & Gamble, accessed 2009)

Media/Entertainment Track
Reference Librarian
National Public Radio
Washington, DC

Provide research for daily news stories and longer term projects using online sources, public records databases, and the Internet; refer customers to appropriate searches and conduct in-depth research and comprehensive literature searches while evaluating and organizing/synthesizing the results for customers; train customers in the use of library resources. (National Public Radio, 2008)

Green Track
Media-Assets Cataloger
Sierra Club
San Francisco, California

Support the club's public and internal communications programs and library by providing access to electronic content materials, for reference and reuse; work on a content management program encompassing an overall media-asset management initiative; develop the protocol and categories for the system and manage records for an expanding number of media assets; create and use metadata and content classification using taxonomies; capture, electronically catalogue, and make available Sierra Club print, graphic, video, audio, and other media assets using asset-management software. (Sierra Club, 2009)

Global Track
Librarian/Documentalist
International Association of Universities (IAU)
Paris, France

Manage and process publications and documents received and online search for information and documents to meet the needs of the association's secretariat; maintain the bibliographical database on higher education (HEDBIB) and create and disseminate subproducts such as acquisition lists; assist in the updating of the database on higher education systems and institutions worldwide (WHED); liaise and build exchange networks with research centers on higher education. (International Association of Universities, 2009)

Resources for Further Information/Exploration

The following resources can help guide you in your career exploration within the field of library and information services. Note that this is not a comprehensive list; there are numerous resources available related to the nuances of the field that are not included. The purpose of identifying key job posting sites and professional organizations is to make you aware of some of the main resources available and to also provide you with gateways to resources that will inform you of the types of careers available in the field.

Professional Organizations Relevant to Library and Information Services

- ALA—American Library Association
  www.ala.org

- ALA Divisions Listings
  www.ala.org/al/Amgrps/divs/divisions.cfm
  - American Association of School Librarians (AASL)
  - Association for Library Collections and Technical Services (ALCTS)
  - Association of College and Research Libraries (ACRL)
  - Association for Library Service to Children (ALSC)
  - Association of Library Trustees, Advocates, Friends and Foundations
  - Association of Specialized and Cooperative Library Agencies (ASCLA)
  - Library Administration and Management Association (LAMA)
  - Library and Information Technology Association (LITA)
  - Public Library Association (PLA)
  - Reference and User Services Association (RUSA)
  - The Young Adult Library Services Association (YALSA)
- AALL—American Association of Law Libraries
  www.aallnet.org/index.asp
- AAHSL—Association of Academic Health Sciences Libraries
  www.aahsl.org
- ALISE—Association of Library and Information Science Education
  www.alise.org
- ARLIS-NA—Art Libraries Society of North America
  www.arlisna.org
- AMIA—American Medical Informatics Association
  www.amia.org
- ASIST—American Society for Information Science and Technology
  www.asis.org
- MLA—Medical Library Association
  www.mlanet.org
- MLA—Music Library Association
  www.musiclibraryassoc.org
- SLA—Special Libraries Association
  www.sla.org

Career Sites Relevant to Library and Information Services

- American Library Association Job List
  http://joblist.ala.org

- Medical Library Association Jobs
  www.mlanet.org/jobs
- Special Libraries Association Career Center
  http://careercenter.sla.org/search
- American Association of Law Libraries Job Hotline
  www.aallnet.org/hotline
- Art Libraries Society of North America Job Net
  www.arlisna.org/jobnet.html
- Association of Research Libraries Career Resources
  http://careers.arl.org
- Global Museum—Museum Jobs
  www.globalmuseum.org
- LibJobs.com
  www.libjobs.com
- Library Journal Job Zone
  http://jobs.libraryjournal.com
- Music Library Association Job Openings
  www.musiclibraryassoc.org/employmentanded/joblist/openings.shtml
- Chronicle of Higher Education—Chronicle Careers
  http://chronicle.com/jobs
- Visual Resources Association Job Opportunities
  www.vraweb.org/jobopps.html

Education and Training

The vast majority of professional librarian positions require a master's degree in library and information services (you'll also see programs called library and information studies or library and information science) from a program or school that is accredited by the American Library Association. You may apply to these graduate programs with any undergraduate major. For a listing of accredited graduate degree programs, visit www.ala.org/ala/educationcareers/education/accredited programs/index.cfm. There are a wide variety of programs available in terms of length (one to two years), format (e.g., campus based or distance/online), and focus or approach (such as interdisciplinary approach or emphasis on practical experience as part of the curriculum).

Be sure to examine a number of programs to determine the best fit for you. While some libraries (e.g., rural or urban areas facing a shortage of candidates) may be open to hiring individuals with alternative degrees and experience, to be well prepared for success and advancement in the field, an accredited graduate degree is essential.

To best prepare for a career as a subject specialist, which is a librarian specializing in a content area such as archaeology, chemistry, or American history, obtaining a master's degree in the subject area as well as a master's in library and information services can be important. To advance to leadership posts in a subject area, a PhD in that subject is often preferred. Career opportunities in special libraries can also be strengthened by obtaining the relevant professional degree. For example, for positions and/or advancement in a law library, it would be beneficial to obtain a JD (Juris Doctor) in addition to the master's in library and information services. A number of graduate schools offer dual or joint degrees that allow a student to obtain two degrees in less time through a combined or coordinated curriculum.

One can find employment in a library with a bachelor's or associate's degree. These positions are typically considered paraprofessional and advancement will be limited. Still, gaining experience in a library setting is an excellent way to determine if this is the right career path for you. Such experience can also strengthen one's application to a graduate program. Libraries will be open to hiring any major, though if you seek employment in a specialized library, certain majors could be helpful. For example, if you majored in biology, that could be an asset if you were to seek employment as a paraprofessional in a life sciences library within a university. Building technical skills as part of your undergraduate studies, in particular with Web 2.0 technologies, will be an asset for paraprofessional library positions as well as good preparation for graduate study in library and information services.

Majoring in education or otherwise obtaining a teaching certificate in your undergraduate degree would be beneficial for those planning to pursue the school library media path, since a teaching certificate is typically required to work as a school librarian. However, some graduate programs offer a means to obtain the teaching certificate as part of a school library media curriculum.

Educational requirements for school media specialists/school librarians vary by state. In some states, school librarians must have a master's in library science including specialized school media coursework as well as a teaching certificate. In other states, students can obtain an undergraduate degree in library science along with a teaching certification to obtain positions as school librarians, with the expectation of obtaining a master's in library science within three years.

While the number of undergraduate programs in library science has decreased over the years, there are a growing number of bachelor's degree programs in information science and informatics. While these majors are not required for paraprofessional library positions, they are options to consider and would open opportunities for other sorts of information-focused jobs as well. In particular, the growth in informatics undergraduate programs points to the overall continued development of information as an academic field and is already becoming a more focused path to prepare for graduate study in information.

References

Davis, Denise M., and Jenifer Grady. 2006. *ALA-APA Salary Survey: Librarian—Public and Academic.* Chicago: ALA-APA.

DeKock, Alisun. 2008. Interview by Kelly Kowatch. December 23.

Frey, Thomas. 2009. "Future Libraries: Nerve Center of the Community." FuturistSpeaker.com, February 22. Available: www.futuristspeaker.com/2009/02/future-libraries-nerve-center-of-the-community/ (accessed August 14, 2009).

Frierson, Eric. 2008. Interview by Kelly Kowatch. December 4.

Hong, Jihae. 2008. Interview by Kelly Kowatch. December 19.

International Association of Universities. 2009. "LIBJOBs Archives." LIBJOBs, January 9. Available: http://infoserv.inist.fr/wwsympa.fcgi/arc/libjobs/2009-01/msg00014.html (accessed August 14, 2009).

Jesella, Kara. 2007. "A Hipper Crowd of Shushers." *New York Times,* July 8. Available: www.nytimes.com/2007/07/08/fashion/08librarian.html (accessed December 23, 2008).

Kavanaugh, K. Nadine. "America's 10 Coolest Public Libraries." MSN City Guides. Available: http://cityguides.msn.com/citylife/cityarticle.aspx?cp-documentid=10444020&page=4 (accessed January 30, 2009).

National Public Radio. 2008. "Careers at NPR." Online application process. Available: http://hostedjobs.openhire.com/epostings/submit.cfm?fuseaction=app.allpositions&company_id=15859&version=1 (accessed October 31, 2008).

Nemko, Marty. 2008. "Best Careers 2009: Librarian." *U.S. News & World Report,* December 11. Available: www.usnews.com/articles/business/best-careers/2008/12/11/best-careers-2009-librarian.html (accessed August 14, 2009).

Procter & Gamble. "Find a Job and Apply." Available: www.pg.com/jobs/sectionmain.shtml (accessed August 14 , 2009).

Sierra Club. 2009. "Sierra Club Careers." Available: www.sierraclub.org/careers/communications/media-assets-cataloger.asp (accessed August 14, 2009).

Sosnowski, Carolyn. 2008. "2008 Salary Survey and Workplace Study." Special Libraries Association, January 5. Available: www.sla.org/content/resources/research/salarysurveys/salsur2008/index.cfm (accessed August 14, 2009).

U.S. Department of Labor, Bureau of Labor Statistics. 2007. "Librarians." *Occupational Outlook Handbook,* 2008–2009 ed. Available: www.bls.gov/oco/ocos068.htm (accessed August 14, 2009).

Additional Source

Wikipedia. "Search Results: Library Services Skills." Available: http://en.wikipedia.org/w/index.php?title=Special%3ASearch&redirs=1&search=library+services+skills&fulltext=Search&ns0=1 (accessed November 2008).

Chapter 4

Human–Computer Interaction

Introduction

Human–computer interaction (HCI) specialists are architects of technology, designing interfaces and user experiences as bridges between human needs and technological solutions. Rather than focusing on technology for its own sake or creating technology first and expecting people to adapt to it, human–computer interaction is a field that focuses on the user, developing solutions that fit the needs of people, considering their behavior and preferences and the context of their situation. Any technical solution created by one person will be inherently biased. Those who pursue a career in HCI learn strategies and techniques to understand and evaluate human needs as objectively as possible, creating design and technical specifications that enable seamless and effortless functionality. Certainly, achieving functionality for a wide range of users is no small feat.

Have you ever opened a new Web page and, after several clicks that don't lead you to what you need, surfed to another site? Has the functionality of a new game or upgraded piece of software left you wondering "Who made this so awkward to use?" Most of us have experienced the challenges of usability, of the level of intuitive functionality of systems, software, Web sites, or products. Talk to family and friends and your list of examples of system flaws and product quirks will quickly grow. Take for example the Amazon Kindle 2. Touted as an improvement to the first Kindle, Wired.com featured a story on users' frustrations with the upgraded version. While the new Kindle offered a thinner, faster product, contrast issues in the text display made it difficult for some users to read text, as with the earlier model. Hundreds of people posted concerns to Amazon or relevant blogs. Yet many users were fine with the text display (Ganapati, 2009). Already there is a new e-reader on the market—Barnes and Noble's Nook, which offers a dual screen with both black and white text display and a color touch screen with browsing capability. With built-in Wi-Fi, an MP3 player, and more, it may well give Kindle some keen competition; time will tell as users put the Nook to the test.

This is the opportunity and the challenge of usability—what is usable for one person is not for the next. Maximizing usability and offering flexible options that enhance usability for individual users is an important aspect of the field of human–computer interaction. Yet it is just one part. The Computer–Human Interaction Interest Group within the Association for Computing Machinery suggests the following working definition of this exciting field: "Human–computer interaction is a discipline concerned with the design, evaluation, and implementation of interactive computing systems for human use and with the study of major phenomena surrounding them" (Hewett et al., 2008).

A blend of cognitive psychology, computer science, engineering, anthropology, and design (and related fields), human–computer interaction focuses on the user and the context of the entire situation that relates to the user and a technology system, tool, or product. The HCI field applies to individual, group, and organizational levels, and includes assessment of needs, design of technology-based solutions, and facilitation of technology adoption and integration to accomplish individual, group, or organizational goals. While many HCI professionals work with software systems and Web interfaces, as technology is embedded into an increasing array of products, they may work with technology within cars, cell phones, kitchen appliances, video games, medical devices, and more, not to mention products or systems not yet imagined.

As technology access and use continues to expand, there are myriad opportunities to focus on particular populations (such as youth or seniors), industries (such as travel and tourism or health and medicine), or format (such as Web sites, mobile devices, or collaborative technologies). Still another specialty area is adaptive technology, which involves creating technology that is accessible for those with disabilities such as visual or hearing impairments.

In the past decade we have witnessed a rapid and exciting evolution of technological advances that have created a rich environment and a heightened need for professionals who specialize in human–computer interaction. These developments have included ubiquitous communication, high functionality systems, mixed media, high-bandwidth interaction, thin displays, embedded computation, group interfaces, and user-tailored functionality (Hewett et al., 2008). In other words, we have seen the progression toward smaller, faster devices that give us rich access to information in most any location, with that information being of high resolution and including words, images, and sound, including tools that allow for information sharing or collaboration and that allow individual users to customize functionality according to individual preferences.

Yet another perspective is expressed by a review of "10 Great Geek Gadgets, Past & Future" on WebUrbanist, a blog focused on culture, design, and art:

> Geeks are living in a golden age—the geeky gadgets we love get smaller, cheaper, and more capable by the day! Cell phones have evolved so fast even last year's models are already un-cool. Go back a few more years—or watch most any '90's sitcom like Seinfeld, and you will be reminded of how things used to be. (WebUrbanist, 2009)

Go back even farther—to the 1970s, and you'll be amazed to see the brick style cell phones (literally the size and shape of a brick) that first came onto the market (WebUrbanist, 2009).

Look into the future, and cell phones are likely to continue to decrease in size, with one prototype featuring small Velcro bands to circle the thumb and pinky finger and a thin phone with number pad and display strapping to the back of one's hand, and another affixing to the palm of one's hand (WebUrbanist, 2009). Currently, developers are exploring the use of mixed and augmented reality to take cell phone functionality to new levels. Researchers at Nokia have created a smartphone that can be pointed toward any location, retrieve geographical coordinates of nearby landmarks, and enable users to retrieve information about locations of interest such as a museum or restaurant (Jonietz, 2007).

Technology advancement is happening so fast it can be hard to keep up—but this is good news for those working in the field of HCI. In the gaming industry, researchers have made a breakthrough in their work on thought controlled games, with the Emotive EPOC headset offering the first Brain–Computer Interface (BCI) for the gaming market, suggesting the future potential for virtual worlds and simulated environments that are increasingly similar to real world experiences (Steere, 2008). Meanwhile, Mozilla Labs has developed Aurora, a concept for the next iteration of the Internet which would remember an individual's patterns of use over time and provide a richly personalized Internet experience. Other technologies in development include a wearable gesture interface for virtual reality applications, and Siftables, which are mini computers that fit in the palm of your hand and allow individuals on screen to interact with one another (DesignReviver, 2009).

Human–computer interaction professionals often work in product engineering or marketing on new products or systems or on upgrades and new versions. They collaborate with engineers and programmers throughout the system or product

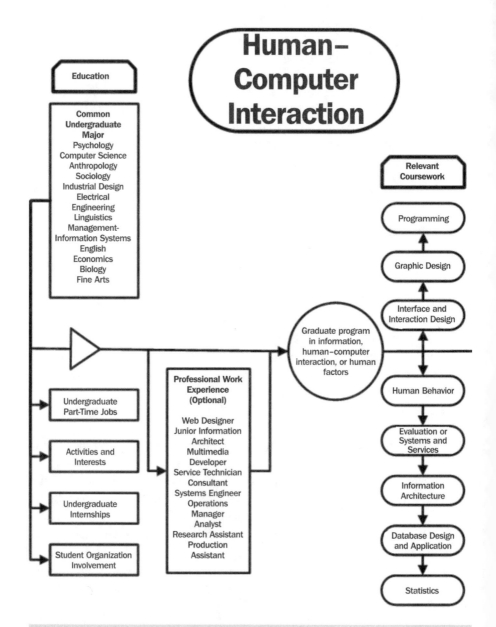

Figure 4. Human–Computer Interaction Career Map
This diagram demonstrates several of the potential paths associated with a career in the field of human–computer interaction.

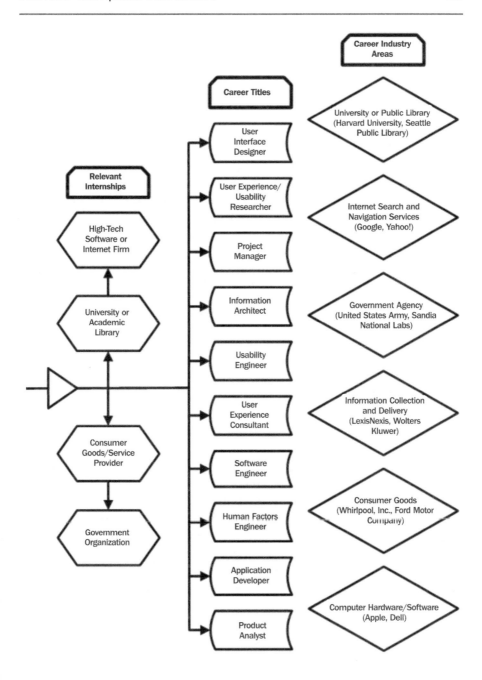

development cycle, conducting user research to inform design, or designing proto-types that incorporate desired functionality. As the product development cycle continues, HCI professionals conduct user testing in labs and in the field and con-tinue to guide the product to its launch. Some will break out on their own as entre-preneurs if they come up with the next big idea or start niche consulting firms. There are also opportunities for HCI work in universities, K–12 education, gov-ernment, consulting, and nonprofit organizations. Those who pursue a PhD could work in corporate research or may pursue a career in academia. While an increas-ing number of people know how to publish a Web site on the Internet, the HCI pro-fessional can create and manage large, complex Web sites that may feature interactivity, multimedia, ecommerce, or all of these and more. They are aware of industry standards for site design as well as for security, privacy, and archiving. Or-ganizations and individuals are using the Internet in increasingly sophisticated ways and need the expertise of trained HCI experts for information architecture, user-experience design, and usability engineering. Think of major Web sites like Amazon, Travelocity, WebMD, and eBay, and you can begin to appreciate the impact and importance of the field of human–computer interaction.

HCI professionals who focus on group or organizational technology needs rather than products and services for individuals guide organizations to effectively integrate new technology to enhance productivity. One of the biggest challenges to organizational technology deployment is helping workers effectively adopt the new technology into their daily practice. Rather than start with the technology it-self, the HCI professional would analyze the needs of the organization and the indi-vidual workers to identify what the issues are and then would choose, adapt, and deploy technology to achieve optimal results. The growth of global work teams has expanded the practice of computer-supported cooperative work, in which technol-ogy that enables real time communication for employees in distant locations is developed and deployed, making distance collaboration increasingly effective.

Some may consider the field of human–computer interaction as fitting better into a book on careers in computer science rather than a book about careers in in-formation. Yet from our perspective, HCI is a perfect fit within the field of infor-mation. The information profession is commonly described as connecting people, information, and technology. Essentially, the interaction of people and computers or computing systems involves information. Information transmitted through technology includes words, numbers, images, sounds—and who knows, maybe someday even smells.

The vast amount of information in the world continues to grow exponentially. The field of HCI is increasingly important as a means to harness information, using technology as a tool, to provide people with quick and easy access to quality information and just the right amount for their needs. This information could be for convenience, such as using an application on an iPhone to identify ingredients needed for a recipe, or be of life or death importance, such as a medical records system that provides quick access to a patient's medical history in the emergency room. Many other information professionals (including librarians, archivists, and search engineers) utilize techniques and concepts of human–computer interaction in their work, and as such the field of human–computer interaction makes an important contribution to the information profession.

Skills and Abilities

For any professional career field, there are required skills and abilities that are important for success. In the field of human–computer interaction (HCI), the right skills and abilities will make you more marketable for a variety of exciting professional positions in a wide range of industries and will provide you with the tool kit for success in landing your dream job.

While positions in HCI vary as far as skill level, experience, and education required, there are common skills, abilities, and characteristics that are highly sought for any type of professional HCI position in any industry.

Outlined in the following sections are both the soft skills and abilities (behavioral/personality traits and characteristics) and hard skills and abilities (technical and career-specific knowledge) that are important for success in the field of HCI. Note that these are the most common skills and abilities; this is certainly not an exhaustive list of all of the valuable skills and abilities that are beneficial for this career field.

> ☑ QUICK FACT!
> HCI professionals must like working with people and have a passion for understanding human behavior.

Soft Skills
- Ability to work in collaboration/be a team player
- Analytical/problem-solving skills
- Ability to communicate (written, verbal, and listening), to achieve:
  - Persuasion
  - Negotiation
  - Empathy
- Motivated/enthusiastic approach to work
- Ability to be creative

- Flexibility/adaptability
- Ability to be entrepreneurial-minded/innovative

Hard Skills

- Evaluation: Observe (and learn from) users as they work with a product before, during, and after the design and development process.
- User experience research: Learn about the people who will use a product and the context in which it will be used.
- Heuristic evaluation: Identify problems associated with the design of user interfaces.
- Contextual inquiry: Observe product use in a field environment.
- Usability testing: Test prototypes on an actual user—often asking the user to talk about his or her thoughts during the experience.
- Interaction design: Define the behavior of products and systems with which a user can interact.
- User analysis: Evaluate the potential users of a system.
- Technical skills (not all are required, but some are helpful and can make you more marketable):
  - Web languages: AJAX, CSS, XML, HTML, PHP
  - Programming languages: Java, Perl, Ruby on Rails
  - Content management systems: Drupal, Joomla, Wordpress
  - Databases: SQL, MySQL, Access, Excel
  - Graphics editing/design: Photoshop, Illustrator, Flash, Visio
- Business management: Learn and understand complex business technologies, business and technical aspects of the Web, working knowledge of industry standards.

☑ QUICK FACT!
A technical background is not always required. Successful HCI professionals must be creative problem solvers, independent of any specific technology.

Overall, the HCI profession seems to be unifying around two career tracks specializing in either research or design-related positions. Those drawn to the research side must have the interest and skills to study and evaluate people in order to inform design. For those drawn to design, they will use their creativity and skills to create prototypes and figure out what ought to be built.

The core of the field of HCI is an understanding of the user and what they need to do and achieve. It is important to have an intrinsic interest and high level of curiosity of people and how they think and behave. Being an effective communicator, listener, and problem solver are critical skills. For example, one must be able to understand not only when it is useful to carry out focus groups, interviews, and/or observations, but also how to carry them out effectively. This is easier said than done and is why real-world experience is crucial to becoming an effective HCI professional. Furthermore, a successful HCI professional is required to speak the language of all stakeholders from diverse groups, from the users, to the programmers, to the designers and business managers. Thus, effective communication skills are essential (Bonard, accessed 2009).

Since the field of HCI is rapidly changing, "soft" skills are sometimes valued even more by employers than specific technical or "hard" skills. It is important to develop transferable skills such as a commitment to learning, problem solving, and critical thinking skills, effective teamwork, a sense of professionalism, and the ability to handle stress and deadlines. These skills are often developed over time and

KEY WORDS TO KNOW

Here are some basic HCI terms that you will see throughout this chapter. For those interested in pursuing this career field, it's a good idea to be familiar with their meaning:

- **usability**: The degree to which something—software, hardware, or anything else—is easy to use and a good fit for the people who use it.
- **user experience design**: A key methodology for carrying out usability. It is about designing the *total user experience*, which consists of all aspects of a product or service as perceived by users.
- **user interface/user design**: The design of systems (Web site, application or device) with the focus on the user's experience and interaction. Goal is to make the user's interaction as simple and efficient as possible.
- **information architecture**: The blueprint that describes how information is organized and structured.
- **human factors**: Involves the study of all aspects of the way humans relate to the world around them.
- **ergonomics**: A discipline that involves arranging the environment to fit the person in it.
- **ubiquitous/pervasive computing**: Technology use that interfaces seamlessly with an individual's daily activities.

are not gained easily. Because they are transferable skills, they easily transcend particular domains of knowledge, which is critical in having the ability to adapt to a world in which change and global cooperation and collaboration are the norm in most industries hiring HCI professionals. Probably the most important factor to success in the field is the ability to think rigorously and have relentless curiosity about how to make products more user friendly.

Specifically, big-picture thinking is critical. HCI professionals need to gain skills and experience in a variety of areas of the entire task and work environment in which systems will be used; they need to deal with constraints and tradeoffs, such as limits on resources and social and organizational pressures; they need to handle work flow, task, and organizational analysis and design; and show teamwork and reflection (Strong, 1994).

Professional Roles

> ☑ QUICK FACT!
> A good HCI professional has a genuine curiosity about how users think and behave.

To better understand the role of HCI professionals, including how they approach their work, it may help to compare and contrast the duties and goals of the most common career pathways. Common duties that cross over most of the widespread jobs include putting others at ease while maintaining objectivity, moderating a focus group, being a good listener, and showing a true interest in people. An overarching theme in many of the HCI career pathways is user-centered design. Generally speaking, some specialize in conducting usability tests or other user research while others practice usability as part of other responsibilities in designing products, services, software applications, or Web sites (Usability Professionals Association, 2009).

- **User Experience Researcher versus Psychologist**
  User experience researchers hunt for an understanding of what it's like to be a member of their target population. Their job is to uncover stories about their users that would be interesting to the designers while accurately portraying the users.
  Psychologists acquire and focus on more generalized knowledge about how humans behave by uncovering abstract facts about human behavior.
- **User Interface Designer versus Graphic Designer**
  User interface designers aim to make the user's interaction as simple and efficient as possible, in terms of accomplishing goals.

Graphic designers seek to make the object or application physically attractive. They plan, analyze, and create visual solutions to communication problems.

- **Web Designer versus Information Architect**
  Web designers focus more on the brilliant use of color, typography, and texture to convey a message.
  Information architects look at the structure of the site from a more objective position and take all perspectives into account while creating certain deliverables: business, technological, and social (user).

Occupational Outlook

U.S. News & World Report selected the field of HCI/usability as one of the best careers in 2009, based on criteria such as job outlook, average job satisfaction, difficulty of the required training, prestige, and pay (Wolgemuth, 2008). Because new, complex products and rapid advances in technology demand the HCI mind-set, not surprisingly, the job outlook for HCI specialists is strong.

☑ QUICK FACT!
Interaction design is poised to become one of the main liberal arts of the twenty-first century (McCullough, 2004).

Many HCI professionals can be found in software and hardware corporations. Other settings include usability consulting firms, advertising agencies, design firms, nonprofit, government/military, or educational institutions. Industries that are showing the most growth right now are health care, government, energy, and green technology. HCI professionals can count on an increased need for their skills in these industries soon.

HCI professionals will typically find themselves being recruited into the marketing or engineering departments within an organization. Within marketing, this role is to ensure a positive customer experience or to improve or defend the organization's brand. Within engineering, this role is more to ensure that the product works properly; will there be bugs that will end up costing more later on? Corporate research departments also recruit HCI professionals, but they are typically staffed by PhD level researchers.

Some of the hottest industries right now are social networking and gaming. As three-dimensional virtual worlds and social networking sites (Blogs, Wikis, Facebook, MySpace, Second Life, and Twitter) continue to grow exponentially, the related career options in these spaces will grow as well. While these technologies improve and more people explore the medium, new and more complex usability challenges will need to be addressed; thus, an increased need for HCI professionals is sure to follow (Nemko, 2007).

☑ QUICK FACT!
Growing opportunities can be found in entertainment, health care, and defense/intelligence.

Positions in research and in academia are fewer and more difficult to come by as so much depends on funding sources, successful grant applications, and availability of academic posts. Industry indicates an ever growing need for more talented HCI professionals. As the importance of HCI has increased in the past decade, the need for students prepared to enter this field has grown as well.

A potential downside of this career is that some companies believe that they can make products without a specifically trained usability expert, so you may have to spend considerable time justifying your service's value. Another drawback is that you may need to make efforts to avoid being typecast as someone who can help design only one kind of product. Despite these challenges, most HCI professionals have high levels of career satisfaction by continually creating systems and products that are easier and thus a pleasure to use, making people's lives easier.

The following is a list of some of the most common HCI job titles and industries that actively recruit HCI professionals (bachelor's and master's level):

- User Experience Researcher, Google (Internet)
- Usability Engineer, Intel Corporation (hardware/IT)
- User Experience Consultant, Booz Allen Hamilton (strategy/technology consulting)
- User Interface Designer, Facebook (social networking)
- Junior Information Architect, Avenue A|Razorfish (interactive marketing/advertising)
- Information Architect, Kaiser Permanente (health care)
- Human Factors Engineer, Lockheed Martin (aerospace/defense)

Other closely related job titles include the following:

- Web Designer: Responsible for the layout, visual appearance, and usability of a Web site
- Technical Writer: Designs, writes, creates, maintains, and updates technical documentation for technical, business, and consumer audiences
- Graphic Designer: Designs and specifies the visible details of a graphic product

- Software Analyst: Problem solve and plan for a software solution
- Market Researcher: Researches information about markets, target markets, and their needs, competitors, market trends, customer satisfaction with products and services, etc.
- Instructional Designer: Creates instructional tools and content to help facilitate learning most effectively. The process consists broadly of determining the current state and needs of the learner
- Industrial Designer: Creates and executes design solutions toward problems of form, usability, user ergonomics, engineering, marketing, brand development, and sales
- Cognitive Psychologist: Focus on human learning, memory, perception, and problem solving, which lends itself well to applications in human–computer interaction
- Ergonomist: Studies human capabilities in relationship to their work demands

While a bachelor's degree certainly qualifies one for most HCI jobs, many organizations prefer or desire an advanced degree (master's or PhD). Faster career advancement into positions such as usability manager, user experience lead, and user research director will typically require an advanced degree. Many

> ☑ QUICK FACT!
> While a master's degree in HCI can *enhance* your ability to get hired, the *key* to getting hired is practical experience.

HCI professionals hold degrees in human factors, psychology, human–computer interaction, industrial engineering, ergonomics, or computer science. Other educational backgrounds include business administration or management, library science, technical communications, graphic design, fine arts, and other social sciences.

It is important to note that in this field, experience is as important as education. Some industries actually value it more. Research indicates that user behavior is remarkably consistent over the years; therefore, the more you have seen and experienced in the workplace, the more accurate your judgments and predictions of future user behavior (Oshlyansky et al., 2007). This places a substantial premium on the value of experience and is why most HCI-related job descriptions require one to two years of experience, even for entry-level positions. While a master's degree is often preferred, the degree alone does not take the place of work experience. Even for master's-level positions, a few years of experience is typically required, while an advanced degree is often preferred.

Salary Information

HCI job salaries have been on the rise over the past few years. According to the *Usability Professionals Association (UPA) 2007 Salary Survey*, the overall average salary of HCI professionals was reported at $83,297. Since 2005, salaries have increased by about $5,000. Increases were seen in all industries and work settings as well as in educational and employment levels (Usability Professionals Association, 2008).

In 2008, entry-level (bachelor's degree, less than a year of experience) salaries for HCI professionals were at $45,901. HCI or usability professionals with 5+ years of professional experience (bachelor's or master's degree) earned about $89,000. The premium on experience in the field has increased in recent years. In 2007, it was about $5,800 per year of experience (Nielsen, 2006).

While advanced education, such as a master's degree in HCI or related field, will yield a higher salary, years of experience in the field tend to result in the highest reported salaries.

- 0–1 years of experience (bachelor's degree): $45,901, junior or entry-level positions
- 2–4 years of experience (bachelor's or master's degree): $61,612
- 5–7 years of experience (bachelor's degree, master's preferred): $82,822, assistant directors, mid-management level positions
- 8–10 years of experience (master's degree or PhD): $97,271, director, manager, lead, and senior-level positions
- 10+ years of experience (master's degree or PhD): low to mid-six figures, director, vice president, principal, senior lead, senior manager-level positions

Profiles—Perspectives of New Professionals

Josh Palay, Interaction Designer
America Online (AOL)
Dulles, Virginia

My path has been a circuitous one. I began with an undergraduate degree in music composition, music theory, and aesthetics from the University of Michigan. After graduating, I worked as a composer and was fortunate to receive a Fulbright Scholarship to Rome for a year. This was the first time after leaving academia where I could fully grasp some of the sacrifices that I would need to make as a musician and a chance to reevaluate my priorities for the future, and so I began looking for a different direction. No matter what direction I was going to choose, it became clear to me that I was going to need a master's degree.

Though I had originally looked to focus on information in migrant communities, through the core classes at the University of Michigan School of Information (SI), I found myself immediately drawn to the human–computer interaction discussions and classes. Leveraging what I learned in my classes, I was offered an internship at Google. After graduating, I accepted a position as an interaction designer at American Online, and this is where I am currently after working for a faculty member as a researcher for a short period.

Overall, my job is best described as being the advocate or ombudsman for the people who come to AOL's pages. I am responsible for designing the information architecture of the pages, finding usability issues within currently deployed pages, and reviewing new visual design to make sure that they appropriately match the vision of the usability team. Additionally, I work with small teams to look for new, innovative, and helpful modules or projects that we could deploy in our pages. Our group defines the layout and presentation of information on AOL's pages, building the core architecture and interaction potentials. It is the skeleton that the development team builds and the structure on which the visual designs are placed. The pages we create become the main source of revenue for the company, so they are treated by management with a great deal of importance.

AOL is currently going through a huge directional change from a service provider to a content provider. As such, there is large emphasis on having solid information architecture and strong usability principles underlying the development. However, there is a parallel and at times conflicting motivation to monetize the AOL properties with ads and sponsorship. Finding the balance between these two issues is at the core of what we are doing currently.

I really love when I can champion a really helpful and innovative feature into one of the products. What is not my favorite is when upper management does not see the same vision as the design team and pushes through products that have poor or even harmful aspects from a user-experience perspective.

The skills I learned in my graduate degree, which included usability testing and interface design, are key to my current job. However, the creativity and problem-solving skills I developed from my undergraduate degree in music composition have been very helpful as well. Furthermore, the ability to convincingly argue your point is one of the most important skills one can have. Similarly, the ability to see the motivations behind other viewpoints is essential. To become a really competitive candidate, I would say it is very nice also to have a skill set that is considered to be a double (user experience and visual design) or triple threat (user experience design, visual design, and programming).

My advice to someone considering this field would be to try to learn as much as you can in a variety of skill sets. The more skills you have (e.g., Photoshop, design interfaces, run usability tests, program in a variety of languages) the better off you will be and the more you can understand what you like doing. (Palay, 2009)

Jessica Duverneay, Information Architect
National Football League (NFL)
Los Angeles, California

After undergrad at Michigan State University, I became an art teacher, which I actually quite enjoyed for a few years. However, I noticed the school media specialist having a lot more fun than most classroom teachers, so I decided, *What the heck, I'll go to library school.* In the end, I attended the University of Michigan School of Information (SI).

In graduate school, my specialization, for about one term, was school library media. I then decided that a career in a public or academic library was a much better fit for my free-spirited personality. I was certain I was going to be a public or special librarian focusing on user outreach and education. However, I continued to feel that another path was tugging at me. I wanted to live in Los Angeles and make enough money for a comfortable lifestyle there with some leftover to send to my family. I wanted to work with people who were more like me. I wanted a work environment that suited my preference for casual clothes and yet would be challenging and exciting to me. Lamenting about this dilemma, an SI alumnus suggested that I enroll in an information architecture (IA) class, which would bridge my skills from library and information services to human–computer interaction.

It was great. I went to both classes offered every day and loved every minute of it. Although I kept looking for jobs in libraries, that internal tugging persisted so I contacted a professor from SI who connected me with an internship and contract work in IA after graduation. While that work wrapped up, I marketed my generalist skills, great attitude about challenges and learning, and landed myself a position as an information architect, drawing on my skills and abilities across human–computer interaction and library and information services.

In my current position, I am responsible for the information architecture of all 32 NFL club sites. My team is rolling all of the club sites, which are currently hosted and run independently by the individual clubs, onto a modular customizable content management system (CMS). My responsibility is twofold. First of all, we are designing the CMS so that I evaluate usability and IA of the individual modules. I critique wire frames, functional specs, and business requirements for each module individually with the developers, designers, project managers, and account managers. As an IA, my job is to make sure the module functions from a user perspective while also meeting the business goals.

The second part of my job is to organize the modules onto homepages and landing pages for the new club sites and communicate user needs to both the developers and the designers, all while battling scope creep, deadlines, and Microsoft Excel. First, we need to make a record of the entire existing site in a legacy sitemap; then, with feedback from the clubs, we propose a new sitemap with labeling and content bucket cleanup, wire frame out the homepage and landing pages, and do as much rogue usability testing as we go. After launch, we make sure everything looks and works as it's supposed to work.

I feel that the whole mind-opening experience and support from people at the School of Information was much more important than any class I took. That said, courses in contextual inquiry, project management, usability testing, and information architecture were all classes that definitely got me hired and made me adequately competent from the first day on the job. Also, utilizing the contacts in my network is basically the sole reason for my current position. It really pays to develop a few strong and meaningful relationships with others in your field, especially with people who have been through it all before.

I recommend that people considering this field do their best to master the following skills: being open to learning new things, which includes everything from software to work flow process; the desire to get it right even if it takes awhile; the ability to quickly process abstract ideas; and the ability to code-switch while talking to very different stakeholders. And, of course, to work in any technology field, it's necessary to have basic computer software knowledge.

I consider the industry outlook to be pretty decent, though with the economy currently being dismal, it is harder to find nice long-term stable jobs. Contract work is in demand, but it may lack longevity. Unless people suddenly stop seeking information on the Internet, I would say we're going to be okay.

My advice is to get an internship, read anything by Jesse James Garret or Peter Moreville, spend a lot of time on the Internet/blogs, and always be thinking about what your favorite Web site is and why it is so fun, easy, and cool to use. Be sure to also equally pay attention to the ones that are not fun, easy, or cool to use. Better yet, make your own Web site. Go to a local meet-up group. Attend the IA Summit (http://iasummit.org) or IDEA (http://ideaconference.org). Ask a bunch of questions. Ask them again. Always ask why. More important, ask, Why not? (Duverneay, 2008)

Jason Withrow, Internet Professional Instructor
Department Chair at Washtenaw Community College and
Owner of Usable Development LLC
Ann Arbor, Michigan

I think the thread tying together my experiences and my career path has been an interest in helping others. As an undergraduate at Capital University, I studied psychology and then I went on to earn a master's degree in psychology in a counseling psychology program at the University of Akron. As I was finishing up that degree, a friend of mine told me about his studies in human–computer interaction (HCI). To me, HCI was a wonderful synthesis of my interest in helping others with my psychology training and my interest in computers.

My first position after graduating from the University of Michigan's School of Information (SI) was as an information architect. In 2001, I moved into an opening as a full-time faculty member at Washtenaw Community College (WCC). Admittedly, other experiences than my studies in HCI helped me gain my current position at WCC. When I was pursuing my master's degree in psychology, I taught multiple sections of Introduction to Psychology, which provided me with the teaching experience that WCC wanted. Yet, the knowledge gained at SI was also a big factor in their hiring decision, as user experience was not an area that any of the existing faculty could address.

Teaching user experience and Web design means keeping up with an ever-changing series of topics. Thus, my materials change to some extent every semester, which requires additional work in comparison to humanities roles where the subject matter is more static. At WCC, the primary challenge is growing the program, including adding new courses as the curriculum evolves and having qualified part time instructors as the number of sections grows.

My desire to remain relevant and to provide the best instruction possible led me first to work part time as a senior business analyst and then to open my own consulting, training, and development company, Usable Development. My goal with Usable Development is to make systems better, so that every user of those systems has an easier time and fewer frustrations.

Usable Development is like any other small company—the workload is too much or too little. It's a good mix of user experience (e.g., usability testing, content inventories, developing site architectures) and building Web sites or Web applications, with all of the various tasks involved there. For Usable Development, the issue is continuing to have a stream of clients and work in the current economy.

The most enjoyable aspect of Usable Development is the work itself, which usually involves creating something new or making an existing system better. Unreasonable or otherwise difficult clients are definitely my least favorite aspect of that job.

In both positions, the knowledge of Web development languages (e.g., xHTML, CSS, JavaScript, PHP, etc.) is critical, as well as the knowledge of user experience methods (e.g., user testing, card sorting, content inventories, heuristic evaluation, personas, etc.). On the soft skills side there is a strong need for good interpersonal skills in order to interact well with students and clients. Being organized is also essential for getting things done on time and being ready for things coming up in the future.

With Web design, there is always movement toward something new and different (and hopefully better). Currently we're in the midst of Web 2.0 and Web sites allowing greater social interaction. In the coming years we'll shift toward Web 3.0 (the semantic Web), with Web sites offering rich information for spiders and other bots and, hopefully, making information retrieval better in a wide variety of ways.

The key for success in this field is to gain practical experience. This does not happen by just having a Facebook or Twitter account but by actually creating something for the Web and evolving it over time as you learn more. My suggestion is to do work for organizations you belong to or just build Web sites for yourself or your friends. Start building your portfolio now and learn something new about Web development every day.

I believe the outlook is strong for the industry. IT positions will continue to experience growth and Web design as well as user experience will make up some portion of those new jobs. Teachers at the community college level have an entry-level salary somewhere in the upper 50s to lower 60s, with a range up into the 80s. Those going into business as a consultant or developer set their own rates, which could range from $50–$125 per hour. Then it's just a matter of how much you want to work and how much work you can find. (Withrow, 2009)

Careers in Human–Computer Interaction: At a Glance

Your career in human–computer interaction can take many directions as you connect your interests and values to the type of functional area and type of organization that you pursue. Here are a few examples of real jobs representing some exciting "tracks" you can follow.

Health Informatics Track
Senior Human Factors Engineer
Baxter International Inc.
Round Lake, Illinois

Provide human factors support to cross-functional program teams responsible for innovating new and improving existing medical devices; lead human factors engineering work and research and designs and executes tests to simulate product use and life for verifying and validating product performance, reliability, and usability; ensure that sound human factors principles are considered and implemented; develop product prototypes to explore and validate user interfaces and demonstration prototypes/technologies. (Device Career Network, 2009)

Corporate Track
User Interface Designer/Developer
PricewaterhouseCoopers LLP
San Jose, California

Develop the most elegant, powerful, useful, and intuitive interfaces possible for a cutting edge text analysis R&D project in its early start-up phases; work with team to elicit, define, and refine requirements (user scenarios); build mock-ups, prototypes, and working models of complex design elements; design, develop, and test .NET-based dynamic applications; attend and contribute to design reviews and code inspections; interact with end users to validate and evaluate software; review and contribute to user documentation. (CHI-Jobs@LISTSERV.ACM.ORG, 2009)

Media/Entertainment Track
Information Architect
Comedy Central
New York, New York

Contribute to the development of new product interfaces, feature sets, and information flows; work with Production, Product Development, Design, and Technology to optimize existing products and templates; contribute to the design of user testing and analysis of results; create detailed wire frames, storyboards, mock-ups, user flows, and presentations to effectively illustrate interfaces, ideas, and architecture; keep abreast of best practices for user interaction and design; implement the user interface design. (Information Architecture Institute, 2009)

Social Justice Track
Web Architect, BeDo Inc.
Atlanta, Georgia

Create our online vision and strategy within the BeDo Inc. mission "Be It! Do It!" which reflects our goal that one day, every citizen on earth will have, at the center of their life, not just work and home but also a third place, a place of purposeful pursuit that improves our world; manage multiple, meaningful projects in the digital realm, with special attention to budgetary constraints and milestones; outline goals and desired outcomes for all digital projects with business goals in mind; work collaboratively on concepts, leveraging a multidisciplinary team and a partnership network; implement and deploy in managing a multidisciplinary team; develop systems for interteam collaboration, including collaboration platforms. (Idealist.org, 2009)

Education Track
Interaction Designer
WestEd
San Francisco, California

Create education-related Web sites and tools for this research, development, and service agency; participate in concept development, user-centered design, and specifications for a wide variety of projects aimed at promoting excellence, achieving equity, and improving learning; work collaboratively to design for Web applications, content-based Web sites, data visualizations, mobile devices, and multimedia presentations; perform requirements gathering, task analysis, personas, user scenarios, information architecture, interaction design, screen layouts, prototypes, observe or conduct usability testing. (Nonprofit Technology Network, 2009)

Global Track
Information Systems Analyst
The Bill and Melinda Gates Foundation
Seattle, Washington

Perform discovery and analysis of the Global Development business processes, user needs relative to the intranet, and translate them into site organization, navigation, and search solutions across the division; perform user, content, and context analysis to understand needs; develop information architecture including taxonomy and metadata models; improve navigation and design of the sites through development of user flows, wire frames, and mock-ups in order to illustrate interfaces and architecture. (Bill and Melinda Gates Foundation, 2009)

Resources for Further Information/Exploration

The following resources can help guide you in your career exploration within the field of Human–Computer Interaction. Note that this is not a comprehensive list; there are numerous resources available related to the nuances of the field that are not included. The purpose of identifying key job posting sites and professional organizations is to make you aware of some of the main resources available and to also provide you with gateways to resources that will inform you of the types of careers available in the field.

Professional Organizations Relevant to Human–Computer Interaction

- ACM—Association for Computing Machinery
  www.acm.org
- AIGA—The Professional Association for Design
  www.aiga.org
- ASIS&T—American Society for Information Science and Technology
  www.asis.org
- SIGCHI—Computer Human Interaction
  http://sigchi.org
- CogSci—Cognitive Science Society
  www.cognitivesciencesociety.org
- CPSR—Computer Professionals for Social Responsibility
  www.cpsr.org
- HFES—Human Factors & Ergonomics Society
  www.hfes.org
- IEA—International Ergonomics Association
  www.iea.cc
- ITG—Internet Technical Group
  www.internettg.org
- LITA—Library and Information Technology Association
  www.lita.org
- SCIP—Society of Competitive Intelligence Professionals
  www.scip.org
- STC—Society for Technical Communication
  www.stc.org
- UPA—Usability Professionals Association
  www.upassoc.org

Career Sites Relevant to Human–Computer Interaction

- Boxes and Arrows
  http://jobs.boxesandarrows.com/jobs
- Creative Hotlist
  www.creativehotlist.com/index.asp
- Computer Jobs
  www.computerjobs.com/homepage.aspx
- Coroflot Jobs
  http://coroflot.com/public/jobs_browse.asp
- Dice
  www.dice.com
- Good Experience Job Openings
  http://goodexperience.com/blog/archives/cat_job_openings.php
- HFcareers.com
  www.hfcareers.com
- Human Factors and Ergonomics Society Career Center
  http://hfesjobs.jobcontrolcenter.com/search.cfm
- Human–Computer Interaction Resource Network Job Bank
  www.hcirn.com/jobs/index.php
- Internet Technical Group Job Bank
  www.internettg.org/post/job_list.asp
- OdinJobs
  www.odinjobs.com
- The Information Architecture Institute Job Board
  http://iainstitute.org/jobboard/jobs/recent.php
- Usability First
  www.usabilityfirst.com/jobs
- UsabilityNews.com Jobs
  www.usabilitynews.com/default.asp?c=2
- Usability Professionals Association Job Bank
  www.usabilityprofessionals.org/usability_resources/jobs

Education and Training

The study of Human–Computer Interaction (HCI) is interdisciplinary, incorporating knowledge from areas including computer graphics, operating systems, programming, communication theory, graphic and industrial design, linguistics, social science, cognitive psychology, and engineering. Thus, students can begin in most any undergraduate major, though taking some coursework in computer science and in psychology is recommended. It can be beneficial, though it is not required, to have a technical major as a base for a career in human–computer interaction, such as a major in computer science or information systems. Some universities offer a bachelor's in human–computer interaction, and there are a growing number that offer undergraduate informatics programs.

However, many students discover the field of HCI while they are studying one of its other related fields, such as psychology, anthropology, art and design, linguistics, or communication. Students may opt to build a base of technical skills while pursuing a major in the social sciences or humanities as another educational path for a career in HCI, and some graduate programs enable students to build technology skills during their advanced studies. Since work experience is highly valued in professional practice, seeking a relevant job for a few years after completing an undergraduate degree is advisable. If a student decides on a career in HCI early in his or her undergraduate program, gaining relevant internship and research experience may be sufficient to proceed directly to a graduate program and into a professional position.

Graduate education in human–computer interaction can open opportunities for more competitive positions and allows for future career advancement. Students will find that a professional master's degree will enable them to reach executive level positions in the field or to take the entrepreneurial path and start their own business venture. Those who are interested in a career in research and teaching can pursue the PhD, working in academia or in high level industry research. In either case, a strong entrepreneurial inclination is important, since faculty and industry researchers must garner substantial research funding to operate labs and produce value-added results through new knowledge and/or marketable applications for real-world problems.

Human–computer interaction programs are still rather young and are quite varied in their approach and focus. It is important to research programs carefully to find the best fit for your needs and interests. HCI programs may be found across the United States and abroad within computer science departments, within information schools, as stand-alone institutes, or in other schools or colleges such as design, engineering, or media arts and sciences. A listing of HCI programs is available online at www.hcibib.org/education/#PROGRAMS.

References

Bill and Melinda Gates Foundation. 2009. "Welcome." Available: www
.gatesfoundation.org/jobs/Pages/job-search.aspx (accessed March 19, 2009).

Bonhard, P. "Reality Bites: HCI in Industry." Accenture User Experience Group.
Available: www-users.cs.york.ac.uk/~pcairns/AI/Bonhard.pdf (accessed April 23,
2009).

CHI-Jobs@LISTSERV.ACM.ORG (February 4, 2009).

DesignReviver. 2009. "The Future of Interface Design." Available: http://
designreviver.com/inspiration/the-future-of-interface-design/ (accessed April 29,
2009).

Device Career Network. 2009. "Advanced Job Search." Available: www.devicecareer
network.com/jobs/job-listing/sr-human-factors-engineer-256974 (accessed April
22, 2009).

Duverneay, Jessica. 2008. Interview by Kelly Kowatch. December 6.

Ganapati, Priya. 2009. "Gadget Lab: Kindle 2's Fuzzy Fonts Have Users Seeing Red."
Wired, April 13. Available: www.wired.com/gadgetla/B2009/04/kindle-2-displa
(accessed April 29, 2009).

Hewett, T., R. Baecker, S. Card, et al. 2008. "ACM Special Interest Group on Computer–Human Interaction." Curricula for Human–Computer Interaction, April 11.
Available: http://sigchi.org/cdg/cdg2.html#2_1 (accessed April 28, 2009).

Information Architecture Institute. 2009. "Mid to Sr-Level Information Architect."
Available: http://iainstitute.org/jobboard/jobs/job.php?id=4446 (accessed March
13, 2009).

Idealist.org. 2009. "Web Architect." Available: www.idealist.org/if/i/en/av/Jo/
B330353-162/c (accessed March 12, 2009).

Jonietz, Erika. 2007. "TR10: Augmented Reality." *MIT Technology Review*, March 12.
Available: www.technologyreview.com/communications/18291/ (accessed April
28, 2009).

McCullough, Malcolm. 2004. *Digital Ground: Architecture, Pervasive Computing, and
Environmental Knowing*. Cambridge, MA: The MIT Press.

Nemko, Marty. 2007. "Usability/User Experience Specialist: Executive Summary."
U.S. News.com, December 19. Available: www.usnews.com/articles/business/best
-careers/2007/12/19/usabilityuser-experience-specialist-executive-summary.html
(accessed April 29, 2009).

Nielsen, Jakob. 2006. "Salary Trends for Usability Professionals." useit, May 8. Available: www.useit.com/alertbox/salaries.html (accessed April 23, 2009).

Nonprofit Technology Network. 2009. "Interaction Designer." nten.org, February 16.
Available: www.nten.org/node/7193 (accessed February 16, 2009).

Oshlyansky, L., P. Cairns, A. Sasse, and C. Harrison. 2007. "The Challenges Faced by
Academia Preparing Students for Industry: What We Teach and What We Do."
British Computer Society. Available: www.bcs.org/upload/pdf/ewic_hc08_v2_
paper58.pdf (accessed April 23, 2009).

Palay, Josh. 2009. Interview by Kelly Kowatch. March 2.

Steere, Mike. 2008. "The Future of Gaming Is All in the Mind." CNN, September 8. Available: www.cnn.com/2008/TECH/science/09/08/Futureofgaming/index.html (accessed April 29, 2009).

Strong, G., with contributions by J. B. Gasen, T. Hewett, D. Hix, et al. 1994. "New Directions in Human Computer Interaction Education, Research, and Practice." Software Engineering Institute. Available: www.sei.cmu.edu/community/hci/directions/ (accessed April 30, 2009).

Usability Professionals Association. 2008. *UPA 2007 Salary Survey.* Bloomingdale, IN: Usability Professionals Association. Available: www.usabilityprofessionals.org/usability_resources/surveys/salarysurvey2007-public.pdf (accessed April 29, 2009).

Usability Professionals Association. 2009. "Resources: About Usability." Available: www.upassoc.org/usability_resources/about_usability/ (accessed April 29, 2009).

WebUrbanist. 2009. "Evolution of 10 Essential Gadgets and Technology." Available: http://weburbanist.com/2009/01/08/the-evolution-of-10-essential-gadgets-technologies/ (accessed April 28, 2009).

Withrow, Jason. 2009. Interview by Kelly Kowatch. April 20.

Wolgemuth, Liz. 2008. "The 30 Best Careers 2009." *U.S. News & World Report*, December 11. Available: www.usnews.com/money/careers/articles/2008/12/11/the-30-best-careers-for-2009.html (accessed April 28, 2009).

Additional Sources

Wikipedia, s.v. "Human-Computer Interaction," Available: http://en.wikipedia.org/wiki/Human%E2%80%93computer_interaction (accessed December 2008).

Wikipedia. "Search Results: Human Computer Interaction." Available: http://en.wikipedia.org/w/index.php?title=Special%3ASearch&redirs=1&search=human+computer+interaction&fulltext=Search&ns0=1 (accessed December 2008).

Chapter 5

Social Computing

Introduction

Social computing specialists are explorers on the frontier of the Internet, inventing and innovating new and better ways of capturing and utilizing the resources of the digital age for human benefit. The growth of social media has been nothing short of phenomenal. Erik Qualman, author of *Socialnomics: How Social Media Transforms the Way We Live and Do Business* (Qualman, 2009a) highlights compelling statistics on social media, including:

- It took 38 years for radio to reach 50 million users . . . for TV it took 13 years . . . for the Internet it took 4 years. . . . Facebook added 100 million users in less than 9 months.
- 80% of companies are using the social networking site LinkedIn as their primary tool to find employees.
- 78% of consumers trust peer recommendations—14% trust advertisements.
- There are over 200,000,000 blogs.
- In the near future we will no longer search for products and services; they will find us via social media. (Qualman, 2009b)

According to Qualman, "Social media isn't a fad, it is a fundamental shift in the way we communicate" (Qualman, 2009b). Simply put, social computing incorporates interaction and collaboration into Web sites, systems, and mobile devices. The resulting systems, known as social media, are new mechanisms for communications, information sharing, and collaboration. Forms of social media include social networking such as Facebook, social bookmarking such as Delicious, social image sharing such as YouTube and Flickr, social news such as Digg, and user generated content through wikis such as *Wikipedia* or through blogs or microblogs such as

Twitter (Nations, 2009). As a whole, social computing is commonly referred to as Web 2.0 technology.

Using social computing tools creates a rich online experience in which an individual might post an update and comment on a friend's photo on Facebook, watch and comment on a YouTube video, vote for an interesting news story on Digg, look for information or contribute content on Wikipedia, share Web sites by tagging them on Delicious, post a blog entry, and send a quick update or Web link on Twitter. But social computing is more than just a new way to contact a friend, share your opinion, or find a new Web site; it has already changed the Internet landscape and its future potential is just beginning to unfold.

One indicator of this potential is the explosive growth of social computing in recent years. Of the Internet user population in the United States, 41 percent were monthly visitors to social network sites in 2008, an 11 percent increase from 2007 (Williamson, 2009). Projections suggest that from 2008–2013, social network users will increase from 79.5 million to 114.6 million, a growth of 44.2 percent. The largest growth is expected from children (61.1 percent) and adults (44.2 percent) (Williamson, 2009). It is estimated that half or more of all Internet users will be regular social media users by 2013 (Williamson, 2009). This rapid growth is generating a new and exciting career trajectory for those who would like to lead the way in the new space of social computing.

In 2008, Facebook became the largest social network in the world with 132 million unique users (Smith, 2008). But just when Facebook seemed to have the corner on the social computing market, Twitter took off. Twitter uses the simple message service (SMS) protocol to enable individual users to send brief (up to 140 character) messages—called Tweets—on the Internet while allowing other users to follow an individual user by receiving his or her Tweets. In April 2009 Twitter's already rapid growth exploded, with 17 million visitors in that month alone—83 percent more than the previous month and 3,000 percent more than the year before (Lipsman, 2009). Celebrity users of Twitter brought significant media hype which fueled the growth; actor Ashton Kutcher became the first individual to reach 1 million Twitter followers, and Oprah Winfrey sent her first Tweet from the set of her talk show (Sutter and Griggs, 2009).

Kutcher's Twitter following was more than an ego boost; he had challenged CNN's breaking news feed to a Twitter duel in which the first to reach 1 million followers would donate 10,000 mosquito bed nets for World Malaria Day. "Ashton's 'Twitter race' is an amazing example of how we can leverage new technology to battle an ancient disease," according to Scott Case, CEO of Malaria No More. "Not only is Ashton helping Malaria No More to raise awareness . . . he's also galvanizing his Twitter army to help end malaria deaths" (Sutter and Griggs, 2009). Social computing indeed has great potential to benefit humankind. Through it we have reached a new era of media democracy where not only individual voices can be heard but where citizens are both creators and consumers of media communications including news and entertainment and where information can be shared rapidly and widely.

Leveraging the power of social computing is of great interest to all sectors of the economy, from business to government to nonprofit and for both internal and external operations. Organizations across the country and around the globe are incorporating Web 2.0 technologies into their internal operations by using blogs to share information and wikis to enhance collaborative work, and they are deploying social media for advertising and public relations and as part of e-commerce operations or service delivery. This transition is increasingly referred to as Enterprise 2.0. It's not just about using Web 2.0 tools in the office but a shift in the paradigm and practice of work in organizations. The controlled, hierarchical flow of information in organizations is giving way to a controlled chaos model of information flow that cuts across the organization in various directions and creates new patterns of communication and collaboration (Nations, 2009).

Companies like Whole Foods Market are making use of social media in their external business operations, and others are following fast. Whole Foods uses Twitter and Tweets about promotions, new products, and even product recalls, while listening to feedback and ideas from customers and generating a sense of transparency and access (Mardesich, 2008). Transparency and access were also key purposes in the use of social media during Barack Obama's presidential campaign and now in his administration. Obama has introduced "Open for Questions" as one of the interactive tools available on WhiteHouse.gov. "Open for Questions" allows individuals to submit questions they would like the president to address, and a public voting system ranks the popularity of questions and determines which questions the president will address in his online town halls, which he conducts on YouTube (Beuker, 2009). Obama has raised awareness and set a bar that other government agencies are beginning to follow by exploring their own ways to deploy Web 2.0 technology.

For example, the Centers for Disease Control and Prevention (CDC) made use of Twitter to communicate about the 2009 swine flu epidemic, and the Environmental Protection Agency encouraged photo submissions from the public via Flickr to celebrate Earth Day, using the categories "people and the environment," "the beauty of nature," and "wildlife." The EPA's stated goal in this project was to "encourage participation and provide maximum public access" (Troiano, 2009).

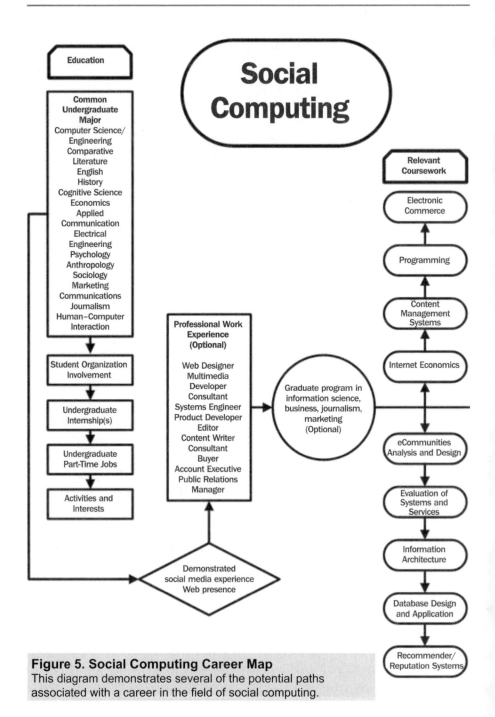

Figure 5. Social Computing Career Map
This diagram demonstrates several of the potential paths
associated with a career in the field of social computing.

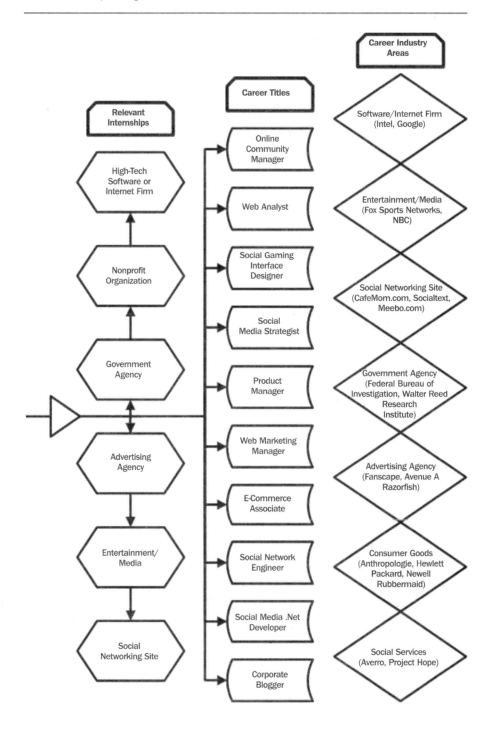

Web 2.0 skills are fast becoming a valuable and transferable skill set in many jobs, and as social computing venues continue to monetize their operations, professional positions in social computing will likely expand. Careers in this area range from technical development, customization, and deployment of social computing systems and tools to managing complex online community environments and developing business and public relations strategies for effective use of social media. A central feature of careers in social computing will be innovation and early adoption of emerging technology, as what is new and hot today will be eclipsed by the next "big thing." Creating the next big thing will be a constant opportunity for entrepreneurial types.

Understanding the needs and preferences of users is important to the success of social computing endeavors, but an even deeper understanding of human behavior is needed, that which has to do with incentives. As with other types of new businesses, many social computing ventures fail. What makes some succeed, especially on the level of Twitter or Facebook? Attention to decision making and motivation is often the "secret sauce." The concept of incentive-centered design addresses these issues in the design and development of social computing systems and tools. Incentive-centered design methods utilize decision making and game theories to evaluate human motivation and predict behavior drawing from psychological, sociological, and economic perspectives. This knowledge is drawn into the design of system features and configurations to maximize effectiveness and to encourage positive behaviors such as participation, honesty, and fairness. A great example of a highly incentivized social computing system is eBay, which relies on good behavior of buyers, sellers, and auction participants to achieve a system with a huge level of participation and a high degree of trust.

Even social computing sites for kids incorporate incentive-centered design concepts. Take Webkinz.com, a virtual world where kids bring their real Webkinz stuffed toys to life in the digital realm. A feat of marketing wizardry, the site provides a safe (no child's identity is revealed) environment that incorporates educational games that allow kids to earn points and purchase food, shelter, clothes, and toys for their Webkinz. Research has shown that kids benefit from online communities that foster social skills, offer learning opportunities, and perhaps most important, build digital literacy, which is already an important life and work skill (Kopytoff, 2008).

Social media has become a key skill set for information professionals of all sorts, but in particular librarians have found these new modes of communication an exciting new means for providing service and helping people engage with the digital age of information. According to Lori Bell, Second Life Librarian and Director of

Innovation for the Alliance Library System, "Libraries of all types need to be evaluating and trying these tools as more and more people participate in virtual worlds and other social networking tools. The growth in the use of virtual worlds has been phenomenal. . . . Libraries need to be where their users are and reinvent some of what they do to meet the information needs people have" (OCLC.org, 2007).

The fast emergence of ubiquitous computing will take social computing to new levels in the near future, enabling seamless and constant access and connection, yet in ways that are shaped by individual preferences and parameters. According to Andrew Lippman, Founding Associate Director at the MIT Media Lab, we are on the verge of a third cloud of computing that will combine mobile devices and social networks to create on-the-fly interaction through intelligent computing (Miller, 2009). For example, a conference call among people who speak different languages would incorporate instantaneous translations enabling high-level global collaboration. In the workplace, SMART Boards would react to people as they approach and allow them to share information from their mobile devices on the screen. Privacy and security will be redefined and managed in new ways as we enter the third cloud computing environment (Miller, 2009).

Social computing is an exciting realm for information professionals with limitless possibilities. Joe Kraus, Google's director of product management, noted during a conference presentation that today users expect all sites to be social, commenting, "Social is a feature, not a destination. . . . Social is the new black" (Smith, 2008). Indeed, social computing is likely to be in style for many years to come, and it is likely to have impact we cannot yet foresee.

Skills and Abilities

For any professional career field, there are required skills and abilities that are important for success. This is certainly the case for the fast-emerging field of social computing. While the right skills and abilities will open doors to a variety of exciting positions in a wide range of industries, a strong interest and belief in the value of social computing on both a professional and personal level is critical for landing your dream job.

Most professional positions in social computing have only recently been developed or have evolved from other fields such as human–computer interaction, computer science, public relations, marketing, and journalism. Not unlike other emerging fields, it is evident that positions in social computing vary in terms of skill level, experience, and education required. Despite these variations and the newness of the field, there are certainly common skills, abilities, and characteristics that are highly sought and that enhance one's marketability for jobs.

Outlined in the following sections are both the soft skills (behavioral/personality traits and characteristics) and hard skills (technical and career-specific knowledge) and abilities that are important for success in the field of social computing. Note that these skills are identified as the most common skills and abilities; this is certainly not an exhaustive list of all of the valuable skills and abilities that are beneficial for this career field.

> ☑ QUICK FACT!
> Excellent writing skills are a must.

Soft Skills

- Ability to communicate (written and verbal), to achieve:
  - Persuasion
  - Negotiation
- Ability to work in collaboration/be a team player
- Relationship management/interpersonal skills
- Analytical/problem solving skills
- Motivated/enthusiastic approach to work
- Ability to be creative
- Ability to be entrepreneurial-minded/innovative

Hard Skills

- Web 2.0: Develop and design Web sites that facilitate communication, information sharing, and collaboration on the Internet.
- Enterprise 2.0: Apply Web 2.0 technologies to business.
- Interactive marketing: Brand a product or service via a conversation facilitated by Internet technology.
- Networking: Build or manage an interconnected system of things or people.
- Public relations: Manage the flow of information between an organization and its constituents.
- Usability: Analyze the potential users of a system.
- Search engine optimization: Optimize one's Web site to get better results in search engines.
- Web application design and development:
  - Web Languages: AJAX, CSS, XML, HTML, PHP
  - Programming languages: Java, Perl, Ruby on Rails
  - Content management systems: Drupal, Joomla, WordPress

- ○ Databases: SQL, MySQL, Microsoft Access, Excel
- ○ Graphics editing: Adobe Photoshop, Adobe Illustrator
- Business management: Understand complex business technologies and business and technical aspects of the Web and have a working knowledge of industry standards.

Social computing is all about collaboration. As organizations continue to integrate Web 2.0 technologies into their overall business strategies, having strong collaboration skills are critical. Just as important is a solid belief in the value of collaboration. Those who aspire to be evangelists for the dominance of communities and the power of the network may find a career in social computing ideal. Career opportunities in social computing are diverse yet tend to be either technical in nature or communications focused. Note, however, that technical positions also require strong communication skills, and communications positions require a solid understanding of the technology driving social computing tools and systems.

> ☑ QUICK FACT!
> Collaboration is what social computing is all about.

Social computing systems must take the everyday user's thoughts and behavior into consideration to meet the organization's goals. In order to design or manage an effective social computing system, it is important to have an intrinsic interest and high level of curiosity about people and how they think and behave as well as knowledge of usability evaluation techniques that capture and apply data and user feedback to system improvements.

While some consider Web 2.0 just the latest addition to the toolkit for public relations and marketing professionals, there are some key differences in the qualities that make someone a good social computing professional compared to mainstream corporate publicists. A corporate blogger, for example, must be more personal than the average corporate PR professional and may need to be available around the clock to respond to anyone who writes about his or her organization. It is also important to understand social computing etiquette. Though social computing demands new skills, many traditional public relations skills are still important. Social computing professionals need to be highly organized with strong analytical skills and exceptional writing skills, including the ability to craft a compelling story.

Proficiency with Web 2.0 skills is essential to becoming a social computing professional. Equally important is having an understanding of how to apply Web 2.0 skills to meet business needs. This means more than just using these tools as a user; it means tracking what messages are working and what's effectively guiding your communications and meeting your business objectives through analytics and search engine optimization, for example. This is what is referred to as Enterprise 2.0. Social computing professionals with proven experience related to business strategy are hard to find. Thus, complementing your educational pathway with business management and marketing knowledge and skills will increase your employment opportunities.

If you are interested in the technical side of social computing—building and developing social systems and applications—then a stronger technical skill set is required. Social software developers and engineers, for example, typically own the end-to-end development and ongoing innovations to manage communities. This includes the design and implementation of solutions, core back-end functionality, front-end feature development, and Web site testing and deployment. Knowledge and skills in SQL, Java, ASP.NET, and PHP would be critical to having the ability to develop effective social software applications.

This is not to say that a computer science or engineering degree is always required to become a social software developer. A degree in a social science, such as social psychology, sociology, informatics, or economics, or in humanities, such as English or a foreign language, can be an alternative path. Again, having programming and technology skills are necessary, but with a strong technical aptitude one can build these skills through courses and work experience. Those who build technical proficiency and stay on top of emerging technologies and practices could qualify for technical positions. It is also helpful to gain some Web application skills and knowledge, such as AJAX, Javascript, and XML (not at the programming level) in order to build cool applications like social bookmarking and social networking sites.

Strong writing skills are probably the most important, yet underrated, skill to have for effectiveness in the field of social computing. Everything that goes on the Web, for instance, should be passed through the hands of someone who has strong editing and proofreading skills. A sharp eye for detail and a deep knowledge of the quality standards and common mistakes that apply to the Web are necessary for any social computing professional who creates or approves content for the Web.

Customer service and relationship management skills are another important skill set for social computing professionals. Strong communication skills are essential for providing effective customer service and maintaining productive relationships and meeting customer expectations. Enthusiasm and advocacy help too, for talking to those customers or stakeholders who don't think they need to contribute information (Williams, 2009). Additionally, social computing professionals must often manage relationships with diverse constituents including clients, vendors, and media representatives.

Specialized social media skills such as professional informality, technical ability (expert user of all social media tools), and the ability to understand a different and dynamic set of user motivations are proving to be essential. Social media literacy skills are of course necessary and expected. Given the rapid rate of technology advancement, staying ahead of trends by being an "early adopter" and evaluating the potential of new social media tools as they emerge will be essential.

Experience in the field is equally if not more important than formal education and training. Currently, it is difficult to find a social computing professional with relevant education, training, skills, *and* real-world experience. A person with 20 years of experience on Madison Avenue, who doesn't know what a Tweet is, would not make an effective social computing strategist, nor would a software developer with outdated programming skills be in demand. In this emerging field, a combination of education, skills, and real-world experience are needed for entry and advancement.

☑ QUICK FACT!
Web 2.0 skills are a must.

KEY WORDS TO KNOW

Here are some additional social computing terms that will be used throughout this chapter. Those interested in pursuing this career field should become familiar with their meaning:

- **social networking**: Term used to describe the way that users build online contacts and interact with these personal or business friends.
- **online communities**: Groups of people that primarily interact through an Internet social network service for social, professional, educational, or other purposes.
- **outreach**: Using social technologies and tools that enable anyone to reach a global audience.
- **access**: Level of openness an organization has to user input and involvement.
- **social media literacy**: Understanding of and ability to use collaborative online tools.
- **e-consultancy**: The business of providing services such as Web page design and marketing advice to companies doing business on the Internet.
- **ubiquitous computing**: Technology use that interfaces seamlessly with an individual's daily activities.

(continued)

(continued)
- **wiki**: Online database used to create collaborative Web sites.
- **blog**: Short for weblog, a type of interactive Web site usually maintained by an individual with regular entries of information, commentary, descriptions, graphics, or video.
- **social bookmarking**: Methods for Internet users to store, organize, search, and manage bookmarks of Web pages on the Internet.
- **user-generated content**: Refers to various kinds of media content, publicly available, that are produced by individual participants.
- **usability**: Refers to how easily users can learn and use a product or system to achieve their goals and how satisfied they are with that process.
- **social software**: Systems that allow users to interact and share data.
- **incentive-centered design**: The art of designing systems or institutions that align participants' (individual) incentives with overall system (social) goals.
- **game theory**: A branch of applied mathematics that analyzes strategy and predicts behavior. (Smogger Social Media Blog, 2006)

Professional Roles

To better understand the role of social computing professionals, including how they approach their work, it may help to compare and contrast the general duties and responsibilities of some of the more common social computing career pathways:

- **Social Software Developer**: Develops, evaluates, and refines social software computer applications to meet the needs of different social contexts; identifies patterns of social interaction and supports new patterns; captures and analyzes data about social interactions.
- **Social Media Strategist**: Manages and oversees all content for blogs from analyzing blog traffic, branding within content areas, and relationship building with external partners and communities.
- **Community Manager**: Manages all aspects of day-to-day community activity, including setting tone, enforcing rules, and hiring and managing remote community contributors; participates in product development for new community initiatives.
- **Public Relations Specialist**: Creates and promotes a positive image for their employer or client; keeps the public informed of current organiza-

tional goals and policies; must be sensitive to the needs, attitudes, and opinions of his or her audience.

- **Social Media Editor**: Expands the use of social media networks and publishing platforms to improve journalism and deliver it to a broader audience of readers.

- **Corporate Communications Specialist**: Manages external and internal public relations by increasing brand exposure through industry editors, media personnel, and journalists; develops deep relationships to maximize quality and frequency of exposure.

- **Interactive Strategist/Marketing Specialist**: Develops, recommends, manages, and implements innovative social media marketing programs; manages client, vendor, and multimedia relationships; conducts industry/product research and production of client pitches; leads social media program execution through coordination across internal and external teams.

- **Corporate Blogger**: Utilizes good general writing and communication skills; addresses the specific writing (and reading) requirements of the blog audience; designs and creates the look of the blog through innovative Web site development and programming skills; designs interface for the corporate blog with the company's general Web site.

Occupational Outlook

The position of social media specialist introduced by such companies as Comcast, General Motors, and JetBlue Airways has become the hottest new

☑ QUICK FACT!
Hottest new corporate job.

corporate job among the new generation of social computing users (Holson, 2009). You can expect to find all types of industries hiring candidates with professional social computing skills and knowledge. Opportunities are opening up in almost every industry. Some industries have established departments with social computing staff, while some smaller companies or companies who are just getting on board with the social computing revolution may have only one social computing expert on staff. The most common industries recruiting for social computing professionals include marketing/PR/advertising, entertainment/media, e-commerce start-ups, information technology, health care, consulting, research, and government.

Expect job opportunities to grow within the government sector. The FBI recently announced a series of new Web initiatives to develop social networking tools that will make it easier for the public to help track down wanted fugitives and missing kids as well as submit tips on terrorism and crime (Hunter, 2009). Even the White House is integrating social media initiatives to reach and empower the public.

Enterprise 2.0 initiatives are a trend to watch for job opportunities. Corporate online communities are expected to grow as more and more corporations realize the value and need to enable employees to jump into communities that are related to their day-to-day activities. By having employees complete their work activities within a community, an enterprise can drive open collaboration as a primary way of working. In a large, globally dispersed workforce, this is critical to relationship management and communication. According to J. B. Holston, President and CEO of NewsGator, there is a view that communities democratize organizations and thus enable innovation and happier employees overall (Mosher, 2009).

Industry sources indicate a growing need for talented social computing professionals. As the importance of social computing continues to increase, so will the need for students prepared to enter various social computing positions. The following are some of the most common social computing job titles and industries that actively recruit professionals (bachelor's and master's level).

> ☑ QUICK FACT!
> Millennials, the generation soon to enter the workforce, will expect some type of social computing when they come into a company.

- Community Manager, Intel (technology)
- Corporate Blogger, Graco (consumer products)
- WebSocial Media Editor, *New York Times* (entertainment/media)
- Consumer Insights/Research Manager, eBay (online auction)
- Social Media Strategist, FBI (government)
- Media Relations Publicist, Zcommunications (interactive media/advertising/PR)
- User Experience Designer, Facebook (social networking)
- Communications Specialist, Goodwill Industries (nonprofit)
- Web Marketing Manager, McGraw-Hill (publishing)
- Social Media Networking Analyst, TechOp Solutions (defense/homeland security)
- Media and Emerging Technologies Librarian, Mount Aloysius College (academic library)

- Marketing Manager, HR Block (finance)
- Social Software Designer, Telligent (consulting)

Salary Information

Given that the field of social computing is fairly
new, there is not an extensive amount of salary data
available. However, there are a few online resources

> ☑ QUICK FACT!
> Expect high salaries!

with salary information for social computing positions (McGary, 2009), and a review of job postings with salary indicated was also used for this salary overview. For most entry-level social computing positions for which managing others is not a function of the job, you can expect to make between $50,000–$75,000 depending on the size and type of organization and the geographic location. For highly technical social computing positions, starting salaries can be expected on the higher end of this scale. For positions where managing others is a function of the job, salaries can be expected at $75,000 and higher (Indeed.com, 2009).

Advanced education beyond a bachelor's degree did not indicate higher salaries, though this may change quickly as the field matures and more graduate level programs offer social computing curricula. Several years of experience with steady advancement resulted in higher salaries—in the low to middle six figures. One of the great things about social computing folks is that they believe in open access to information and are sharing salary information within their communities. Until there are more established salary standards for social computing positions, salaries can be benchmarked against positions such as software developer, usability engineer, PR specialist, Web content coordinator/manager, communications specialist, or public affairs specialist. Here are some examples of social computing positions and associated salaries:

- Community manager—entry-level, bachelor's degree, and a few years of experience: $50,000–$85,000.
- Corporate blogger—entry-level, bachelor's degree, with a few years of experience: $50,000–$75,000.
- Public relations specialist—entry-level, bachelor's degree, with a few years of experience: $52,100. Public relations managers, bachelor's degree, with more than five years of experience and managing others can expect a salary at around $72,900. Public relations vice president can expect high salaries of $125,000 and up (Valle, 2008).

- Corporate communications specialist—entry level with a few years of experience can expect a salary in the range of $75,000. Corporate communications managers/directors average $115,000. Senior VP of corporate communications salaries can be expected at $150,000.
- Social/Web application developer—entry level, bachelor's degree, with a few years of experience can expect a salary of about $75,000.

Profiles—Perspectives of New Professionals

Kelly Ripley Feller, Social Media Strategist
Intel—Social Media Center of Excellence
Portland, Oregon

After getting my degree in communication and political science from the University of Michigan, I embarked on a marketing career that spanned multiple states and industries, from travel and organic foods to health care and high technology. I spent many years managing various forms of marketing until I discovered my passion for writing. I joined SAS Software where I was an editor for their online publication BetterManagement.com.

After managing marketing for Intel for a couple years, my boss asked me to venture into the virtual world Second Life to assess its business potential for Intel. While I remained unconvinced of Second Life as a platform for business, I stayed in the world and began writing a blog about my experiences there. That was my introduction to social media.

The realm of social media marketing is somewhat like the Wild West; folks are running a bit haphazardly as they try to make sense of this new social and online environment. To help put some structure around how Intel employees can use these tools to benefit the company, Intel created the Social Media Center of Excellence. As a member of this small but mighty team (only three people), I develop strategies, guidelines, and programs that help Intel make use of social tools and technology to connect with our customers in a different way.

I spend much of my time training other employees on the best ways to use Twitter, for example. Just this week I completed the draft of Intel's overall strategy for Facebook. Today I will attend an all-day meeting focused on how Intel will track metrics differently in this new environment, monitoring things like online conversational buzz, re-Tweets, and earned and word-of-mouth media. It's a fantastically fun job, but it's quite challenging to be one of a few people with expertise in this area.

Most companies know they have to include social media in their marketing plans, yet companies continue to struggle with ways to do this effectively. Tracking the business value of these online social efforts remains one of the greatest hurdles companies face as they look to justify investments in this space. The big question on the minds of executives is, "Will we sell more products if employees are on Twitter?" At Intel we are working hard to identify the quantifiable benefits of social media marketing, from earned (word-of-mouth) media to influencing buzz.

One of the second major issues we're working to address is to help the company scale its efforts. Right now there are a few foot soldiers in the social space who really understand the milieu. However, to be successful we must engage more people at the company across the board and enable more employees to go forth and get online.

I am extremely lucky to work in the exciting and ever-changing field of social media marketing. My favorite aspects of my job are tackling the big problems, like how to measure the effectiveness of our efforts and what Intel should do with our Facebook presence. Yet my real passion lies in being a social media practitioner, someone who engages in social media on the company's behalf. I struggle to find the time to write blog posts (one of my favorite things to do), Tweet, and engage with customers online. My least favorite aspects are managing the details required for the implementation of software projects.

Since I'm one of the few who do what I do professionally (there are a plethora of consultants in this space), one perk is that I often get asked to speak at various conferences. Another benefit is that I often get to try out new products so that I might publicize them (like free access to Intel's Wimax solution). I am also lucky in that my organization has a huge impact on the company as a whole. We recently wrote social media guidelines (www.intel.com/sites/sitewide/ en_US/social-media.htm) that provide guidance to employees who wish to participate online on the company's behalf. Additionally, we're working to implement software that will track online buzz about Intel and its many brands. We anticipate that this will impact the entire company.

Since I spend much of my time writing and speaking in public, my degree in communications has been immensely beneficial. I am able to process my ideas into thoughtful conclusions and present them in an engaging way. My job also requires me to think strategically as I work to understand how specific issues might affect the company at a global level. On a daily basis I'm faced with issues that require me to consider all sides of an issue and how it might be perceived by the media, shareholders, and the public at large. Because I work for Intel, I also must possess a solid grasp of hardware and software technology in order to support Intel's marketing objectives.

Social media is one of the fastest growing arenas in technology marketing. It rather resembles the climate of the Internet bubble back in the early 1990s. However, research actually backs up the trend. Research conducted by Intel indicates that nearly 70 percent of consumers consult social networks before buying a computer. Additionally, in this challenging economic climate social media is seeing a 40 percent increase in spending on everything from marketing expertise to software technology. I anticipate this trend to continue as companies realize the importance of this new and growing field. From data analysts to Web developers, job candidates with proficiency with various Web technologies will be in high demand.

There is no shortage of information for students interested in this field. However there are many people who understand social media in theory but lack real on-the-job experience. I suggest that those who are interested in this area read blogs, subscribe to Twitter feeds of several social media experts, and read several books that provide terrific background into this growing area. These books include *Groundswell* by Charlene Li and Josh Bernhoff, *Personality Not Included* by Rohit Bhargava, *Wikinomics* by Tom Davenport, and *Satisfied Customers Tell Three Friends, Angry Customers Tell 3,000* by Pete Blackshaw.

As mentioned, the outlook for careers in this field is very positive. I believe it is one of the fastest growing areas in technology. Professionals in this area probably can expect to make close to six figures once they gain some experience in this area. The greatest opportunities, I believe, lie in the area of data analytics and Web development. After all, someone not only must create the platform and applications that help facilitate these social networks but someone else must also make sense of the data and insights that are gleaned from all of these online conversations. (Feller, 2009)

Jackie Cerretani Frank, User Experience Researcher
Facebook
Palo Alto, California

In the late 1990s, I became interested in making Web sites, so I got a book on how to write HTML and a copy of Photoshop and taught myself. My first client was the supervisor of my Americorps internship. My second client was an organic farm that traded me vegetables to first build and then maintain their Web site. Word of my skills spread in my community, leading to paid gigs, and eventually I found myself running my own Web and graphic design studio.

However, by 2006, two things became clear to me: first, the one-woman-band model of Web design, where I did all of the consultation, information architecture, marketing, planning, design, coding, and maintenance of a site, was becoming outdated. Not only had my clients' technical desires started to exceed my skill set, but I realized that I wanted to focus my expertise so I could work on more complex projects with multidisciplinary teams. It also became clear to me that I had a particular interest in user experience, and I wanted to learn how to better understand users so that I could make sites that fit users' needs and behaviors. As a result, I decided to return to graduate school at the University of Michigan School of Information to augment my design skills with a strong theoretical background and an arsenal of user research techniques, making me a competitive candidate for jobs with the complexity and collaboration I was looking for.

Simply put, Facebook has changed the way people communicate, keep in touch, cultivate relationships, and even enact social change. Its contribution has been enormous for being on the scene only a few short years—I think we won't know the true extent of its influence until we can look back from years out and see how much it has changed us.

Being a user researcher makes the work I do incredibly diverse. I consult with teams all over the company, meaning I get to contribute to Facebook's evolution on a number of fronts. The teams I work with are comprised of designers, developers, project managers, and others, meaning I get to hear and integrate the perspectives of a lot of different people. Finally, I talk to hundreds of users, from a huge range of backgrounds. All of this keeps my work both challenging and engaging.

My current work at Facebook has two main components. The first is helping design teams fine-tune ideas by providing usability feedback throughout the design process. This includes methods like user tests, heuristic analysis, card sorts, and interviews. The second is user research, which is less tied to a current design process and more exploratory: trying to understand users' thoughts, behaviors, expectations, motivations, and norms around a product. This is accomplished using methods such as interviews, surveys, ethnography, and observation. My team dedicates significant effort to keeping up on new methods and research coming from academic and industry sources and to thinking about how we can adapt existing methods to the unique circumstances at Facebook.

The projects we work on influence the lives of hundreds of millions of people, not only in how they keep in touch with their friends or share information, which is significant, but also in situations like the recent elections in Iran, where dissenters used Facebook to get information out when main news outlets were being shut out. Also, the company is very high profile, which lends an exciting gravitas to the work I do. If we don't get something right, we can expect to see it written up in *The New York Times*. Finally, Facebook is extremely agile, innovative, and open to new ideas—if you throw something really good on the table, it's got a fighting chance of actually getting built. What is the only downside of working at Facebook? Almost everyone I know is a user, and since they know I work here, they tell me all of their problems in hopes that I can fix them. It can be hard not to be able to help every one of them, especially when they're your friends.

There are several skills that are essential to my job. Technical skills include research design, experience with research methods, an understanding of statistics, the ability to interview well, problem solving, strategic thinking, and experience in design and coding. Personally, I feel that an innate sense of curiosity, humility, the ability to listen, boldness, willingness to collaborate, and a critical mind are essential to being a successful user researcher.

I think the best way to prepare yourself for a job in this field is to take advantage of the many opportunities to learn beyond your classes, which are often yours for the taking if you just volunteer. In that vein, some of my most useful experiences were the research projects I worked on in collaboration with professors and PhD students, and the project I worked on for the CHI conference Student Design Competition with four of my peers. These experiences challenged my assumptions and deepened my ability to use the skills I'd learned in my classes.

Also, get involved early with volunteering, jobs, internships, or personal projects. Make sites or apps for other people and practice usability techniques on them. Find an internship with a company doing usability. Get involved in research projects at your university, so you can learn best practices. Also, be a voracious learner— read academic papers, white papers, blogs, and articles. Go to talks and presentations. Listen and think about the perspectives of your peers. Not only will this knowledge make you more competitive for jobs and further study, but it will also make you better at what you do, giving you success in the long term. (Frank, 2009)

Ryan Buckley, Owner
Scripped and B2G Media
Boston, Massachusetts

I always had the entrepreneurial bug. I was big on computing as a middle school student during the mid-1990s, staying after school to do special projects with the computer teacher. I then became more interested in social issues, particularly the environment. In high school, I started a few clubs and really blossomed in college. This was just before "going green" became a savvy thing to do. After college at the University of California–Berkeley I dabbled in consulting and headed off to Harvard University's Kennedy School of Government and MIT's Sloan School of Management, where I concurrently rediscovered my entrepreneurial interests and was able to combine them with media and politics. This is how Scripped and B2G came to be.

Scripped (www.scripped.com) is an innovative and easy-to-use screenwriting software. For the professional or budding screenwriter, this Web site provides the community of filmmakers, producers, distributors, and agents access to scripts. Screenwriters are part of an online community in which messages can be sent, articles posted, and discussions developed. With Scripped, we're tackling the Hollywood studio system. Our goal is to become the largest repository of screenplays on the Internet. We'll use this content to become a virtual development department for studios and other clients.

B2G (www.b2gmedia.com) is even more in the social computing realm as a company that provides social media and Web strategy consulting services for business to government (B2G) specialists. In B2G, we tackle the political technology question and look at ways politicians can become better representatives of the people by using social media. We write and deliver reports to clientele ranging from police officer associations to candidates and other start-ups.

Our impact on the world is significant. With Scripped, we give hope to amateur writers. Our business model revolves around identifying the best talent, so we have to treat them all like they're the best. For many, it means getting that screenplay out of their system that's been bugging them for ten years. We get e-mails from teachers saying how they use it for writing classes and the kids love it. For B2G, we make public organizations and officials more accessible to the public. We use social technology to bring them closer to the people, and it feels good from our side, too.

The best part of my job is that I get to chose what I do. It's a double-edged sword. I eat what I kill, so to speak, and when I don't make deals I get really nervous. When things go well, though, you feel like you're on top of the world. Like you're the boss—and you really are. So it's a mixture of euphoria and despair. Right now I'm still a novice, but I look forward to the trials that lie ahead. I think that's what defines an entrepreneur in the social computing space. However, the perks are great: I take a break and play tennis in the middle of the day, every day. I take calls in my living room. I meet with people all over San Francisco. I have a nice story to tell. I think that's the biggest benefit. I'm proud of what I do.

However, I have to make money. As an entrepreneur, cash flow is king, and while I own one venture, the other has investors who require progress on the revenue front. It also is nerve-wracking to live day to day. You have to get used to uncertainty and be able to stomach a drought. In short, my responsibilities are to continue making steps and hope that they're moving forward.

Every day, I write and I outline nearly all day. My success with B2G came from being able to write very nice, compact proposals. People in the business and government world respond to tight writing, and this has always been a critical skill of mine. Soft skills are equally important. You have to be good on the phone. No one will work with you or want your product if you can't put them at ease at first on the phone and then in person. So in general, to own a business and be CEO, communication is key, even in the field of social computing.

Mobile is the hot field right now. It's all about mobile right now in the political technology space. B2G is working on an app that will make it very easy for fieldworkers doing canvassing (door to door information and donation gathering) to get more information quickly and process credit cards on the spot. Scripped is working on ways to make scripts accessible to mobile devices and help studios see the light in Internet-based sourcing opportunities.

My advice to the budding social media entrepreneur is to go online. It's all there, and don't be afraid to ask if you don't see what you're looking for. Ask bloggers, ask people on Facebook, ask authors of regular newspapers. E-mail addresses are all over the place, and sometimes it's just below the surface. Be bold in your approach to the Internet. You get to make it what you want.

Coming out of this recession, I believe both the online media and political technology fields are ripe for the picking. I'm excited about the 2010 race and the role that B2G will play in it. I'm excited about getting Scripped more notoriety as we complete our first Web production. We're leveraging social media as much as we can and learning by doing and watching others.

I need a minimum of $5,000 a month to cover taxes, rent, and student loan payments. I wouldn't be doing what I'm doing for less than $60,000. Other CEOs I know make closer to $100k, but if you're starting out and lucky enough to get an angel or venture capitalist to back your company (and cover your salary), you're looking at somewhere in the $70k–$90k range. In the long run (and two years is long), you're looking at salaries not much larger than this but at stock portfolios of rapidly increasing size. The payout comes all at once, and you cannot count on it. So spend your money wisely. (Buckley, 2009)

Careers in Social Computing: At a Glance

Your career in social computing can take many directions as you connect your interests and values to the type of functional area and type of organization that you pursue. Here are a few examples of real jobs representing some exciting "tracks" you can follow.

Consulting Track
Social Media Research Analyst
Crimson Consulting
San Francisco, California

Identify and monitor global conversations about clients' products and services; lead our clients to a deeper understanding of how social media audiences (blogs, forums, communities) are responding to their products and influencing others; monitor and profile the conversation landscape using a social media monitoring tool—including who are the biggest influencers and how they are influencing others; understand the conversation topics, topic trends—such as what they are saying about client's products, what is the overall sentiment, and what the implications are/what role the client could take in the conversation; provide recommendations based on social media research, analysis, and results. (LinkUp, accessed 2009)

Media/Entertainment Track
Community Manager
Songkick
London, United Kingdom

Monitor and participate in discussions on Songkick and elsewhere on the Web; think critically about what our community needs and work with the design team to implement new features and tools for them; creatively and proactively assist our users; identify and engage key users, ensuring the team knows about all feedback; rule-set and moderate within the community; track and analyze trends in community conversation and activity; establish metrics and report; prioritize bugs for quality assurance; suggest new killer features to product development; advise on how to communicate with our users in our copy and e-mails; be a highly visible team member and key ambassador for Songkick—you'll attend events on our behalf—and brainstorm offline events that will bring our community together. (Songkick, accessed 2009)

Green Track
Social Networking Web Developer
SustainLane
San Francisco, California

Work with our engineering, creative, and marketing teams to support social networking and other media (green information sharing platforms); utilize strong skills in standards-based XHTML and CSS, professional level Javascript, and experience with server-side scripting languages like JSP and PHP; create and improve user interfaces, use user testing and site analytics in an iterative process as well as understand Web site goals and metrics. (Dice, accessed 2009)

Social Justice Track
Web Producer
Center for Democracy and Technology (CDT)
Washington, DC

Manage our online presence and advise and assist with our online campaigns; shape an online strategy to improve capacity for online advocacy; oversee migration to new Drupal CMS; implement content strategy for CDT's Web site; manage existing content, including updates; develop summaries of material to make content easier to find and understand; monitor and build Web site traffic; engage constituents through the use of innovative Web tools and social media; design and implement interactive tools for use on CDT's Web site as well as externally; maintain and utilize our CRM to engage and inform mailing lists; design, create, and distribute multimedia packages; create graphics and new Web sites for Web campaigns and Web site. (Nonprofit Technology Network, accessed 2009)

Global Track
Web 2.0 Social Media Web Developer
CACI International
Washington, DC

Support the Knowledge Management Action Team on the Communities @ State program and the Diplopedia wiki; communicate and coordinate effectively with eDiplomacy staff, offices, and bureaus and with state personnel in federal agencies and personnel working for foreign diplomatic missions; provide strong technical and creative support in the troubleshooting of existing Web-based technologies and development of new solutions; help with content-management duties on eDiplomacy Web sites; help with editorial functions of the Diplopedia wiki; train users on Movable Type and Media Wiki. (Simply Hired, accessed 2009)

Resources for Further Information/Exploration

The following resources can help guide you in your career exploration within the field of social computing. Note that this is not a comprehensive list; there are numerous resources available related to the nuances of the field that are not included. The purpose of identifying key job posting sites and professional organizations is to make you aware of some of the main resources available and to also provide you with gateways to resources that will inform you of the types of careers available in the field.

Professional Organizations Relevant to Social Computing

- ACM—Association for Computing Machinery
  www.acm.org
- Special Interest Group on Electronic Commerce (SIGEC)
  www.sigecom.org
- Special Interest Group on Computers and Society (SIGCS)
  www.sigcas.org
- ASIS&T—American Society for Information Science and Technology
  www.asis.org
- SIGCHI—Computer Human Interaction
  http://sigchi.org
- Association for the Advancement of Artificial Intelligence
  www.aaai.org
- Economic Science Association
  www.economicscience.org
- CogSci—Cognitive Science Society
  www.cognitivesciencesociety.org
- CPSR—Computer Professionals for Social Responsibility
  www.cpsr.org
- ITG—Internet Technical Group
  www.internettg.org
- STC—Society for Technical Communication
  www.stc.org

Career Sites Relevant to Social Computing

- Boxes and Arrows
  http://jobs.boxesandarrows.com/jobs
- Creative Hotlist
  www.creativehotlist.com
- Dice
  www.dice.com

- Good Experience Job Openings
  http://goodexperience.com/blog/archives/cat_job_openings.php
- Internet Technical Group Job Bank
  www.internettg.org/post/job_list.asp
- OdinJobs
  www.odinjobs.com
- Social Media Jobs
  www.socialmediajobs.com
- LinkedIn Jobs
  www.linkedin.com/jobs

Education and Training

Given that social computing is an emerging field, specific curricula to prepare social computing professionals are still emerging as well. At the graduate level, information schools or iSchools have been adding coursework related to social computing, and faculty in these programs are conducting exciting research that continues to advance this branch of the information profession. At the University of Michigan (a leading iSchool), social computing is a specialization option within the Master of Science in Information program and within the undergraduate Informatics program.

To learn more and review a list of iSchools, visit www.ischools.org. Social computing and social media are also being incorporated into the curriculum of library and information science (LIS) programs, some of which are iSchools. All accredited LIS programs may be found through the American Library Association Web site at www.ala.org. In addition to iSchools, at both the undergraduate and graduate level, coursework focused on social computing or social media may be found in programs or departments such as human–computer interaction, computer science, engineering, communication studies, media studies, and journalism.

For example, The Massachusetts Institute of Technology (MIT) offers a program in media arts and sciences that includes social media coursework. Rochester Institute of Technology has developed coursework in social media, and the University of Sunderland in the United Kingdom has opened a master of arts program in public relations that includes a focus on the use of social media in public relations. Enterprise 2.0 and social media is also a new topic of study within MBA programs but is not yet fully represented in the MBA curricula.

Training in Web and programming languages that support the development and design of social computing applications is available at community colleges as well as universities including online or distance learning programs. However, broader understanding and interdisciplinary study at the undergraduate and graduate level is quickly becoming important for professional positions and for career advancement. Training and development firms are beginning to offer workshops, seminars, and courses on social media, though these are mainly targeting executives or communication professionals who seek to quickly build basic knowledge of how to apply social media to business operations.

References

Beuker, Igor. 2009. "Obama's Extreme Social Media Marketing Skills." ViralBlog, April 18. Available: www.viralblog.com/social-media/obamas-extreme-social-media -marketing-skills (accessed May 15, 2009).

Buckley, Ryan. 2009. Interview by Kelly Kowatch. August 11.

Dice. "Social Networking Web Developer." Available: http://seeker.dice.com/ jobsearch/servlet/JobSearch?op=101&dockey=xml/0/e/0ec19834d0c446cc2e3d8d 1adcd4faea@endecaindex&c=1&source=21&cid=simplyhired (accessed June 2, 2009).

Feller, Kelly Ripley. 2009. Interview by Kelly Kowatch. June 14.

Frank, Jackie Cerretani. 2009. Interview by Kelly Kowatch. August 5.

Holson, L. M. 2009. "Tweeting Your Way to a Job." *New York Times*, May. Available: www.nytimes.com/2009/05/21 (accessed May 21, 2009).

Hunter. 2009. "The FBI's New Social Media Strategy." Mediabistro.com WebNewser, May 19. Available; www.mediabistro.com/webnewser/political_web/the_fbis_new _social_media_strategy__116875.asp (accessed May 2009).

Indeed.com. 2009. "National Salary Trends." Available: www.indeed.com/salary/ (accessed May 15, 2009).

Kopytoff, Verne. 2008. "Kids Gain Valuable Skills from Time Online." SFGate.com, November 20. Available: http://sfgate.com/cgi-bin/article.cgi?f=/c//A2008/11/20/ BUKE147TA1.DTL (accessed May 15, 2009).

LinkUp, "Social Media Research Analyst." Available: www.linkup.com/results.php #q=Online%20community%20manager&l=&c=&d=25&m=normal&p=25&sort= r&tm=ALL&page=1&jobHash=abc3779d177641b62d2fbe84b3018f18 (accessed May 22, 2009).

Lipsman, Andrew. 2009. "Twitter.com Quadruples to 17 Million U.S. Visitors in Last Two Months." The comScore Blog, May 12. Available: http://blog.comscore.com (accessed May 15, 2009).

Mardesich, Jodi. 2008. "Business Uses for Twitter." Technology.inc.com, September. Available: http://technology.inc.com/networking/articles/200809/twitter.html (accessed May 20, 2009).

McGary, M. 2009. "Social Media Salaries." MizzInformation, April. Available: www .mizzinformation.com/2009/04/social-media-salaries.com (accessed May 2009).

Miller, Ron. 2009. "The Third Cloud and the Future of Social Computing." DaniWeb IT Discussion Community, April 5. Available: www.daniweb.com/blogs/ entry4208.html (accessed May 15, 2009).

Mosher, Barb. 2009. "Enterprises Want Social Computing, Not Just Another Facebook." CMSWire.com, April. Available: www.cmswire.com/cms/enterprise -20/enterprises-want-social-computing-not-just-another-facebook-004074.php (accessed May 15, 2009).

Nations, Daniel. 2009. "What Is Enterprise 2.0?" About.com Web Trends. Available: http://webtrends.about.com/od/office20//Aenterprise-20.htm (accessed May 15, 2009).

Nonprofit Technology Network. "Web Producer." Available: www.nten.org/node/ 7255 (accessed February 16, 2009).

OCLC.org. 2007. "Libraries and Social Networking." *Nextspace; The OCLC Newsletter* 7 (September). Available: www.oclc.org/nextspace/007/1.htm (accessed May 15, 2009).

Qualman, Erik. 2009a. *Socialnomics: How Social Media Transforms the Way We Live and Do Business.* Hoboken, NJ: John Wiley and Sons.

Qualman, Erik. 2009b. "Statistics Show Social Media Is Bigger Than You Think." Socialnomics Social Media Blog, August 11. Available: http://socialnomics.net/ 2009/08/11/statistics-show-social-media-is-bigger-than-you-think/ (accessed October 21, 2009).

Simply Hired. "Web 2.0 Social Media Web Developer." Available: www.simplyhired .com/a/jobs/list/q-social+media%20developer (accessed June 26, 2009).

Smith, Justin. 2008. "Intriguing Trends in Social Networking Growth during 1H 2008." Inside Facebook, July 27. Available: http://insidefacebook.com/2008/07/27/ intriguing-trends-in-social-networking-growth-growth-during-1h-2008/ (accessed May 15, 2009).

Smogger Social Media Blog. 2006. "An A–Z Guide to Web 2.0 Jargon." Available: http://smogger.wordpress.com/2006/12/30/social-media-literacy-an-a-z-guide-to -web20-jargon (accessed May 2009).

Songkick. "Community Manager." Available: www.songkick.com/jobs/ (accessed May 12, 2009).

Sutter, John D., and Brandon Griggs. 2009. "Oprah, Ashton Kutcher Mark Twitter 'Turning Point'." CNN.com, April 17. Available: www.cnn.com/2009/TECH/04/ 17/ashton.cnn.twitter.battle/index.html (accessed May 15, 2009).

Troiano, Nick. 2009. "EPA Marks Earth Day on Flickr." Socialgovernment.com, April 17. Available: http://socialgovernment.com (accessed May 20, 2009).

Valle, Elena del. 2008. "The Official PR Salary and Bonus Report." Hispanic MPR.com, July 5. Available: www.hispanicmpr.com/2008/07/25/pr-2008-salary-bonus-report -offers-market-insights-by-region-specialty/ (accessed May 2009).

Williams, Neil. 2009. "Beyond Cut and Paste: The Professional Skills Every Government Web Publisher Should Have." Mission Creep, April 26. Available: http:// neilojwilliams.net/missioncreep/2009/beyond-cut-and-paste-the-professional- skills-every-government-web-publisher-should-have/ (accessed May 2009).

Williamson, Debra Aho. 2009. "Social Networks: Five Consumer Trends for 2009."
eMarketer, February. Available: www.emarketer.com/Reports/All/Emarketer_
200566.aspx (accessed May 15, 2009).

Additional Sources

Wikipedia, s.v. "Social Computing," Available: http://en.wikipedia.org/wiki/Social_
computing (accessed January 2009).

Wikipedia. "Search Results: Social Computing." Available: http://en.wikipedia.org/
w/index.php?title=Special%3ASearch&redirs=1&search=social+computing&
fulltext=Search&ns0=1 (accessed January 2009).

Chapter 6

Information Systems Management

Introduction

Information systems managers are gurus of organizational effectiveness in the digital age, harnessing information for planning and decision making and aligning information problems with technology solutions to increase efficiency and accuracy in organizational operations. From managing networks for optimal computing capability to leading comprehensive information management strategy development, information systems managers are playing an increasingly pivotal role in achieving organizational success. Across all types of organizations, including corporate, government, education, and health care, information systems managers are helping to realize the potential of the information revolution, one organization at a time.

A global survey of 1,527 chief information officers (CIOs) supports the value-added focus of IT (information technology) in organizations, identifying top priorities including business process improvement, reducing enterprise costs, improving workforce effectiveness, virtualizing server/storage, and collaborating technologies (Ericson, 2009). According to Mark McDonald, group vice president and head of research for the leading information technology research firm Gartner EXP, "Organizations are going to meet the challenges they face in the economy by being very decisive in how they use their resources. The success of many decisions relies on having a strong set of information" (Ericson, 2009). McDonald continues, "You take process improvement, cost and workforce effectiveness and put them together with business intelligence, and that is a recipe for changing the way you work" (Ericson, 2009).

Another IT management research firm, Enterprise Management Associates, released IT management trends and technologies for 2009. Its chief operating officer

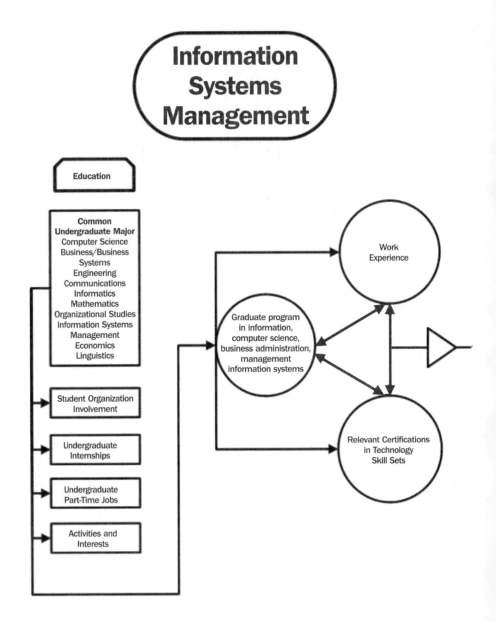

Figure 6. Information Systems Management Career Map
This diagram demonstrates several of the potential paths associated with a career in the field of information systems management.

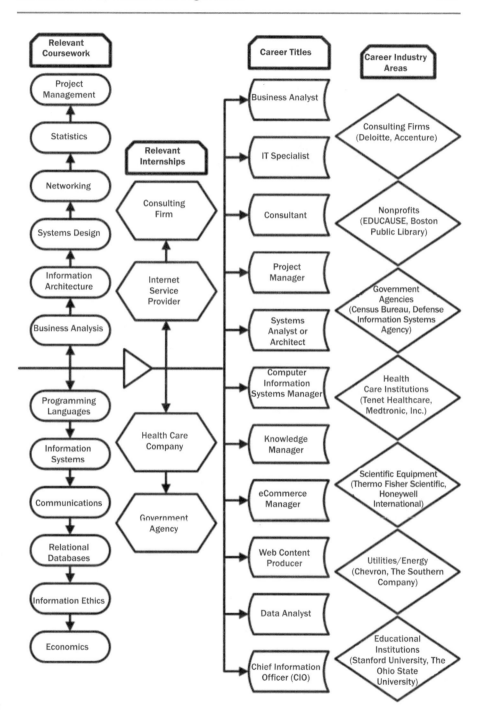

Dan Twing stated, "While there are obvious concerns surrounding the global economy, we expect that IT management initiatives will continue to gain corporate support and will have a positive impact on the business performance of the enterprise" (Kostek, 2009). Among the trends are green IT, IT governance, and security. Each of these trends relates to cost reduction as organizations turn to IT to help them weather the current economic storm. While the IT department is not a revenue source, investing in information systems management including IT is becoming central to organizations' efforts to remain financially solid or to gain an edge on the competition (Kostek, 2009).

Green IT is fast becoming a smart business strategy. While some organizations' green IT efforts will be motivated by their interest in the environment, the cost savings aspects of sustainability initiatives from increased return on investment and reduced power consumption will drive others to get on board as well. Similarly, IT governance is an investment that ties to lean business operations. While IT always helped different departments with their information technology needs, now a comprehensive information systems management approach is taking IT to a new level, implementing integrated systems for resource management, accounting, and project and portfolio management, increasing agility and nimbleness in decision making and project implementation. With a heightened need to stay on track and avoid pitfalls, risk management including IT security is another trend that connects with organizations' efforts to work smarter. Security threats continue to rise, and as cloud computing and virtualization become central features in organizational IT, new paradigms for security are emerging (Kostek, 2009).

Breadth and depth are both important when it comes to information management needs in today's organization. According to research conducted by Accenture, a global management consulting, technology services, and outsourcing company, organizations are moving toward enterprise-wide strategic approaches to information management. "The broad management of data (quality, security, governance) has had limited attention but will be critical in the next three years. In particular, analytics is highlighted as a future area of focus, with organizations increasing their investments in business intelligence and data warehousing as well as data management and architecture" (Accenture, 2007).

The shift to Web 2.0 and cloud computing has not only impacted individual consumers of the Internet but has triggered a transformation of the workplace as we know it. According to Kishore Swaminathan, Accenture's chief scientist, "We can expect a series of major technology trends to usher in an era of highly flexible and elastic capabilities that will allow businesses to stretch, change, and expand at will. . . . Such an era will add urgency to all aspects of data management as a result of maturing of technologies to extract intelligence from data" (Swaminathan, 2009). In the future, then, the Internet will be the center of IT and information management activities for business rather than huge software programs, creating flexibility and fostering swifter change from one tool to the next. Technology and information management will become increasingly tied to business operations, and the advancement of highly integrated systems will allow businesses to use data to inform decisions in increasingly sophisticated ways, including the use of data visualization tools and mashups that will afford employees direct access to live data as they need it (Swaminathan, 2009).

While the opportunity of technology to advance information systems management to new levels is great, truth be told, implementing these changes is a difficult challenge. Guiding large scale change in the way people use systems in their work is a major undertaking. Not only must the system be highly intuitive and usable for a wide range of individuals, but the proper incentives are critical to forward significant and lasting changes in behavior. The emerging field of incentive centered design addresses these very issues. At the University of Michigan School of Information, incentive centered design (ICD) is defined as "the art of designing systems or institutions that align participants' (individual) incentives with overall system (social) goals" (University of Michigan School of Information, 2009). Jeff Mackie-Mason, Arthur W. Burks Collegiate Professor of Information and Computer Science and Associate Dean for Academic Affairs at the University of Michigan has established the methodology of ICD, describing it as a process of "discovering and developing principles and methods for creating or improving information and communication systems, treating human motivation and responsiveness to incentives as central to the design problems and their solutions" (University of Michigan School of Information, 2009).

Clearly organizations are in need of creative and innovative information systems managers with interdisciplinary training across the fields of information, technology, and business in order to understand intertwining issues and lead organizations to reap the benefits of technology in the fast evolving information age. Those with technical know-how and the ability to lead and inspire others to move with or ahead of the changing enterprise landscape will be highly valued and will have added value to their organizations, resulting in lasting impact.

Skills and Abilities

For any professional career field, there are required skills and abilities that are important for success. In the field of information systems management (ISM), the right skills and abilities open doors to a variety of exciting professional positions in a wide range of industries and will provide a tool kit for success in landing your dream job.

While positions in ISM vary as far as skill level, experience, and education required, there are key skills, abilities, and characteristics that are highly sought for any type of professional ISM position in any industry. Outlined in the following sections are both the soft skills and abilities (behavioral/personality traits and characteristics) and hard skills and abilities (technical and career-specific knowledge) that are important for success in the field of ISM. Note that these are identified as the most common skills and abilities; this is certainly not an exhaustive list of all of the valuable skills and abilities that are beneficial for this career field.

> ☑ QUICK FACT!
> Management insights, technology perspectives, and strong communication skills will make you a top candidate in the eyes of ISM recruiters.

Soft Skills

- Ability to communicate (verbal and written), to achieve:
  - Negotiation
  - Persuasion
  - Presentation
- Ability to work in collaboration/be a team player
- Strategic or systems thinking skills
- Leadership capabilities
- Analytical/problem solving skills
- Flexibility/adaptability

Hard Skills

- Business systems management: Have working knowledge of complex business technologies, of business and technical aspects of the Web, and of industry standards.
- Project management: Deliver and manage projects, from planning, organizing, and managing resources to bring about the successful completion of specific project goals and objectives.
- Technical knowledge and skills: Dependent on the nature of the position and career pathway, not all are required, but some are commonly mentioned in many job postings as desirable, particularly for the more technical ISM jobs such as systems analyst or computer information systems manager:

- Database management: SQL, MySQL, Access, Excel
- Operating systems: Linux
- Programming: JAVA, C++, PHP, Ruby on Rails, J2EE, .Net
- Web languages: HTML, CSS, AJAX, XML, PHP
- Product design/development: Generate ideas, develop concepts, and test and manufacture or implement a physical object or service; improve an existing product or develop new kinds of products.
- User experience design and research: Collect and analyze data about the people who will use a product or system and the context in which it will be used.
- Security: Ensure the confidentiality, integrity, and availability of systems, networks, and data through the planning, analysis, development, implementation, maintenance, and enhancement of information systems security programs, policies, procedures, and tools.
- Systems analysis: Apply analytical processes to the planning, design, and implementation of new and improved information systems to meet the business requirements of customer organizations.
- Network services: Plan, analyze, design, develop, test, assure quality, configure, install, implement, integrate, maintain, and/or manage networked systems used for the transmission of information in voice, data, and/or video formats.
- Data management: Plan, develop, implement, and administer systems for the acquisition, storage, and retrieval of data.
- Systems administration: Plan and coordinate the installation, testing, operation, troubleshooting, and maintenance of hardware and software systems.

ISM professionals require a broad range of skills. Generally speaking, the field of information systems management is a blend of information systems, technology, and business management. The field is multidisciplinary, drawing from business, economics, psychology, and sociology for effective design, and from computer science for the engineering of systems. Overall, the profession has two purposes: the use of information systems to solve business problems and the management of technology, which includes product development.

While advanced technical skills aren't required for all ISM jobs, they are essential for computer and information systems managers who must have a solid understanding of technology and must be able to communicate effectively with diverse constituents including IT, line managers, and customers. Systems administration skills are important for these positions.

Many ISM jobs involve planning, coordinating, and directing research to improve the company's operations. The person working in this capacity must have a good understanding of computer systems as well as a firm grasp of business principles in order to be successful. ISM professionals need a keen understanding of people, management processes, and customer needs. Some employers look for managers who have experience with the specific software or technology used in the organization as well as a background in either consulting or business management. The expansion of ecommerce has elevated the importance of business insight, and, consequently, many information systems managers are called on to make important business decisions.

Strong project management skills are extremely important as the management of technical projects is an integral component of almost any ISM position. Knowledge of general business management is also important, such as having an understanding of how a business functions, how it earns revenue, and how technology relates to the core competencies of the business. As a result, some organizations now prefer to give these positions to people who have spent time outside of purely technical fields (U.S. Department of Labor, Bureau of Labor Statistics, 2009). Furthermore, because it is critical that there is a match between system user and system goal, incentive-centered design skills should be a fundamental building block within the ISM field. Careful attention to individual incentives can lead to vast improvements in information systems (University of Michigan School of Information, 2009).

Soft skills are just as important as hard/technical skills in the ISM field. ISM professionals must possess strong interpersonal, communication, and leadership skills because they are required to interact not only with staff members but also with people across and outside of their organizations. They must possess team skills to lead and work on group projects and other collaborative efforts. Strong problem-solving and analytical skills are essential as well. ISM professionals must apply appropriate problem-solving methodologies to the analysis and solution of problems. They must be able to effectively evaluate issues related to information systems and work productivity.

Effective analytical skills should reflect a systems thinking approach to business problems and solutions. An ISM professional must demonstrate skills in systems analysis appropriate to the management of information systems projects. Big-picture and strategic thinking is critical, as ISM professionals must be able to conceptualize and manage the design and implementation of high quality information systems. Equally important are strong interpersonal skills; many ISM professionals coordinate activities of diverse groups of people from top management executives, departmental managers, equipment suppliers, and other contractors (Career Overview, 2009). ISM professionals must be able to communicate effectively using oral, written, and multimedia techniques. They must also be able to effectively lead, collaborate with, and motivate cross-functional teams to deliver on-time products and meet goals.

> ☑ QUICK FACT!
> Information systems managers must have a keen understanding of how individuals in organizations relate and make decisions.

KEY WORDS TO KNOW

The following are some key ISM terms that you will see throughout this chapter. If you are interested in pursuing this career field, it's a good idea to become familiar with their meaning:

- **information systems**: A tool for managing and processing information, typically computer-supported.
- **information systems management**: The planning, acquisition, development, and coordinated use of tools that facilitate information processing, analysis, and business operations.
- **systems approach**: A framework of thinking that is based on the belief that the component parts of a system can best be understood in the context of relationships with one another and with other systems rather than in isolation.
- **incentive-centered design**: The art of designing systems that align users' incentives with overall system goals.
- **information security**: The protection/safeguarding of information and information systems from harm and destruction. This type of security goes beyond the network—it applies to the organization as a whole.
- **IT security**: Refers to the protection of an organization's network—the hardware, software, and overall network of an organization—from harm and destruction (virus, hacking, etc.).
- **user experience design**: An effort to intentionally facilitate the experience a person has as a result of his or her interactions with a particular product, service, or system.
- **information economics**: Provides a foundation for understanding systems and individual behavior.

Professional Roles

The role of the information systems manager is multifaceted. To better understand the range and scope of ISM professional roles it may help to compare and contrast the duties and goals of the most common ISM career pathways. Common duties that crossover most ISM positions include planning, coordinating, and facilitating the technology and information management activities of an organization. Additionally, information systems managers interpret and help determine both the technical and business goals of an organization in consultation with top management and make systematic plans for the accomplishment of these goals. Therefore, a strong understanding of both technology and business practices are the foundation for success in any professional ISM role.

Common career pathways:

- Systems analysis and design
- Applications development
- Systems architecture development
- Data warehousing and data mining
- Systems integration
- Product and technology management and/or development
- Business analysis
- Information systems project management
- Information technology sales/marketing

Common roles:

- **Systems Analyst**: Attempts to provide a bridge between the business requirements and the technical definition of the IT solution.
- **Business Analyst**: Collects data and information and creates reports to detail business requirements and support decision making.
- **Project Manager**: Coordinates scheduling, work flows, and budget requirements for specific projects. Guides and tracks all phases of the project alongside key players in the process, including clients, technology specialists, consultants, and sales representatives.
- **IT Consultant**: Focuses on advising businesses on how best to use information technology to meet business objectives. In addition to providing ad-

vice, IT consultants often implement, deploy, and administer IT systems on businesses' behalf.

- **Systems Architect**: The high-level designer of a system, provides the engineering view of the users' vision for what the system needs to accomplish.
- **Computer Information Systems Manager**: Supervises the programming, support, and analysis departments of an organization. Works with all phases of computer activities including planning, developing, implementing, and managing computing systems.
- **Management Information Systems Directors**: Oversees all resources and systems within a firm. Leads and coordinates the many services available to employees, including the help desk, and makes valuable suggestions to technological practice as it relates to software and hardware development.
- **IT Director**: Manages computing resources for an organization.
- **Chief Information Officer (CIO)**: Provides high level leadership for processes and practices supporting the flow of information in an organization.
- **Chief Technology Officer (CTO)**: Provides high level leadership for technology infrastructure, manages and plans technical standards, and oversees IT activities for an organization.

The following is a list of some of the most common job titles and industries that actively recruit ISM professionals (bachelor's and master's level):

- Business Analyst, Abbott Labs (pharmaceutical/health care)
- Systems Analyst, Department of Defense (government)
- Chief Technology Officer (CTO), Microsoft (technology)
- Chief Information Officer, Motorola (consumer products)
- IT Director, Yahoo! (technology)
- IT Consultant, Booz Allen Hamilton (consulting)
- Technical Architect, MasterCard (financial)
- eCommerce Consultant, Amazon.com (e-commerce)
- Project Manager, State Farm Insurance (insurance)
- Systems Designer, Penn State University (academic/education)

Occupational Outlook

Companies realize more than ever the importance of staying competitive and increasing efficiency by continuing to install sophisticated computer networks and launching complex intranets and Web sites. Thus the outlook for ISM professionals remains strong. With the increasing importance of technology in the workplace, it is not surprising that the employment of information systems management professionals is expected to grow faster than the average for all occupations through the year 2016 (U.S. Department of Labor, Bureau of Labor Statistics, 2009). The most active industries recruiting for ISM professionals are technology, e-commerce, marketing, consulting, government, defense, insurance, and financial services.

A fast growing area within information systems management is security. With more and more business being carried out over computer networks, security will continue to be a critical issue. As hackers become more sophisticated and viruses become more complex and destructive, organizations need to understand how their systems are vulnerable and how to protect their infrastructure and Internet sites. Organizations of all types will increasingly hire security experts to fill key roles in their information technology departments because the integrity of their computing environments is of utmost importance.

With the explosive growth of electronic commerce and the capacity of Web 2.0 technology to create new relationships with customers, the role of the ISM professional will continue to evolve. Those who have experience in Web applications and Internet technologies will become increasingly vital to their organizations and will be in the best position to achieve the potential of highly integrated and advanced information systems to achieve optimal organizational success.

Salary Information

Earnings for ISM professionals vary by specialty and level of responsibility. Depending on specialty and skill area, approximate annual salaries for ISM professionals range from $47,000 for the bottom 10 percent to $140,000 for the top 10 percent. Average earnings ranged from $75,000–$85,000 (Career Overview, 2009).

The Robert Half Technology 2010 Salary Guide (Robert Half Technology, 2010) lists the following annual salary ranges for information systems management positions:

- IT Manager and technical services manager: $62,500–$89,250
- Chief technology officer (CTO): $101,000–$180,000
- Chief security officer: $97,500–$150,000

According to the Bureau of Labor Statistics' *Occupational Outlook Handbook*, 2008–2009 Edition, median annual earnings of managers were $101,580. The middle 50 percent earned between $79,240 and $129,250. ISM professionals with a bachelor's degree or higher along with a few years experience can expect salaries at the middle to higher end of these ranges. High level leadership positions such as CTO or CIO earnings can be found in the top percent of the ranges. Leadership positions require advanced degrees along with substantial work experience and proven ability in the field. Additional incentives for becoming an upper-level manager are the many associated benefits such as stock option plans, bonuses, and expense accounts (U.S. Department of Labor, Bureau of Labor Statistics, 2009).

Profiles—Perspectives of New Professionals

Elizabeth Larson, Sr. Knowledge Manager
Syngenta
Research Triangle Park, North Carolina

Having a solid education provided a backbone for my career path. However, my career path has been shaped by understanding the challenges that an organization faces and assessing ways that I can best address these needs.

At Syngenta, I oversee the knowledge management, research, and library functions for a research division within the company. I am responsible for developing the knowledge management strategy for my group and am involved with various projects to implement this strategy. Prior to my current role, I also oversaw program execution and communication and recruitment for a global leadership development program. I acted as a change agent to streamline operations and knowledge management processes, which resulted in efficiencies in program delivery. I also managed day-to-day operations and rectified human resource, technology, and operations questions with participants. I developed knowledge management systems to manage recruiting workflow, communications, and program tracking. Last, I directed communication strategy and branding with country

HR leaders and business unit leaders to improve program positioning and communication flow.

Since I am now in a new role, there are elements of change that are associated with implementing changes in behavior. I have been able to make gradual changes to implement processes and educate individuals regarding information products and knowledge sharing strategies. I can say that I am sought out for my experience in navigating the organization and am looked to for advice on various projects.

Syngenta, as an organization, continues to grow and develop its own identity following a spinout nine years ago. Being a part of a research-based organization, it is critical to embed processes that capture, preserve, and reuse the intellectual capital of the organization. This needs to be done delicately to allow for innovative thinking not to be stifled. Within my unit, I am exposed to a variety of areas and projects that have provided me additional growth opportunities to expand my interpersonal, technical, and managerial skills. Much of my informal learning has come through personal interactions with colleagues in my organization and within my personal network. However, a challenge to being a part of a collaborative environment is the volume of meetings and limited time to complete projects. This frustration is balanced by opportunities to travel globally as part of my work and meet with colleagues outside of the United States, which enhances my understanding of global business knowledge.

My educational background includes a combination of English, communication, marketing, and information science studies from the University of Michigan School of Information. I focused my master's degree studies initially on special libraries and supplemented the curriculum with business electives. While this training provided initial entry into the marketplace, my ongoing education and training have been pivotal to my development. I have taken advantage of developing my knowledge in project management, time management, presentations, technology training, coaching and leadership, industry training, and company knowledge to complement my formal education.

For those who are considering entering the field of knowledge management, I find that the skills that are most critical include business aptitude, change management, communication skills, leadership and coaching training, and technology competence. Organizations will continue to evolve based on different business models and needs. While I believe that trends are short lived and can be easily outpaced by the latest and greatest technologies, information professionals need to continue to evolve and not be tied to a physical location, collection of materials, or traditional values. Individuals need to have broad skill training and be prepared to adapt to new environments. The ability to position the value of your skills is critical.

I recommend to readers that they think about the skills that they feel will be helpful for an organization so problems can be solved for them. It isn't enough to show up and expect there to be a suitable career path already in place. You may need to build your own career path.

I feel that knowledge management continues to evolve. Those of us working in this field need to move away from the focus on tools and focus on changing behavior to allow individuals to work smarter while preserving the "corporate brain." Change management programs take time and are often undervalued in an organization when the effects are not immediately measurable. (Larson, 2009)

David Hsiao, Analyst
Accenture
Detroit, Michigan

I've always enjoyed learning and working with computers and technology. Even though I graduated from the University of California–Berkeley with a degree in bioengineering, I took several programming courses and learned other computer related skills in my free time. However, I did not want to be a pure program developer. Instead, my interests lay in how to use technology to improve daily lives and make work easier and more efficient.

My day-to-day responsibilities at Accenture include meeting with clients to gather business requirements and holding internal meetings to translate these requirements into technical terms. Depending on the different phases of a project, my responsibilities can range from writing design deliverables to the actual development work (programming), such as customization of "off-the-shelf" products.

As a global and highly diverse company, our overall strategy is to try to help organizations streamline their workflow process, converting the existing process from manual process to automatic. Accenture is trying to help organizations consolidate different groups/divisions/branches together and utilize technology to improve the communication among different units within the organization.

I like the fact that what I am doing is actually contributing to an organization and that the impact reaches as many as thousands of people. As the project goes from development to production, I can see the progress and the hardship that the project overcomes when the system finally goes live—with people actually using it. I travel weekly to other cities depending on the projects to which I am assigned.

The programming skills I learned from my undergraduate years and also in the University of Michigan School of Information (SI) definitely helped me become familiar with the technical side of my work functions. The hands-on projects and client-facing experience learned from SI also provided me with more confidence in different meetings and presentations.

Since the company is essentially a technology consulting firm, being technically inclined helps me to grasp new technical ideas faster. However, as a consulting company working on client sites, the ability to deal with difficult situations and help or guide the client to gain the most from the technology is also essential.

One trend in the future is to consolidate different legacy systems into one centralized system for easier management and more efficient communication. With the heavy reliance on electronic files and systems, the ability to retain, retrieve, and modify information securely becomes very important (including in legal terms).

We all know that systems are very powerful, but only when they are used correctly. In addition, all systems have limitations, and knowing those limitations can guide design changes or improvements. Therefore, for anyone considering this field, I would suggest that familiarity with technology is a must. Knowing what is going on behind the scenes (in the back-end system) definitely helps when trying to design a solution.

During the downturn of the economy, my company was not immune from impact. However, I would imagine as the economy starts to pick up, organizations will have more need to upgrade or convert existing systems to cope with growth. The starting salary for someone with no experience will probably range from $50k to $60k depending on location. However, salary often jumps as much as 20 percent during promotional year (every two to three years). In addition, when changing from a consulting company to corporate environment, salaries are also known to increase. (Hsiao, 2009)

David Dworin, Consultant
Gallup
Chicago, Illinois

At Gallup, I entered as a consulting specialist, helping to implement and analyze employee and customer surveys. I currently lead an internal initiative around improving our processes and internal consulting capabilities. About 80 percent of my time is spent managing what we now call a Consulting Resource Center but which has had a number of other names over the past 18 months. I'm helping the organization improve the quality of its consulting by focusing on improved execution of our projects. Over the past year this has included changing expectations around project management and leading process improvement activities; in the future, this will involve working on how we build capability around research, analytics, and change management.

On an average day, I'll spend time coaching consultants on the use of our best practice project management tools, conduct strategic analysis for our executives, follow up with the teams behind a process improvement workshop I've led, help our business development group plan and scope projects, and connect with operations managers about how they can better support our consulting work. Like most jobs, it varies a lot from day to day.

The other 20 percent of my time is spent leading projects, primarily in our human capital consulting area. This involves the implementation of our employee engagement measurement programs (the Q12), our selection research tools, and our leadership development programs. In addition to helping clients get the solutions up and running in their organization, I'll conduct and deliver analysis from the data we've gathered and help them develop high impact training programs to drive organizational change.

Like most companies, we're dealing with a downturn in business-to-business spending that has severely hurt our growth plans. At the same time, the problems we faced before the recession haven't gone away. Over the past few years we've embarked on a change from a survey research company into a consulting firm, and this change isn't complete yet. We still struggle every day with what it means to be a "research-based consulting firm" and how we're going to accomplish this. At the same time, many aspects of our culture that made us successful up to this point, such as a focus on individual achievement and quantitative performance measurement, may not be the things that will help us thrive as a consulting firm, where we need to be more collaborative and measure performance in the abstract.

In my own role, my job is to transform the organization from a survey research company into a world class consulting firm, and I measure impact based on the progress toward that goal. Because I don't have strong quantitative measures, I rely heavily on the qualitative perceptions of others, especially our senior executives and thought leaders.

Within our clients, our goal is to change the way organizations relate to their people and to their customers, and where we're successful we create a fundamentally different experience for everyone involved. We define impact by the difference we make in those interactions as measured by our own surveys and, more importantly, by the difference we make in the bottom lines or other key metrics of the organizations we partner with.

Overwhelmingly, my favorite part of my job is the level of flexibility I have to set my own direction and execute against it. My firm's leadership has placed on me a high level of trust that allows me to continuously initiate and execute projects that will align with the organization's interests, and this has allowed me the freedom to work when, where, and how I want.

Every day I get to try new things and experiment within the sandbox of one organization, where I have the flexibility to make mistakes, recover, learn, and innovate. Within reason, I also rarely get told "no" when I ask for things like tools or software. I've worked in other organizations where you had to fill out five forms in triplicate just to get Internet access, and that just isn't the case here.

More than any set of experiences, my biggest asset has been the diversity of experiences. A strong background in the social sciences from Michigan State University taught me how to synthesize a lot of information into a compelling case and communicate it effectively. A basic understanding of computer science and programming has allowed me to credibly communicate with our technology and operations groups where other consultants failed. Most important for my consulting work, the economics courses I took in graduate school at the University of Michigan School of Information gave me a solid foundation for understanding systems and individual behavior, and the information economics and incentive design courses especially gave me a keen understanding of how individuals in organizations relate and make decisions.

The most important skills in my job are an affinity for systems thinking, an ability to communicate and build trust with lots of different groups, and a sense of humor. Computer skills are helpful, but they are more of an added bonus than a necessity. I suggest to anyone who might be interested in this field to learn to communicate effectively and think critically in a structured way. Read extensively and widely.

Organizations always have a dearth of strong leaders and solid people managers, so anyone with these talents will always be in high demand. I think project management, especially outside of technology, will also continue to be in high demand, though from my experience there's a huge difference between strong project managers and the merely mediocre.

It's hard to tell right now what the employment outlook is for the field, but while consulting has been fairly hard hit in the recent economic downturn, it tends to recover well along with the rest of the economy. Because of the natural churn in the business, there are always openings, and smaller to midsize firms are actually thriving in this environment as they're able to react quicker than the larger and more established firms. (Dworin, 2009)

Careers in Information Systems Management: At a Glance

Your career in information systems management can take many directions as you connect your interests and values to the type of functional area and type of organization that you pursue. Here are a few examples of real jobs representing some exciting tracks you can follow.

Health Informatics Track
Community Health Information Systems Manager
St. Luke's Episcopal Health Charities (SLEHC)
Houston, Texas

Provide leadership and oversight on the development of community health information endeavors, including development of opportunities for new projects and data sources, initiatives, and partnerships and supervision of related staff, student interns, and fellows; provide leadership and oversight for all Web activities, including the Community Health Information System, the Community Resource Directory, Project Safety Net, the Breast Health Resource Mapping Project, and Preschool for All and the SLEHC Website in general, which houses these components and includes information for the SLEHC work domains. (St. Luke's Human Resources, accessed 2009)

Government Track
Knowledge and Issues Strategist
Ohio Public Employees Retirement System (OPERS)
Columbus, Ohio

Conduct and support research into a wide variety of issues related to retirement, which is used to formulate strategic messages to constituent groups that are linked into consistent threads; develop and implement cataloging systems as well as preserve the freshness and accuracy of cataloged items; manage and maintain various information sources and extract information on a daily basis for immediate, presentational, and archival use; produce original research, content compilation, reporting, and the analysis of current and proposed retirement policies; serve as a resource for information mining requests; work closely with Web Content/Design Specialist, Webmaster, Portal Content Manager, or other information technologist to design, feed, and maintain a readily accessible portal for filing, cataloging, storing, and retrieving information in various formats; research and identify new sources of information relevant to the retirement industry and issues that may be affected by political, social, and environmental factors. (Ohio Public Employees Retirement System, accessed 2009)

Media/Entertainment Track
Media Asset Management Functional Lead
Fox Filmed Entertainment
Los Angeles, California

Lead efforts associated with the implementation and support of the media asset management component of Fox's digital vault and support of Fox's enterprise wide marketing collateral repository, including business process mapping, requirements gathering, design, testing, training, and documentation; perform analysis and design of applications based on customer needs; lead development and testing activities, developing new complex features and functions for software applications; assist infrastructure group with configuration and deployment of new systems; develop comprehensive business processes flows, application security modeling; serve as a coach to contractor resources, to ensure that project processes and procedures are followed and adapted to support project goals. (Fox Filmed Entertainment Human Resources, accessed 2009)

Green Track
Environmental Planner/Data Specialist
Houston-Galveston Area Council
Houston, Texas

Collect, process, quality assure, analyze, and distribute water quality and other environmental data generated through the Clean Rivers Program including obtaining the water quality data from local partners and subcontractors; assist Clean Rivers staff with water quality monitoring field work; process data; perform Q/AQC and manage the water quality database; prepare specially formatted data files and related data for delivery to TCEQ and other funding agencies; analyze water quality data, prepare reports and presentations for local technical groups; maintain sections of the Clean Rivers Program Web site; manage multiple subcontracts with local governments and laboratories. (Houston-Galveston Area Council, accessed 2009)

Social Justice Track
Manager, Multimedia Design (Web)
Teach for America
New York, New York

Amass and develop resources; cultivate community through discussion boards, forums, and social networking; curate a space for knowledge development through wikis, showcasing the stories of classrooms across the country and creating online workshops and courses; creatively collaborate with content and multimedia designers to identify Web-based solutions including eLearning courses, Flash modules, and the creation of proprietary Web pages and sites, managing to successful completion multimedia projects; update/overhaul a variety of existing proprietary internal Web sites, managing all aspects of Web site development, including working with outside vendors, front end coding, quality assurance testing, support inquiries, and maintenance; administering and supporting existing data systems including current eLearning course platform and Teaching & Learning Lab site (built on Drupal). (Mediabistro.com, accessed 2009)

Global Track
Information Systems Officer
Office of Information and Communication Technology
United Nations
New York, New York

Manage projects involving feasibility studies, systems analysis, design, development, and implementation of new, moderately complex systems; develop detailed system and other functional specifications and user documentation for major systems; provide specialized advice to users, analyzing users' requirements and translating these into new applications; determine application systems integration and linkage issues; maintain, upgrade, or enhance existing user systems; troubleshoot and provide continuing user support; develop and maintain computer programs that require integration of many interrelated systems and program elements; ensure appropriate data security and access controls considering both local and wide area issues; organize and perform unit and integrated testing, designing, and utilizing test bases; assist users in acceptance testing. (United Nations Human Resources, accessed 2009)

Resources for Further Information/Exploration

The following resources can help guide you in your career exploration within the field of information systems management. This is not a comprehensive list; there are numerous other resources available related to the nuances of this field that are not included. The purpose of identifying key job posting sites and professional organizations is to make you aware of some of the main resources available and to also provide you with gateways to resources that will inform you of the types of careers available in the field.

Professional Organizations Relevant to Information Systems Management

- ACM—Association for Computing Machinery
  www.acm.org
- AITP—Association of Information Technology Professionals
  www.aitp.org
- ASIS&T—American Society for Information Science and Technology
  www.asis.org
- ASAPM—American Society for the Advancement of Project Management
  www.asapm.org
- CPSR—Computer Professionals for Social Responsibility
  www.cpsr.org
- DAMA—Data Management International
  www.dama.org
- IACIS—International Association for Computer Information Systems
  www.iacis.org
- IEEE—Institute of Electrical and Electronics Engineers
  www.ieee.org
- IPMA—International Project Management Association
  www.ipma.ch
- ISA—Instrumentation, Systems and Automation Society
  www.isa.org
- ISOC—Internet Society
  www.isoc.org
- ITG—Internet Technical Group
  www.internettg.org
- PMI—Project Management Institute
  www.pmi.org
- STC—Society for Technical Communication
  www.stc.org

Career Sites Relevant to Information Systems Management

- ComputerWork.com
  www.computerwork.com

- devBistro
  www.devbistro.com
- Dice
  www.dice.com
- Icrunchdata
  www.icrunchdata.com
- Just Project Manager Jobs
  www.justprojectmanagerjobs.com
- Nonprofit Tech Jobs
  www.nten.org/jobs
- Tech-Centric.net
  www.tech-centric.net
- Internet Technical Group Job Bank
  www.internettg.org/post/job_list.asp
- OdinJobs
  www.odinjobs.com
- Wired Jobs
  http://jobs.wired.com

Education and Training

Information systems management positions typically require at least a bachelor's degree, with relevant majors including but not limited to informatics, computer science, engineering, business, marketing, economics, and psychology. Most people working as professional information systems managers accrue a few years of relevant work experience before taking on this role (JobMonkey.com, 2009). Those planning to pursue ISM positions directly from college should pursue relevant internships and part time jobs to build experience, ideally in the particular industry or type of organization in which they hope to work professionally.

Individuals who seek continued career advancement will typically need a master's degree in information systems management or management information systems, information or information science, business, economics, computer science, engineering, or related degree (Career Overview, 2009). Career advancement for ISM professionals will also require the development of advanced technical knowledge and skills as well as high-level communication and organizational skills. For top leadership positions, employers prefer a graduate degree with technology as a core component. This type of preparation will continue to be critical for the field as more information systems managers are making important technology decisions as well as business decisions for their organizations.

A few ISM professionals may be able to secure positions with an associate's degree, but they must have substantial work experience and must have acquired additional training and skills on the job. Certainly, associate's degree programs can lead to a number of technical positions within an information systems or IT department. Given the varied educational options to enter this field, a college search tool such as Petersons.com may be useful in searching for potential academic programs at the associate, undergraduate, and graduate level. For continued success in this field, ongoing professional development and updating of technical skills will be important.

Technical certification programs abound in the information systems management and IT arenas. Highly regarded certifications are offered by CISCO and Microsoft, and a range of professional associations also offer training and certification. It is important to be a wise consumer of any educational program, since the needs of employers change rapidly and certification programs can be created quickly and easily. It is advisable to check with employers of interest about their preferred certifications for various positions or seek this information through professionals working in positions of interest.

References

Accenture. 2007. "Accenture CIO Survey: Information Management Trends." Available: www.accenture.com/ciosurveyim (accessed June 28, 2007).

Career Overview. 2009. "Computer Information Systems Manager Careers, Jobs and Employment Information." Available: www.careeroverview.com/computer-infor mation-systems-manager-careers.html (accessed June 2009).

Dworin, David. 2009. Interview by Kelly Kowatch. May 28.

Ericson, Jim. 2009. "Gartner: BI, BPM Top Priorities in 2009." Information Management Online, January 15. Available: www.information-management.com/news/ 10002406-1.html (accessed July 2, 2009).

Fox Filmed Entertainment Human Resources. "Media Asset Management Functional Lead." LinkUp Job Search Engine. Available: www.linkup.com/results.php?q= information%20systems%20management&l=&m=normal&c=&list=&d=25&t[10] =advertising&t[13]=arts,%20media%20and%20publishing&t[14]=publishing&t [15]=tv,%20film%20and%20video&t[16]=writing%20and%20editing&p=25&sort =r&tm=ALL&page (accessed June 29, 2009).

Houston-Galveston Area Council. "Community Health Information Systems Manager." LinkUp Job Search Engine. Available: www.linkup.com/results.php?q= information%20systems%20management&l=&m=normal&c=&list=&d=25&t[12] =agriculture,%20forestry%20and%20fishing&p=25&sort=r&tm=ALL&page=1& jobHash=ea7d0eef0de416a629de3dabbface632 (accessed June 29, 2009).

Hsiao, David. 2009. Interview by Kelly Kowatch. May 26.

JobMonkey.com. 2009. "High Paying Jobs." Available: www.jobmonkey.com/highpayingjobs/info-systems-managers.html (accessed June 2009).

Kostek, Jessica. 2009. "Information Technology—EMA Outlines 12 Hot IT Management Trends to Watch for in 2009." TMCNet.com, January 15. Available: www.tmcnet.com (accessed July 2, 2009).

Larson, Elizabeth. 2009. Interview by Kelly Kowatch. May 28.

Mediabistro.com. "Job Listing: Resources, Teach for America Human." Available: www.mediabistro.com/joblistings/jobview.asp?joid=90416&page=1 (accessed June 29, 2009).

Ohio Public Employees Retirement System. "OPERS Career Listings." Available: www.opers.org/about/employment/careers/listings/Knowledge-Strategist-052109.htm (accessed June 29, 2009).

Robert Half Technology. 2010. *2010 Salary Guide*. Menlo Park, CA: Robert Half Technology.

St. Luke's Human Resources. "Community Health Information Systems Manager." LinkUp Job Search Engine. Available: www.linkup.com/results.php#q=information%20systems%20management&l=&m=normal&d=25&c=&sort=r&p=25&tm=ALL&page=1&jobHash=2c06d636cdd9e66c2cc61d2683ee997c (accessed June 29, 2009).

Swaminathan, Kishore S. 2009. "An Everything-Elastic Business." *Information Management Magazine*, June. Available: www.information-management.com/issues/2007_59/data_management_analytics (accessed July 1, 2009).

United Nations Human Resources. "Information Systems Officer." LinkUp Job Search Engine. Available: www.linkup.com/results.php#q=information%20systems%20management&l=&m=normal&d=25&c=&sort=r&p=25&tm=ALL&page=2&jobHash=098d45f29c1b92bce33a8df80d9e2435 (accessed June 29, 2009).

University of Michigan School of Information. 2009. "Incentive Centered Design (ICD) Specialization." Available: www.si.umich.edu/msi/icd.htm (accessed July 3, 2009).

U.S. Department of Labor, Bureau of Labor Statistics. 2009. "Computer and Information Systems Managers." *Occupational Outlook Handbook*, 2008–2009 ed. Available: www.bls.gov/oco/ocos258.htm (accessed June 2009).

Additional Source

Wikipedia. "Search Results: Information Systems Management." Available: http://en.wikipedia.org/w/index.php?title=Special%3ASearch&redirs=1&search=information+systems+management&fulltext=Search&ns0=1 (accessed February 2009).

Chapter 7

Information Policy

Introduction

Information policy professionals are advocates for access and protectors of privacy, balancing the challenges and opportunities of the information age and shaping the structural elements of our digital society to reap rewards and deter detriment for individuals, organizations, governments, and nations. Most people can relate to the information and technology issues present in daily life, such as spam, security of personal data in online transactions, and proper handling of medical records. Information policy professionals help address and manage these challenges and much more.

The incredible growth of information and speed of technological advancement in society have resulted in a significant need for information policy experts who can guide decisions that will have local, national, and international impact. Priority information policies identified in a global survey include information and communication technology (ICT) research and development, improving online government activities, spreading broadband, raising ICT skills and employment, increasing the use of ICTs, and supporting digital content development (Organisation for Economic Co-operation and Development Information Technology Outlook, 2008). According to the Center for Democracy and Technology, "The Internet has tremendous potential to promote free expression and individual liberty online. But will future Internet technologies maximize this potential for freedom?" (Center for Democracy & Technology, 2007).

Congress continues to introduce bills to address spam, or unsolicited electronic mail, yet they are up against the interests of a huge industry, represented in part by the Direct Marketing Association. Finding a real solution to the privacy issue of names being sold from one organization to another for direct marketing continues to be evasive and presents a continuing challenge for policymakers. The prevalence of mobile devices continues to grow and brings many benefits, from enabling communication in an emergency, to allowing quick response on important business decisions, to expanding small business operations in developing countries. Yet mobile devices also bring privacy concerns such as the prominence of location applications and services.

While mobile devices are one thing requiring policy attention in our networked world, the "Internet of Things" is the topic of a report from the European Commission (EC) which highlights the ubiquitous computing path we are fast following. Viviane Reding, the European Union's Commissioner for Information Society and Media, purports that "over the next decade, connected devices could multiply a thousand times . . . from cars connected to traffic lights that fight congestion, to home appliances connected to smart power grids [that track] electricity consumption, or connected pedestrian footpaths that guide the visually impaired" (Hanson, 2009).

Ubiquitous technology will bring amazing conveniences and nontrivial benefits to individuals (personalized reminder systems and automated health monitoring, for example), yet the concept of "Big Brother is watching" starts to raise concerns for those regarding trust and accountability for how technology and information will be managed when it is a seamless part of countless objects with which we interact.

Another compelling privacy issue requiring careful attention is medical record privacy. While the Health Insurance Portability and Accountability Act (HIPAA) provided comprehensive regulations related to health information as of 2003, there are exceptions and gray areas that have required additional attention. In 2009, President Obama signed the American Recovery and Reinvestment Act, which places limits on health marketing and the sale of medical records, sets standards for policies on health information access and security, and requires tracking of individuals who access patient records (Electronic Privacy Information Center, 2009b).

A technology advancement ripe with policy issues stems from the amazing growth in the use of social media, raising both privacy and intellectual property concerns. Considerable discussion and debate continues regarding the terms of use and privacy controls of popular social networking sites such as Facebook. A likely trend in information policy development, Facebook offered its users a "governance vote" to include participants in the decision to implement a new "Facebook Principles and Statement of Rights and Responsibilities" (Ullyot, 2009). For a social media site to be successful, users need to be comfortable with and trusting of policies and practices. Users also need to be aware that what they post to a social site may then be owned by that site, and policies of use and reuse vary from one site to the next.

In fact the Internet has brought a whole new set of issues related to intellectual property. According to the World Intellectual Property Organization, "In this new and rapidly changing environment, information and knowledge are increasingly the source of value; hence the intellectual property system—the body of law protecting creations of the mind—is crucial in maintaining a stable and equitable foundation for the development of the digital society" (World Intellectual Property Organization, 2009). For years now the Recording Industry Association of America has battled against illegal downloading of music, which violates copyright law. In 2009 a case against a Boston University graduate student resulted in a $675,000 fine for downloading 30 songs. While protecting intellectual property is of course important, many continue to call for a change in the music industry's business model and consider the current guidelines for damages excessive. Meanwhile, the defendant and his lawyer, Charles Nessum, professor and founder of the Berkman Center for Internet Society at Harvard University, created a Web site called "Joel Fights Back" to explain the case and advocate for system change that is more in tune with the digital age (Beja, 2009).

Certainly, promoting intellectual freedom is an important aspect of professional practice for all information professionals. Yet while some governments do not uphold intellectual freedom, even in democratic societies, the digital divide creates unequal access between those with ready access to technology and those without. National and international associations for the library and information science profession include intellectual freedom as a core responsibility of library and information professionals. Intellectual freedom as a core value drove the development of the Internet as we know it and is central to the open source software movement and the growing use of social media. Yet who is in charge of decisions about the Internet, new media, and technology development and access?

It turns out there is another sort of divide—one between policymakers and technology professionals. Private companies and technical standards groups are making decisions about Internet standards and architecture without much if any input from governments or public entities and with little input from the public. Meanwhile, those in a position to make information or IT policy decisions do not have the technical knowledge to fully understand the impact of their decisions, which can have serious consequences (Center for Democracy & Technology, 2007). Information policy organizations are working to address these concerns, such as the Center for Democracy and Technology's Internet Standards, Technology and Policy Project aimed at increasing dialogue and collaboration across stakeholders, including information technologists, legal experts, politicians, and policy advocates (Center for Democracy & Technology, 2007).

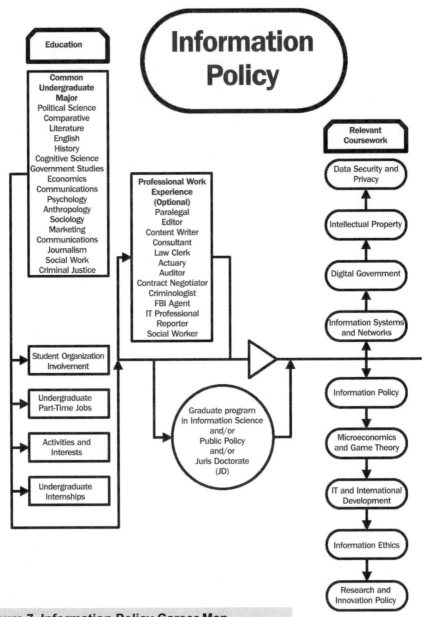

Figure 7. Information Policy Career Map
This diagram demonstrates several of the potential paths asociated with a career in the field of information policy.

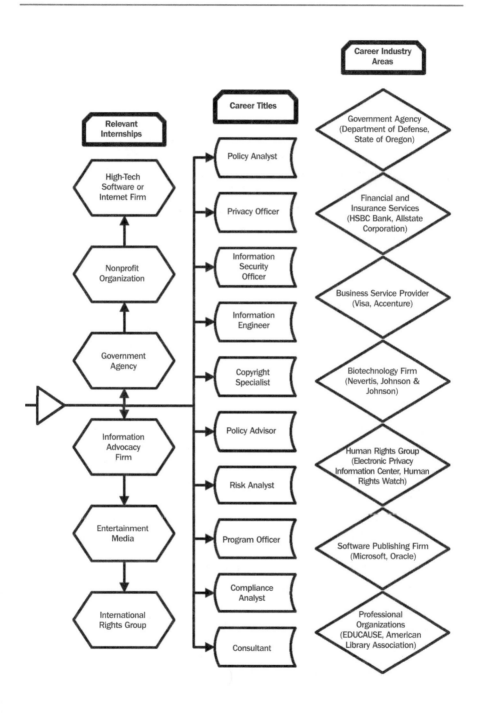

Governments are working hard to catch up with and capitalize on the benefits technology offers in governing the information society. President Barack Obama has brought a renewed focus to digital governance in the United States, initiating a new cybersecurity plan with significant attention to privacy issues while also initiating significant efforts toward creating more transparency in government. Obama's open government initiative is led by Beth Noveck (2009), law professor and author of *Wiki Government: How Technology Can Make Government Better, Democracy Stronger, and Citizens More Powerful*. Noveck states, "The Federal CIO Council is moving toward really radical data transparency—transparency that's consistent with legal requirements, security, privacy, etc.—to help provision more and better government data to the public so it can be mashed up, visualized, and used by people to create useful social applications or drive more accountability" (Towns, 2009).

Digital governance initiatives have the potential to create unprecedented impact in developing countries and if deployed effectively may empower marginalized communities in efforts to improve services and raise the collective standard of living. For those motivated to chart the path through the maze of information issues around us and who are captivated by the opportunity to harness the power of technology for human benefit, a career in information policy at this pivotal point in the emergence of the information age could bring remarkable rewards.

Skills and Abilities

For any professional career field, there are required skills and abilities that are important for success. In the field of information policy, the right skills and abilities will make you more marketable for a variety of exciting professional positions at all levels in a wide range of industries and will provide you with the tool kit for success in landing your dream job.

While positions in information policy vary as far as skill level, experience, and education required, there are key skills, abilities, and characteristics that are highly sought for any type of professional information policy position in any industry. Outlined in the following sections are both the soft skills and abilities (behavioral/personality traits and characteristics) and hard skills and abilities (technical and career-specific knowledge) that are important for success in the field of information policy. Note that these are identified as the most common skills and abilities; this is certainly not an exhaustive list of all of the valuable skills and abilities that are beneficial for this career field.

☑ QUICK FACT!
Demonstrated integrity is highly valued in this field.

Soft Skills

- Ability to communicate (written and verbal), to achieve:
  - Persuasion
  - Negotiation
  - Presentation
- Problem solving/analytical skills
- Interpersonal/relationship management skills
- Ability to work in collaboration/be a team player
- Flexibility/adaptability

Hard Skills

- Information and data analysis: Identify the underlying principles, reasons, or facts of information by breaking down information or data into separate parts.
- Project management: Deliver and manage projects, planning, organizing, and managing resources to bring about the successful completion of specific project goals and objectives.
- Business management: Advise about and respond to the business needs of an organization. Understand the strategic vision and mission of an organization.
- Network services: Plan, analyze, design, develop, test, assure quality, configure, install, implement, integrate, maintain, and/or manage networked systems used for the transmission of information in voice, data, and/or video formats.
- Data management: Plan, develop, implement, and administer systems for the acquisition, storage, and retrieval of data.
- Technical knowledge and skills: Dependent on the nature of the position and industry, not always required, but mentioned in many job postings as desirable, particularly for IT policy, systems analysis, and network security position:
  - Database management: MySQL, SQL, Access, Excel
  - Operating systems: Linux
  - Programming: JAVA, C++, PHP, Ruby on Rails, J2EE, .Net
- Competitive intelligence: Define, gather, analyze, and distribute information about products, customers, competitors, and any aspect of the environ-

ment needed to support executives and managers in making strategic decisions for an organization.

- IT standards: Know cooperation agreements, or specifications, that make networked computing possible.
- Social media: Know how to navigate and create online content created by people using highly accessible and scalable publishing technologies such as blogs, wikis, podcasts, and social networking sites, and online communities such as Facebook, Myspace, and LinkedIn.
- Research: Observe, receive, and otherwise obtain information from all relevant sources.

Effective communication and complex problem solving and analytical skills are probably the most critical skills to being an effective information policy professional. Information policy professionals collect and compile information, especially statistical data, to help explore issues and explain the solution they propose. They evaluate outcomes by determining whether an existing policy has been effective and consider the costs and benefits of potential actions to advocate for the most appropriate one. They communicate information to diverse constituencies including policymakers, the media, academia, and the public. Producing reports, proposals, presentations, and guides for these diverse audiences is a common task for most positions. Furthermore, writing for Web sites, blogs, and social media resources is becoming increasingly common in the profession.

Strong relationship management skills go hand in hand with communication skills. To be an effective information policy professional, developing constructive and cooperative working relationships with others and maintaining them over time is crucial. Effective negotiation and persuasion skills are equally important as information policy professionals often bring others together to reconcile differences and must persuade others to change their minds or behavior.

While a technical background is not required for most information policy jobs, to be marketable and successful in the field you must be up to date on emerging technology trends and be able to apply new knowledge to the job. While a computer science background isn't necessarily required for most information policy jobs, a strong ability to use computers and computer systems to program, write software, set up functions, enter data, or process information are often listed as desirable for IT policy, systems analysis, and/or network security positions. Furthermore, for most information policy jobs, having a thorough knowledge of IT standards within specific industries is critical. For example, Section 508 of the Rehabilitation Act is a law that applies to all federal agencies when they develop, procure, maintain, or use electronic and information technology to ensure accessibility for all employees and members of the public with disabilities (Section 508, 1973). Compliance to IT standards varies by industry; therefore, it is critical for any information policy professional to have expert knowledge in this area.

As with all emerging technologies, social networking is advancing rapidly, and information policy professionals need to remain aware of the security risks associated with it. Skills and knowledge of social marketing tools and technologies are becoming more and more important as many organizations have integrated social media into their overall business plans, which in turn is leading to a greater need for information policy and security measures.

KEY WORDS TO KNOW

Listed here are some key information policy terms that you will see throughout this chapter. If you are interested in pursuing this career field, it's a good idea to be familiar with their meaning:

- **information security**: Protecting information and information systems from unauthorized access, use, disclosure, disruption, modification or destruction; protecting the confidentiality, integrity, and availability of information.
- **information privacy**: The relationship between collection and dissemination of data, technology, the public expectation of privacy, and the legal and political issues surrounding them.
- **risk management**: The active process of identifying, assessing, communicating, and managing the risks facing an organization to ensure that an organization meets its objectives.
- **cybersecurity**: Protection of a computer's Internet account and files from intrusion by an unknown user.
- **information and communications technology (ICT)**: A generic name for all of the technologies involved with communicating with computers.
- **compliance**: Conforming to a specification or policy, standard, or law that has been clearly defined.
- **intellectual property**: Legal property rights over creations of the mind, both artistic and commercial, and the corresponding fields of law.
- **digital governance**: Refers to governance processes in which information and communications technology (ICT) plays an active and significant role.
- **assurance**: Refers to professional services that improve the quality of information.

Professional Roles

Information policy professionals often have an educational background in information, law, economics, business, public policy, or other social sciences. They often specialize in a particular domain in the field such as intellectual property, IT standards, media and telecommunications, information privacy and security, competition and antitrust, research and innovation policy, or digital governance (University of Michigan School of Information, 2009). Information policy professionals not only work in leading Fortune 500 companies, various public sector organizations, federally funded agencies, defense organizations, information assurance, and risk management, but also find opportunities to work with management and technology consulting firms (Carnegie Mellon Heinz College, 2009). To better understand the range and scope of information policy professional roles it may help to compare and contrast the duties and goals of a few of the most common job roles:

- **Policy Analyst**: Overall function is to provide policymakers with research and analysis around an issue to make sound decisions. They identify and prioritize current policy issues and their consequences, clarify policy objectives relevant to issue to identify potential conflicts in terms of objectives and interests, identify viable policy options, develop criteria and indicators to assess progress toward policy objectives, design effective strategy to obtain support to ensure effectiveness, and advocate policy options in a clear, persuasive way.

- **Privacy Officer**: Overall function is to develop and manage privacy-compliance activities within an organization such as implementing policies and procedures, conducting educational programs, and auditing and administering privacy program reviews. Organizations that transmit or maintain protected/confidential data, such as health, financial, and personal information, are required to have privacy officers on staff.

- **Information Security Officer**: Responsible for the development and delivery of a comprehensive information security and privacy program. Provide assurance that information created, acquired, or maintained by an organization is used in accordance with its intended purpose; protect information and its infrastructure from external or internal threats; and provide assurance of compliance standards and regulations regarding information access, security, and privacy.

The following is a list of some of the most common job titles and industries that actively recruit information policy professionals (bachelor's and master's level):

- Junior Policy Analyst, SAIC (technology)
- Information Security Officer, Kaiser Permanente (health care)
- National Policy Analyst, Department of Defense (government)
- Enterprise Risk Management Consultant, Deloitte Services (consulting)
- Employee Privacy Specialist, McGraw-Hill (publishing)
- Copyright Specialist, University of Michigan Library (academic/university)
- Chief Privacy Officer, Facebook (social media)
- Information Security Engineer, Intel (technology)
- Information Policy Analyst, Department of Homeland Security (government)

Other closely related job titles include:

- Consultant
- Researcher
- Research analyst
- Systems analyst
- Economist
- Intelligence officer
- Risk/compliance analyst

Occupational Outlook

From intellectual property to IT standards, telecommunications to privacy, security, and digital governance, information policy has emerged in recent years as a dynamic and fast-growing field—and a key shaper of the information landscape of the future (University of Michigan School of Information, 2009). A strong and growing need for information policy professionals exists across all sectors and industries, particularly in government, military/defense, and health care. Not surprisingly, the U.S. Department of Homeland Security has a high demand for information policy professionals at the local, state, and federal level, and this demand

> ☑ QUICK FACT!
> Watch for growing opportunities in cybersecurity, social media, and health care.

continues to increase. Because government has such a high demand for information policy professionals, it is not surprising that the top cities for information-policy-related jobs are in Washington, DC, and Arlington, VA, followed by New York, NY, Atlanta, GA, and McLean, VA (Indeed.com, 2009).

A rapidly growing area within information policy across all industries is security, specifically cybersecurity. According to the U.S. Bureau of Labor Statistics, jobs in the field of computer and cybersecurity should have favorable projections over the next decade. With more and more business being carried out over computer networks, security will continue to be a critical issue. As hackers become more sophisticated and viruses become more complex and destructive, organizations need to understand how their systems are vulnerable and how to protect their infrastructure and Internet sites. Organizations of all types will be in need of hiring more information security experts to fill key roles because the integrity of their computing environments is of utmost importance (U.S. Department of Labor, Bureau of Labor Statistics, 2009). As social media becomes heavily integrated into many organizational business plans, the social computing domain is another growth area where information policy opportunities will be on the rise. Additionally, under this current administration, another area for growth in this career field will be evident in health care, specifically within bioinformatics, as information privacy and security will be key concerns and initiatives that will require capable professionals to address them effectively.

Salary Information

> ☑ QUICK FACT!
> An advanced degree and proven ability in the field will yield high earnings.

Earnings for information policy professionals vary by specialty, level of position, level of education, and industry. The U.S. Bureau of Labor Statistics does not classify information policy analysts as a separate occupation and, therefore, does not have specific data on their earnings (U.S. Department of Labor, Bureau of Labor Statistics, 2009). We can, however, look at salary data associated with research analysts, systems analysts, political scientists, and economists, among other related titles, to get an idea of salary earnings in the field.

Across all industries, information-policy related jobs can expect earnings in the range of $48,820–$85,760. Average earnings for bachelor's or master's level positions are $64,650. Information policy professionals with an advanced degree and significant work experience can expect high earnings in government: $93,000–$145,000. Entry-level policy-related jobs (bachelor's degree and minimal work experience) within government can expect earnings in the range of $35,000–$40,000 to start. Across all industries, an advanced degree at the master's or PhD level, along with proven ability in the field, will yield higher earnings and career advancement into senior, chief, and director roles. The Robert Half Technology (2010) *2010 Salary Guide* indicates that chief security officers can expect a salary in the range of $97,500–$150,000. A bachelor's degree with no work experience may start at entry-level, junior, or assistant policy roles and can expect salaries around $40,000.

Profiles—Perspectives of New Professionals

Alex Kanous, Operations Manager
University of Michigan Data Sharing & Intellectual Capital
Knowledge Center
Ann Arbor, Michigan

I first became acquainted with the future codirectors of the Data Sharing & Intellectual Capital (DSIC) Knowledge Center while interning for them while a graduate student at the University of Michigan School of Information (SI). After my internship, I was offered the operations manager position and asked to contribute to the Knowledge Center grant proposal because of both my law and information policy background. (I obtained a JD from Michigan State University College of Law and a master of science in information [MSI] degree with information policy specialization at SI after a bachelor's from Oakland University in Rochester, Michigan.) The MSI was deemed valuable because the education I received at SI not only dealt with highly current issues but also was broad enough that there was confidence in my ability to respond to myriad, and often unfamiliar, issues. The legal educational experience was seen as helpful for interpreting the complex regulatory and legal landscape that DSIC operates in.

As the operations manager for the DSIC Knowledge Center, I am responsible for the day-to-day management of the project. This means monitoring spending constrained by budget allowances, working with and managing subcontractors, and maintaining and updating the center's wiki and forums. However, as the Knowledge Center is comprised of a small staff, I am also required to function as a subject matter expert in particular domain areas of knowledge. In this role I also engage with members of the research community, respond to substantive questions submitted to our forums or via phone and e-mail, and sit on nearly daily teleconferences with a wide variety of stakeholders.

The DSIC Knowledge Center is a component the National Cancer Institute's (NCI) cancer Biomedical Informatics Grid (caBIG) Project, a network initiative facilitating the sharing of data and knowledge by the constituents of the cancer community including researchers, physicians, and patients. The goal is to connect this community via an interoperable infrastructure and develop tools for the collection, analysis, and dissemination of information related to cancer research and care. However, an effective tool for sharing data is only one component of the network envisioned, and barriers arising from legal, regulatory, ethical, contractual, and cultural concerns must be addressed. This is the domain area of the DSIC Knowledge Center. We engage caBIG participants to educate them and help them navigate these obstacles; develop recommendations for policies, standards, and best practices; and draft comments on proposed policies and guidelines.

What I love most about my job is knowing that I am working on a project that is not only currently relevant but is aimed at easing the burdens on health care professionals and researchers in treating and seeking out a cure for a scourge of a disease. Not a day goes by without some news item being reported that reaffirms this relevance. However, tackling these issues is a complex, messy affair at times and the concerns and interests that must be reconciled can often make the process a frustrating and disheartening one. Ideally, if the Knowledge Center is able to engage with the community at the level it aims to, it will provide sufficient guidance to navigate a complex regulatory, legal, and ethical environment and promote an evolution in health care and research culture toward comprehensive data sharing and cooperation, all toward the end goal of accelerating the discovery of a cure for cancer.

Because of the multiple hats that I wear, I employ a wide variety of skills. I think this is common for most employees in small nonprofits. So while I utilize the skills harnessed in law school and SI to evaluate a policy proposal, I am also responsible for content management on the center's wiki, authorizing user privileges on our forums, and occasionally acting as a graphic designer.

Bioinformatics, which is the field that the DSIC Knowledge Center most closely follows and interacts with, is going to increasingly demand capable professionals. One need only look at the substantial funding the current administration has made available for the implementation of electronic medical record systems to realize that there will likely be a community responsible for developing these systems, ensuring their cross-institutional interoperability, and navigating the accompanying complex regulations and legal concerns for a long time to come.

Individuals interested in the policy side of this type of work would be best served by having a diverse educational experience. A law degree would be helpful, particularly if health law courses were pursued, and information policy experience should include exposure to health care and research concerns. Alternatively, programs in public health, particularly those that offer in-depth exposure to the relevant regulatory environment, would be a good companion to an information policy degree.

The outlook for my particular position is difficult to predict simply because of the grant-funded nature of it. However, this domain is of great current relevance, and I'm confident that at the conclusion of this project the experience I will have gained will serve me well in finding my next endeavor. As my job is a grant-funded position, it's relatively difficult to use it to approximate the salary expectations of work of this type. That being said, my own job search while still at SI suggested that policy positions for individuals with both a policy education as well as some subject matter expertise, whether through an additional graduate level degree or substantive work experience, could expect to start somewhere around $65,000+. Depending on the particular path taken from such jobs and how soon one could move into a leadership role, a $100,000+ salary after ten years of work would be reasonable. (Kanous, 2009)

Peter Transburg, Programme Officer
United Nations World Food Programme
Democratic Republic of Congo

My interest in international humanitarian work stems largely from my childhood experience of growing up in the Democratic Republic of Congo (then Zaire). My parents, who have spent most of the past 25 years teaching in Congo and Tanzania, are a source of inspiration to me and have played an enormous role in shaping who I am and what I do for work.

Already with international development work in mind, I got a bachelor's degree in anthropology and sociology from Wheaton College and pursued several overseas internship and work experiences, including the Peace Corps in Ghana, West Africa. As I returned from the Peace Corps, I searched for a graduate degree program that would help me harness my experiences and prepare me for a career in the international development sector. The University of Michigan School of Information (SI) seemed an odd choice for this career path, but it was in 2001 during a 15 minute wait for a Web page to open in a small cybercafé in rural Ghana that I was struck by the potentially revolutionary role that information and communication technology (ICT) could play in international development work.

SI provided me with ample opportunities to study, research, and practice my rather narrow interest amid the regular coursework. Professors put me to work on projects that incorporated ICT and community and international development, and I used the summer between my two years of study to do an internship with the

United Nations in Geneva. In 2005, after I graduated, the United Nations World Food Programme (WFP) saw potential amid my international experience, language skills, and information degree and offered me a job managing food assistance programs in central Mozambique. Over time, my role with WFP in Mozambique changed to communications, reporting, and information management at the national level.

In early 2009, I took a job as WFP Programme Officer in the Ituri District suboffice in northeastern Democratic Republic of Congo (DRC). Here, I am responsible for the management of food assistance programs for over a quarter of a million poor and war-displaced people in a geographical area bigger than California. I coordinate with other UN agencies, military peacekeeping officers, and nongovernmental organizations with whom WFP partners in all humanitarian actions. I negotiate agreements, plan interventions, manage budgets, and lead a team of food security experts on field missions to monitor and evaluate ongoing food assistance projects—an activity that is complicated by the tenuous security situation in the area. And, of course, my workdays also involve the normal, routine things of office life: e-mails, paper filing, power outages, more e-mails, hosting charitable celebrity visits, report writing, attending meetings to determine when we'll hold future meetings, swatting malaria-laden mosquitoes, and more e-mails.

I love the satisfaction that my work is making a critical difference in people's lives. I enjoy living and working with colleagues from around the world and the opportunity of using French as my daily language. One of the most rewarding parts of the job is the chance to talk directly with WFP beneficiaries about their lives, a task that is possible and enjoyable because I can do it using Lingala, the language I learned while living in Congo years ago as a kid. Conversely, the insecurity in the region is a drain on energy and morale. Constantly anticipating armed militia attacks in the areas where we work and the possibility of harmful threats even in the town where I live is difficult to get used to.

My education prepared me well for working in the field of international humanitarian work. Particularly pivotal were the internships that I did, including a six-month development internship in Peru during my senior year of college and the graduate research work and UN internship I did as part of my time at SI. There is no question that these experiences and especially the UN internship caught the eye of WFP when they were looking for qualified candidates. Furthermore, strong cross-cultural and multilanguage communication skills are essential to my work. Being able to work effectively with a wide range of people—donors, beneficiaries, military personnel, local staff, and international colleagues from all over the world—requires tact, tolerance, and a lot of listening and learning.

Managing a team requires patience, confidence, and good organization of activities, time lines, and budgets. Also, one of the big challenges I faced when I assumed my current role was establishing a structured electronic records system for my unit and training the staff on proper file naming, version control, and general information management. A relatively transient staff within the international humanitarian field makes records management all the more important for preserving institutional memory, but the reality is that few people have not the slightest notion about information management, either conceptually or practically. My SI-honed skills in this area have been instrumental to bringing order to several ad hoc file dumps.

For others considering jobs in the international development sector, having a useful second language (French, Spanish, Arabic, Russian, Portuguese) is key—go live in a country to immerse yourself in learning another language. Also, do as many volunteer experiences or internships as you can, even if unpaid (they most likely will be in this field). Use all of the opportunities you can through your high school or university to gain overseas experience. Take advantage of the programs offered at your school—you will not regret doing them, but you might regret not doing them. After college, your options for structured practical engagement programs will be more limited. I also suggest working as a Peace Corps Volunteer.

Despite our best efforts, hunger and poverty will always be with us, but we can minimize their reach and effects. The humanitarian and development fields constantly need new ideas and new energy to ensure that assistance is provided and received in a holistic, inclusive, and empowering manner. As a result, humanitarian organizations are always hiring, and the range of skills required to do the work is wide, including finance, logistics, management, monitoring and evaluation, research, and a wide range of sector-specific expertise including nutrition, water management, child protection, information management, and even Web development.

The standard UN base salary for my professional position (P3 level) is around US$55,000 per year. In addition to this base salary, each duty station includes several other allowances, depending on the cost of living and the hardship/danger level, which can as much as double the base salary. In five years, I can reasonably expect to earn US$65,000 per year (plus allowances) as a program officer with WFP. Combine that with a paid annual trip to my home country, six weeks of vacation every year, and the satisfaction that a hungry family had a meal today due, in part, to my work, and it ends up being a very rewarding job. (Transburg, 2009)

Timothy Vollmer, Assistant Director
Program on Public Access to Information
American Library Association Office for Information Technology
Policy
Washington, DC

I've been interested in law and policy since I was an undergraduate student pursuing degrees in sociology and legal studies from the University of Wisconsin–Madison. For some time, I thought I'd like to attend law school, but my growing personal interest in information science, coupled with my work at both the Madison Public Library and Wisconsin State Law Library, prompted me to apply to library/information science graduate programs instead. At that time, many schools were offering unique, evolving classes around such topics as information policy, copyright, and digital libraries. The University of Michigan School of Information (SI) was at the top of that list. While attending SI, I was able to participate in the school's Alternative Spring Break Program and completed a weeklong internship at the American Library Association's (ALA) Office for Information Technology Policy (OITP) in Washington, DC. There, I conducted a brief investigation and prepared a short issue paper on online copyright filtering for the office. I enjoyed the work and later followed up with the office to inquire about employment prospects just when OITP was looking to hire an information technology policy analyst. I interviewed and was offered the job; I've since been promoted to Assistant Director of the Program on Public Access to Information.

My day-to-day tasks vary quite a bit, depending on the issue or project at hand. For the most part, I'm involved with research and writing, whether it be policy briefs, blog posts on our District Dispatch site, or helping prepare comments to agencies such as the Federal Communications Commission or U.S. Copyright Office. Since ALA is a member-based organization, we work closely with several committees and with members directly. We conduct conference calls with member groups and coalitions of which we are a member within Washington, DC. Personally, I attend many events, hearings, and conferences pertinent to our mission and report back to the larger ALA Washington Office. I also participate in panel discussion and meetings, where appropriate, to contribute to the dialogue and ensure that the library and public interest voice remains to be heard.

Some of the key issues that the Office for Information Technology is currently involved with are copyright (both domestic and international), library policy surrounding traditional cultural expressions, public policy considerations of mobile devices and libraries, broadband access for public libraries, e-rate simplification and education, research into the "future of libraries," and general telecommunications policy.

The broad array of projects and the work with our fantastic members make this job great. The work is always fast paced and exciting, and we get to work on timely and pertinent issues. Drawbacks include navigating the bureaucratic maze of working in a large nonprofit organization and sometimes feeing like much of our work is making sure bad things don't happen. Having to be on the defensive all of the time can limit the scope of innovative new projects we're able to address. However, being located in Washington, DC, provides a wealth of interesting talks, events, and conferences around technology and policy, most for free, which is a great perk to this position. It's also encouraging to work alongside so many smart individuals and organizations that genuinely care about improving information access and rights for the public.

The impact of the American Library Association is significant. The ALA is the largest library association in the world, with over 65,000 members. And, as we are a membership-based organization, ALA members look to the Washington Office, comprised of OITP and the lobbying arm called the Office of Government Relations, to be a strong voice for the library community inside the beltway.

If you are interested in information policy and technology, get involved in student groups that focus on information policy, or elsewhere, such as Students for Free Culture, the Open Access Movement, or others. Keep abreast of what's going on by following organizations you are interested in through social media and blogs. If you are interested in ALA, join the student chapter and consider joining one of the many committees within the organization.

Coursework in public policy, government, project management, etc. are important for a position such as mine, but really the key is personal interest and drive, and participating in valuable experiences such as internships. In my experience, potential employers want to see that students are intimately involved in projects. Therefore, opportunities similar to my summer internship and SI's Alternative Spring Break program are invaluable. Writing and editing skills are extremely important and often involve some technical and legal analysis. And obviously, communication is central, since we collaborate with so many different entities, both public interest organizations in DC and hundreds of members on committees, offices, and divisions within ALA. Openness, flexibility, and political sensitivity are also essential, since situations and avenues for action can change so quickly.

For many nonprofit organizations, including ALA's OITP, the workload is partially determined by grant funding. It's clear that grant-issuing foundations have suffered huge losses to their endowments due to the economic downturn over the past year, so it remains to be seen whether the foundations supporting public interest and nonprofit groups will be forced to scale back their programs. That said, talented and thoughtful policy analysis will continue to be required in Washington and elsewhere.

The salaries for nonprofit and public interest positions such as policy analyst are often somewhat lower than analogous government or corporate positions. However, the five-year outlook may be in the $50,000–60,000 range, and the ten year more near $75,000–85,000. (Vollmer, 2009)

Careers in Information Policy: At a Glance

Your career in information policy can take many directions as you connect your interests and values to the type of functional area and type of organization that you pursue. Here are a few examples of real jobs representing some exciting "tracks" you can follow.

Health Informatics Track
Information Security Governance Analyst
Kaiser Permanente
Oakland, California

Support governance and relationship management activities within the Information Security Organization by supporting compliance and the Principles of Responsibility by maintaining the privacy and confidentiality of information, protecting the assets of the organization, acting with ethics and integrity, reporting noncompliance, and adhering to the applicable federal, state, and local laws and regulations, accreditation and licenser requirements, and Kaiser Permanente's policies and procedures. (Kaiser Permanente Human Resources, accessed 2009)

Corporate Track
Policy Analyst
Google Inc.
Washington, DC

Work on U.S. public policy issues and government affairs for Google. Key issues will include those relating to privacy, content regulation, freedom of speech, advertising, intellectual property, and general technology policy. With the rest of the Google's Public Policy team, work to advance public policy positions and related activities reflecting the goals and values of the company. Research new policy positions for review by Google's policy and management teams; work with industry and public interest partners to advance Google's policy agenda; work with broad cross-functional teams to implement and engage in public policy initiatives; assist in the management of relationships with key lawmakers and their staff; support strategies to communicate policies to key constituencies in the U.S. and worldwide. (Google Human Resources, 2009)

Media/Entertainment Track
Rights Clearance Specialist
GreenLight, a Division of Corbis
Los Angeles, California

Work closely with Project and Clearance Managers in formulating and executing strategy plan for clearance phase; have a total command of project for negotiations with clearance entities; communicate with other clearance specialists in GreenLight group to leverage and share knowledge—coordinate united strategies in approaching clearance entities across multiple projects; respond to concerns and issues of talent representatives, acting as liaison between clearance entities and media packaging project management team; modify agreements to talent representatives' specifications within parameters of project; coordinate with Rights Clearance Administrator in securing all documentation for given project. (EntertainmentCareers.net, accessed 2009)

Public Interest Track
Internet Public Interest Opportunities Program, Clerkship
Electronic Privacy Information Center
Washington, DC

Learn about the legislative process, public interest litigation, the Freedom of Information Act, online activism, and emerging Internet issues; actively participate in valuable programs in Internet law, policy, and legislation; attend weekly seminars led by eminent scholars and practitioners in the field of Internet policy; experience firsthand the new and exciting intersection between Internet law and public policy; research, draft, and submit memoranda on critical issues regarding legislation, government oversight, litigation, and collaboration. (Electronic Privacy Information Center, 2009a)

Global Track
Foreign Service Diplomatic Security Special Agent
United States Department of State
Global opportunities

Administer and manage U.S. diplomatic mission security programs at overseas posts to include protection of personnel, facilities, and sensitive information along with the U.S. Marine Security Guard and contract local security guard programs;

conduct investigations to include criminal investigations, personnel investigations, counterintelligence and counterterrorism inquiries, and investigative work in preparing for court appearances; conduct or implement projects or programs involved with the safeguarding of classified and sensitive information and materials as derived from Presidential Directives or Executive Orders; assess security threats against U.S. interests and diplomatic installations and personnel abroad as well as investigating hostile intelligence attempts to subvert U.S. personnel and interests overseas. (U.S. Department of State, 2009)

Resources for Further Information/Exploration

The following resources can help guide you in your career exploration within the field of information policy. Note that this is not a comprehensive list; there are numerous resources available related to the nuances of the field that are not included. The purpose of identifying key job posting sites and professional organizations is to make you aware of some of the main resources available and to also provide you with gateways to resources that will inform you of the types of careers available in the field.

Professional Organizations Relevant to Information Policy

- AALL—American Association of Law Libraries
  www.aallnet.org
- ABA—American Bar Association–Technology
  www.abanet.org/tech/ltrc
- ACSA—Applied Computer Security Associates
  www.acsac.org/acs/A
- ACM—Association for Computing Machinery
  www.acm.org
- AIPLA—American Intellectual Property Law Association
  www.aipla.org
- AIPPI—International Association for the Protection of Intellectual Property
  www.aippi.org
- ANSI—American National Standards Institute
  www.ansi.org
- APPAM—Association for Public Policy Analysis and Management
  www.appam.org/home.asp

- APSA—American Political Science Association
  www.apsanet.org
- IAPP—International Association of Privacy Professionals
  www.privacyassociation.org/index.php
- ISN—International Relations and Security Network
  www.isn.ethz.ch
- ITechLaw—International Technology Law Association
  www.itechlaw.org
- SCIP—Society of Competitive Intelligence Professionals
  www.scip.org
- SLA—Special Library Association
  www.sla.org
- The Policy Studies Organization
  www.ipsonet.org/index.asp
- WIIS—Women in International Security
  http://wiis.georgetown.edu
- WIPO—World Intellectual Property Organization
  www.wipo.int

Career Sites Relevant to Information Policy

- DevJobs
  www.devjobsmail.com
- Public Service Careers
  www.publicservicecareers.org
- Special Libraries Association (SLA) Career Center
  http://sla.jobcontrolcenter.com
- TechCareers
  www.techcareers.com
- Foreign Policy Association Job Board
  www.fpa.org/jobs_contact2423/jobs_contact.htm
- Policy Jobs (some posts require membership)
  www.policyjobs.net
- Coalition on Human Needs Job Announcements
  www.chn.org/jobs
- Foundation Center Jobs
  http://foundationcenter.org/pnd/jobs

- Hillzoo.com Jobs
  www.hillzoo.com/jobs
- National Conference of State Legislatures Job Listings
  www.ncsl.org/Default.aspx?TabID=305&tabs=1027,78,589#1027
- Opportunities in Public Affairs
  www.opajobs.com
- Roll Call Jobs
  www.rcjobs.com/jobs
- Hill Jobs
  http://corporate.cq.com/wmspage.cfm?parm1=57
- Conservative Jobs.com
  www.conservativejobs.com
- USA Jobs
  www.usajobs.gov
- Global Risk Jobs
  www.globalriskjobs.com
- BankInfoSecurity Career Center & Job Board
  http://careers.bankinfosecurity.com
- Educause Job Opportunities
  www.educause.edu/jobs?tid=16500&page_id=38

Education and Training

While there are relevant positions in information policy for those with a bachelor's degree, to obtain professional level information policy positions and continued advancement opportunities, a graduate degree is typically necessary. At the undergraduate level, helpful majors include information science, public policy, prelaw, political science, computer science, and communications. Taking technology courses will provide important understanding of terminology and technical issues. Seeking relevant internships will provide important experience that will significantly enhance one's marketability for a full time job after graduation.

Graduate education options include information, information policy, library and information science, public policy, or law. The Juris Doctor (JD) would of course be essential for those who want to practice law as part of an information policy career, such as serving as a legal counsel in an information or technology organization or specializing in intellectual property within a law firm or corporate law office. Some law schools will have stronger offerings related to information policy than others, so it is important to investigate which schools have faculty experts and courses in information policy. Similarly, review the course offerings and faculty research areas within schools of information, library and information science programs, or schools of public policy to see which offer courses or specializations in information policy.

Another option is to seek universities that have both a strong information school and a strong public policy or law school and pursue a dual degree. Typically, dual degrees involve double counting of some credits, reducing the amount of time required to complete two degrees rather than one by as much as a year. For those interested in intellectual property, including patents and technology transfer, an undergraduate degree in a science or engineering field combined with graduate study in law, information, or public policy would be ideal.

Gaining relevant internships will be essential to make one's foray into the field of information policy. Potential internships may be found in information policy organizations, government agencies, think tanks, consulting firms, with senators or members of Congress who are on relevant committees, or with professional associations related to technology or library and information science or related to information policy areas such as intellectual property, antitrust, or security.

References

Beja, Marc. 2009. "Jury Orders Boston U. Graduate Student to Pay $675,000 for Illegal Downloads." *The Chronicle of Higher Education: The Wired Campus*, August 1. Available: http://chronicle.com/blogPost/Jury-Orders-Boston-U-Graduate/7551/ (accessed August 5, 2009).

Carnegie Mellon Heinz College. 2009. "MSISPM Careers in Information Security and Assurance." Available: www.heinz.cmu.edu/school-of-information-systems-and-management/information-security-policy-management msispm/careers/index .aspx (accessed July 2009).

Center for Democracy & Technology. 2007. "Internet Standards, Technology and Policy Project." Available: www.cdt.org/standards/ (accessed July 23, 2009).

Center for Democracy & Technology. 2009. "The Dawn of the Location Enabled Web." Available: http://cdt.org/publications/policyposts/2009/12 (accessed July 23, 2009).

Electronic Privacy Information Center. 2009a. "Jobs/IPIOP." Available: http://epic .org/epic/jobs.html (accessed August 14, 2009).

Electronic Privacy Information Center. 2009b. "Medical Record Policy." Available: http://epic.org/privacy/medical (accessed July 31, 2009).

EntertainmentCareers.net. "Corbis Human Resources." Available: www.entertainment careers.net/id/?id=98095 (accessed July 14, 2009).

Google Human Resources. 2009. "Google Jobs." Available: www.google.com/support/ jobs/bin/answer.py?answer=160366 (accessed October 12, 2009).

Hanson, Wayne. 2009. "Yogurt Talks, the Chips Are Silent: Europe Outlines Actions to Promote 'Internet of Things'." *Government Technology,* June 18. Available: www .govtech.com/gt/696307?topic=290183 (accessed July 31, 2009).

Indeed.com. 2009. "Policy Analyst Salaries." Available: www.indeed.com/salary?q1= Policy+Analyst+%2440%2C000&l1= (accessed July 17, 2009).

Kaiser Permanente Human Resources. "Kaiser Permanente Job Opportunities." Available: http://kp.taleo.net/careersection/external/jobdetail.ftl?lang=en&job=29394 (accessed July 17, 2009).

Kanous, Alex. 2009. Interview by Kelly Kowatch. May 27.

Noveck, Beth Simone. 2009. *Wiki Government: How Technology Can Make Government Better, Democracy Stronger, and Citizens More Powerful.* Washington, DC: Brookings Institution Press.

Organisation for Economic Co-operation and Development. 2008. "OECD Information Technology Outlook 2008." Available: www.oecd.org/sti/ito (accessed July 25, 2009).

Robert Half Technology. 2010. *2010 Salary Guide.* Menlo Park, CA: Robert Half Technology.

Section 508. 1973. "Section 508: Rehabilitation Act." Available: www.section508.gov (accessed July 2009).

Towns, Steve. 2009. "Beth Noveck on the Future of Government Transparency." Government Technology, July 6. Available: http://govtech.com/gt/699280?topic= 117673 (accessed July 31, 2009).

Transburg, Peter. 2009. Interview by Kelly Kowatch. June 9.

Ullyot, Ted. 2009. "Results of the Inaugural Facebook Site Governance Vote." Facebook Blog, April 23. Available: http://blog.facebook.com/blog.php?post= 7914652130 (accessed July 31, 2009).

University of Michigan School of Information. 2009. "Information Policy (IPOL) Specialization." Available: www.si.umich.edu/msi/ipol.htm (accessed July 2009).

U.S. Department of Labor, Bureau of Labor Statistics. 2009. *Occupational Outlook Handbook,* 2008–2009 ed. Available: www.bls.gov/oco/ (accessed July 31, 2009).

U.S. Department of State. 2009. "Diplomatic Security Special Agent." Available: http://careers.state.gov/specialist/opportunities/secagent.html (accessed August 14, 2009).

Vollmer, Timothy. 2009. Interview by Kelly Kowatch. July 25.

World Intellectual Property Organization. 2009. "About. Electronic Commerce Programs and Activities." www.wipo.int/about-ip/en/studies/publications/ip_ ecommerce.htm (accessed July 21, 2009).

Additional Source

Wikipedia. 2009. "Search Results: Information Policy." Available: http://en.wikipedia .org/w/index.php?title=Special%3ASearch&redirs=1&search=information+policy &fulltext=Search&ns0=1 (accessed March 2009).

Chapter 8

Information Analysis and Retrieval

Introduction

Information analysis and retrieval (IAR) professionals are the wizards of search and data, masterminding the mathematical magic of search engines, designing intuitive information systems, and interpreting masses of data using elegant visualizations. While it is hard to think of a more talked about technology topic right now than search, given the power of Web analytics and the potential of network analysis and data visualization, these terms are also likely to become part of our daily vocabulary and common in our daily work.

Search engine development examines how to understand and interpret questions from users and builds technology using algorithms and natural language processing techniques to effectively mine information from an unlimited number of dynamic sources. Connecting the indexed information with the queries and doing so in an intuitive manner is where the magic of search engines unfolds. Certainly, Google has been a dominant leader in the search industry and has spawned related specialties for which IAR professionals have ideal skill sets, such as search engine optimization and search engine marketing, which focus on helping organizations maximize their visibility and traffic from search engine results. Other companies are working hard to catch up with Google. With the introduction of Microsoft's Bing search engine in 2009 along with the Yahoo!–Microsoft search partnership, the search industry is heading toward an era of greater competition and, certainly, continued growth.

The major search providers as well as up-and-comers are working hard to advance search technology to gain (or to keep, in Google's case) a competitive edge in the market. While Bing is similar to Google in a number of ways, it attempts to improve the search experience by providing a sample of the information on the links provided as one's mouse moves over the link text, and it provides a set of related search results that may expedite finding the best source. The next step in advancing search is to provide direct answers to questions, and new search engines on the scene have made this the focal point of their functionality. For example, Wolfram Alpha refers to itself not as a search engine but as a "computational knowledge engine" and provides direct responses to questions including data and graphics in its results. Enter any two stocks on Wolfram Alpha and the results do not point you to sources of information as Google would but provides information directly including latest trades, a financial data summary, a recent returns chart, a relative returns graph, performance comparisons, and projections including the optimal portfolio's expected yearly return and volatility.

Another new search engine using semantic search is Yebol, which launched soon after Microsoft's Bing. According to the press release announcing its arrival, "Yebol utilizes a combination of patented algorithms paired with human knowledge to build a revolutionary Web directory for each unique query and each user. Instead of the common 'listing' of Web search results, Yebol automatically clusters search results into highly concentrated and well-organized groups of term-specific categories. Yebol seamlessly combines searching and browsing capabilities" (Landis, 2009).

The new emphasis on seamless search results is more human centered, focusing on what an individual's goal or need is for the information being sought. Andrew Tomkins, chief scientist for search at Yahoo! described the direction of search technology this way:

> I like to think of search as the place people start for a lot of things they want to do. Sometimes, they get their answer and they're done. Other times, it's part of a process that may take months to complete, like buying a house or researching high-def televisions. The next generation of search will be about understanding the task a user has in mind and changing the way search operates to get those things done. (Newcomb, 2008)

While search engines are rapidly evolving, the boon of mobile devices brings another set of opportunities for those focusing on search and information retrieval. Given the small screens and keypads of mobile devices, typing and even screen tapping can be a challenge. Enter sound recognition as search technology. Giving a cell phone or car voice command system a command to search for information via the Internet is already on the horizon, but beyond that it is likely that millions of objects could have a speech recognition chip that connects to the

Internet via wireless connection, creating search engines out of all sorts of everyday items, such as a kitchen appliance or a toy (Boland, 2009).

Add voice-over Internet protocol (VOIP) capability and a person could make a phone call from a voice search and wireless enabled object. Imagine seeing an item of interest on television, then asking your watch to search for best price options on the Internet and then asking to connect by phone to place an order. Or consider the benefits of this technology for an emergency room doctor who could give a voice command to retrieve side effect information on a particular drug while evaluating a patient. A partnership between Sensory Inc. and Google already enables users to connect with local businesses with voice commands through a wireless mobile device (Boland, 2009). Focusing on search in one's career today is akin to being on the front end of the automobile industry or at the onset of the personal computer industry. The search industry is already strong, yet in years to come its scope and impact is likely to greatly expand.

Another fast-growing area in information analysis and retrieval is Web analytics. At one point, e-commerce was viewed as a separate sort of business activity and limited to certain kinds of organizations and products. Today, almost all organizations engage in e-commerce as part of their business operations—if not for online transactions then certainly for advertising and marketing. Having an effective Web site has become essential, and Web analytics allows for fast and deep analysis of a Web site's performance in terms of visits, click throughs, user demographics, and more. The better the Web analytics tool, the better a company is able to make timely decisions and quick adjustments to enhance business results. In a 2009 interview with Forbes.com, Anthea Stratigos, chief executive of the media research and advisory firm Outsell Inc., commented on the firm's annual marketing study, which "predicts $65 billion will be siphoned away from traditional advertising channels in 2009 and spent instead on companies' own Web sites and Internet marketing" (Smillie, 2009). Stratigos stated, "The marketing dollars companies now spend on their own sites is equivalent to all TV ad revenue for the year. . . . Most (companies) have invested in page content, Web analytics, search engine optimization, site design, and social networking platforms" (Smillie, 2009).

Web analytics is also increasingly used for internal business operations. Given the challenge of staying ahead of the competition with products and services, enhancing organizational efficiency and improving business decision making can give organizations an edge in terms of outcomes (Enge, 2008). Dashboard systems are enabling user friendly, real-time data analysis on key performance metrics. One screen graphic display is akin to a car's dashboard, with gauges and signals that allow up to the minute access to key information across functional areas, giv-

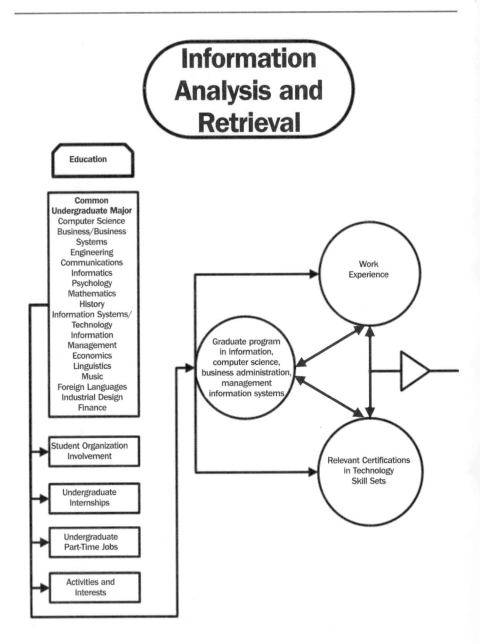

Figure 8. Information Analysis and Retrieval Career Map
This diagram demonstrates several of the potential paths associated with a career in the field of information analysis and retrieval.

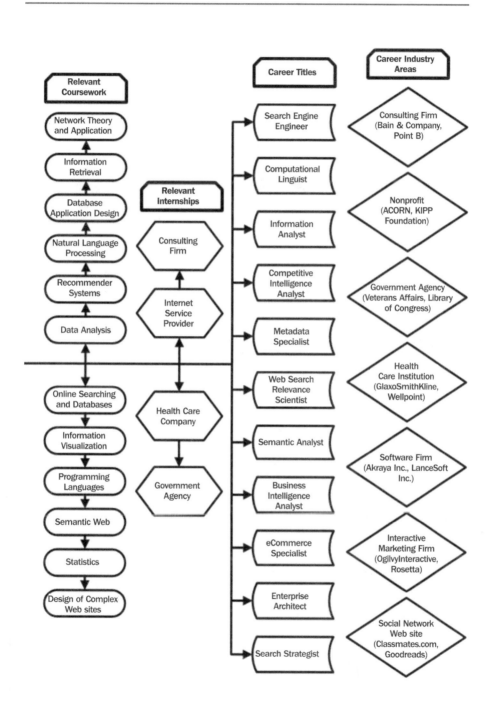

ing the "big picture" and including options to drill down for details on areas of interest. IAR professionals not only work on designing and implementing Web analytics tools, they help organizations make the best use of such tools.

As technology advances, Web analytics advances too. Digital signage is a new marketing strategy that places smart bar codes on products. If a consumer takes a picture of the bar code with their smartphone, they are linked to a Web site with more information on the product (Guruswamy, 2008). Widgets are self-contained components of interactive Web content that can be accessed from a Web site or mobile device. For example, an online Maybelline advertisement includes a widget that, when downloaded, enables a user to do photo touch-up that gives the effect of one of their products. Digital signage and widgets provide robust data for Web analytics, and as their use expands, the challenge will be for Web analytics to remain manageable given the loads of data available (Guruswamy, 2008).

The enormous increase in the production and availability of information in our world is both an amazing opportunity and a formidable challenge. Information analysis and retrieval offers a means to process or mine huge volumes of data either for an important nugget of information, such as a key medical research result, or to illuminate trends and patterns out of stores of data, such as comparing the current economic crisis with previous downturns. Increasingly, data visualization tools provide exciting graphic representations of such data, including visualizations of networks such as those created through social media. Analyzing the patterns of online communities can help build understanding of what makes them work effectively and what impact they have. For example, pattern analysis of social media during the 2008 presidential election could impact planning for social media use in the next campaign.

Information analysis and retrieval applies technology to make information accessible to people in exciting and meaningful ways. Most any content or interest area has a need and an application for IAR, from the iTunes music store to the Web-based Medical Information Retrieval System (WebMIRS) developed at the National Library of Medicine. For those with technical and quantitative skills and a desire to apply ingenuity and innovation in advancing real-world information solutions for the benefit of people and organizations, IAR offers unlimited possibilities.

Skills and Abilities

For any professional career field, there are required skills and abilities that are important for success. In the field of information analysis and retrieval (IAR), the right skills and abilities will make you more marketable for a variety of exciting professional positions in a wide range of industries and will provide you with the tool kit for success in landing your dream job.

While positions in IAR vary as far as skill level, experience, and education required, there are key skills, abilities, and characteristics that are highly sought for any type of professional position in any industry. Outlined in the following sections are both the soft skills and abilities (behavioral/personality traits and characteristics) and hard skills and abilities (technical and career-specific knowledge) that are important for success in the field of information analysis and retrieval. Note that these are identified as the most common skills and abilities; this is certainly not an exhaustive list of all of the valuable skills and abilities that are beneficial for this career field.

> ☑ QUICK FACT!
> Attributes needed for the field include strong analytical skills, IT savvy, and project management know-how.

Soft Skills

- Ability to communicate (verbal and written), to achieve:
  - Persuasion
  - Negotiation
  - Presentation
- Complex analytical problem solving skills
- Ability to work in collaboration/be a team player
- Relationship management/interpersonal skills
- Flexibility/adaptability
- Leadership capability

Hard Skills

- Information and data analysis: Identify the underlying principles, reasons, or facts of information by breaking down information or data into separate parts.
- Project management: Deliver and manage projects, planning, organizing, and managing resources to bring about the successful completion of specific project goals and objectives.
- Data mining: Analyze data in order to determine patterns and their relationships to predict future consumer behavior.
- Data management: Plan, develop, implement, and administer systems for the acquisition, storage, and retrieval of data.

- Business intelligence: Use skills, technologies, applications, and practices to help a business acquire a better understanding of its commercial context.
- Technical knowledge and skills:
  - Programming Languages: C++, .NET, Java, Perl, Ruby on Rails, unix, python
  - Web Applications: HTML, Java, Javascript, AJAX, CSS, XML, PHP
  - Databases: SQL, MySQL, Access, Excel
- Web analytics: Collect, report, and analyze site visitor behavior data through specialized software applications such as Google Analytics and WebTrends.
- Market research: Systematically collect and evaluate data regarding customers' preferences for actual and potential products and services.
- Statistical analysis: Use this mathematical science to collect, analyze, interpret or explain, and present data.

IAR professionals are expected to have the knowledge to make managerial-level decisions in such areas as business and market intelligence, data mining of structured records, and information retrieval. Essential skills include natural language processing, database design, information retrieval, and network analysis (University of Michigan School of Information, 2009). Successful IAR professionals will offer a strategic perspective, sound business judgment, deep analytical capabilities, and a collaborative working style. They will possess strong intellectual curiosity and have the drive for achieving practical business impact. The most critical skills to develop for this field are strong communication skills (both written and presentation), interpersonal, and complex analytical problem-solving skills. Strong technical, math, and statistical skills are equally important.

While a technical educational background isn't always required for IAR jobs, a strong technical and quantitative skill set is often preferred, and knowledge and skills in Web and software tools and applications is listed as required on most IAR-related job postings. The IAR field is multidisciplinary, drawing from computer science, information, mathematics, library science, business, cognitive psychology, linguistics, statistics, and physics. While technical aptitude and skill is important, an effective IAR professional must have the leadership ability and communication skills to effectively manage complex technical and knowledge management solutions, including consensus building and problem solving in a team environment.

Successful IAR professionals must possess the ability to translate and conceptualize statistical information to determine user trends and to analyze Web navigation and user habits. Web analytics is a common career pathway in the field of IAR, and the ability to merge market research and information technology is essential to improving the user experience while increasing return on investment for a business. Therefore, an IAR professional will benefit from industry-specific technical and business knowledge. Web sites ranging from simple "Mom and Pop" to complex e-commerce operations rely on Web analytics to measure user experience and behavior such as the number of visitors that browse the site per day, which pages they viewed the most, how they arrived at pages, on which keywords they searched to arrive at pages, etc. The ability to research, track, and analyze user behavior is critical to the success of any online business, and, therefore, IAR connects directly to the bottom line (Niznik, 2009).

IAR professionals contribute to specific business goals and objectives. They collect, analyze, and present data findings on customer demographics, preferences, needs, and buying habits to identify potential markets and factors affecting product demand. They measure and analyze data pertaining to customer satisfaction as well as forecast and track marketing and sales trends. They gather data on consumer opinions and competitors and analyze their prices, sales, and method of marketing and distribution, often collaborating with marketing and IT professionals, statisticians, pollsters, and other professionals.

KEY WORDS TO KNOW

The following are some key information analysis and retrieval terms that you will see throughout this chapter. If you are interested in pursuing this career field, it's a good idea to be familiar with their meaning:

- **search engine optimization (SEO)**: The process of improving the volume or quality of traffic to a Web site from search engines via "natural" (organic or algorithmic) search results.
- **search engine marketing (SEM)**: A form of Internet marketing that seeks to promote Web sites by increasing their visibility in search engine result pages.
- **natural language processing**: A field of computer science and linguistics concerned with the interactions between computers and human (natural) languages.

(continued)

(continued)

- **information retrieval**: The science of searching for documents, for information within documents, and for metadata about documents as well as that of searching databases and the Internet.
- **metadata**: "Data about data," of any sort in any media.
- **taxonomy**: The practice and science of classification.
- **metrics**: Standards of data measurement.
- **e-commerce**: The buying and selling of products or services over electronic systems such as the Internet and other computer networks.

Professional Roles

Information analysis and retrieval professionals can pursue a diverse set of career paths from search engineer, language engineer, information analyst, to Web analyst and often specialize in a particular domain in the field such as Web analytics, data visualization, competitive intelligence, or information retrieval. To better understand the range and scope of IAR professional roles, it may help to compare and contrast the duties and goals of a few of the most common jobs.

- **Natural Language Engineer**: Evaluates to measure one or more *qualities* of an algorithm or a system, in order to determine whether (or to what extent) the system answers the goals of its designers or meets the needs of its users. Tasks might include text and data analysis, machine translation, information retrieval, speech analysis.
- **Web Analyst**: Analyzes, tracks, and reports Web site data to advance business understanding of Web site users' behavior and site experience. Provide insight on how to optimize Web site design, content, campaigns, and sales. Provide decision makers with the information they need to maximize marketing, sales, administrative efficiencies, and overall business efforts.
- **Data Mining Analyst/Engineer**: Prepares data, conducts data analysis, data cleaning, knowledge extraction, and interpretation.
- **Search Engineer**: Build search engines and Web sites that return the most relevant results to searchers. Augment and manage the data behind search functionality to enhance the user interface providing greater search functionality.
- **SEM Specialist**: Manages a company or client marketing campaign including setup, support, reporting, and analysis on search projects. Responsible for understanding company or client goals and expectations as well as all

department deliverables and must be able to clearly convey and explain search engine best practices.

- **Market Research Analyst**: Research market conditions in local, regional, or national areas to determine potential sales of a product or service. Gather information on competitors, prices, sales, and methods of marketing and distribution. Use survey results to create a marketing campaign based on regional preferences and buying habits.

- **Competitive Intelligence Analyst**: Contributes to intelligence collection, analysis, and communication and helps drive the market insight mission for company by way of directed networking and outreach.

- **Enterprise Search Architect**: Lead architectural design, implementation, and integration of enterprise search components that provide world-class search functionality for Web sites, structured data, and federated external content.

While a bachelor's degree is typically required for some entry-level IAR jobs, increasingly, positions are indicating a need for a few years of experience and/or a master's degree in the area of information, computer science, linguistics, statistics, or library science. An advanced degree may lead to faster career growth into management, director, senior, and lead IAR roles. Pursuing a more research-focused career pathway, such as a research or information scientist, will typically require a PhD in information, computer science, or a related degree.

The following is a list of some of the most common job titles and industries that actively recruit information analysis and retrieval professionals (bachelor's and master's level):

- Natural Language Engineer, Monster.com (Internet)
- SEO Engineer, Comerica Bank (financial services)
- Data Mining Analyst/Engineer, Think Resources (energy)
- Research Engineer–Search Analytics, Conductor Inc. (analytics vendor/ consulting)
- SEO Analyst, MTV Networks (entertainment)
- Information/Data Analyst, Nationwide Insurance (insurance)
- Search Strategist, Blue Cross Blue Shield (health care)
- Competitive Intelligence Researcher, Department of Homeland Security (government)

- SEM Consultant, PricewaterhouseCoopers (consulting)
- SEO & Marketing Manager, Heifer International (international nonprofit)
- Search Engineer, Amazon.com (e-commerce)

Other closely related job titles include:

- Project manager
- Web designer
- Web developer
- Systems analyst
- Software developer

Occupational Outlook

> ☑ QUICK FACT!
> Skilled IAR professionals are in high demand—and will continue to be in high demand for years to come.

According to the U.S. Bureau of Labor Statistics' *Occupational Outlook Handbook*, 2008–2009 Edition, employment growth in IAR-related occupations is projected to be faster than average. Bachelor's degree holders may face competition for employment in this field. Among bachelor's degree holders, those with good quantitative skills, including a strong background in mathematics, statistics, survey design, information, and computer science, will have the best opportunities. Job opportunities should also be strong for jobseekers with a master's or PhD degree in information, computer science, marketing, linguistics, business technology, or statistics. PhD holders should have a range of opportunities in many industries, especially in consulting firms. For all IAR professionals, growth industries include marketing, consulting, computer systems design, software publishing, financial services, health care, advertising, insurance, and government (U.S. Department of Labor, Bureau of Labor Statistics, 2009).

As companies continue to expand their online marketing and business goals, the need for IAR professionals will continue to increase. For example, full-service interactive agencies such as Rosetta and Avenue A|Razorfish have developed entire departments whose focus is on analytics and search engine optimization. Opportunities in government agencies, such as the Department of Homeland Security, FBI, and CIA, are growing as the need for professionals who know how to analyze and retrieve data instantaneously continues to be a top priority for national security. IAR jobs can also be found in academic, research, and public libraries. Web search engines are direct IAR applications, so it's not surprising that companies such as Google, Yahoo!, and MSN actively recruit IAR professionals. In addition, globalization of the marketplace creates a need for more IAR professionals who can analyze foreign markets and competition and who speak a second language in order to work in overseas locations.

The search industry is hot and has exploded into the mainstream over the past few years. Businesses are falling over themselves to get seen by online searchers, and they will pay big bucks to search engines for the privilege (Jordan, 2007). At this time, there are many more jobs than there are skilled IAR professionals to fill them. This extreme demand means that SEM and SEO professionals can pick and choose their jobs. According to Gartner, a leading information technology research and advisory company, the need for IAR talent currently outweighs supply by at least 2 to 1. In a few years organizations will need three times as many professionals on their analytics staff as they do today as they launch a bevy of e-business services focused on wireless and business-to-business deployment. This means that some companies will be willing to pay high salaries for qualified analysts. Highly skilled professionals are actively recruited by head hunters on a regular basis. Experts in select specialties such as pay-per-click advertising (a subset of SEM) are currently enjoying even higher demand than usual, as advertisers outbid one another to have their site shown for popular keyword searches on Google, Yahoo!, and MSN (Jordan, 2007).

Advances in technology are making massive data sets common in many scientific disciplines, such as astronomy, medical imaging, bioinformatics, chemistry, remote sensing, and physics (Grossman et al., 2001). To find useful information in these data sets, scientists and engineers are turning to data mining professionals to find useful information to help solve problems, design systems, and develop products that make a direct and measurable business impact. Given these advances, look for growing IAR opportunities in the realm of natural language processing, data and text mining, as well as in analytics in both academic and corporate research departments. Keep in mind that these types of career opportunities are typically at the PhD level.

Salary Information

Earnings for information analysis and retrieval professionals vary by specialty, level of position, level of education, and industry. The U.S. Bureau of Labor Statistics does not classify information analysis and retrieval as a separate occupation

☑ QUICK FACT!
Excellent income and flexible work hours are sure to lead to job satisfaction.

and, therefore, does not have specific data on their earnings (U.S. Department of Labor, Bureau of Labor Statistics, 2009). We can, however, look at salary data associated with related titles such as research analyst, data and systems analyst, market researcher, and software engineer, among other related titles, to get an idea of salary earnings in the field.

Across all industries, IAR related jobs can expect earnings in the range of $42,190–$112,510. Entry-level bachelor's positions will start at the lower end of this scale. Positions requiring substantial years of experience as well as a master's degree or PhD will find salaries at the middle to high end of this range. Overall average earnings for entry-level information retrieval jobs can be expected to fall within the range of $52,000–$72,000 (Indeed.com, 2009). The more technical positions requiring a master's degree or PhD such as natural language engineer, data mining analyst, or Web analytics expert, combined with longevity in the field, will yield higher earnings. For positions requiring a PhD, six-figure salaries can be expected.

In addition to higher earnings, flexible work options are another benefit of this field. For example, the work for most SEO or SEM professionals is mainly done online; therefore, they often have the freedom of choice to work for an employer, to work from home, and/or to freelance. Many SEO/SEM freelancers end up hiring workers and starting their own company due to the massive demand. The skills in SEM are portable and global. You do not need to be at a desk or in an office all day. With the Internet as the universal equalizer, you can service clients in any country in the world, in many different languages. You can compete with one person shops and Fortune 500 companies on the same playing field. The flexibility and growth of the search industry, combined with exciting job opportunities and high salaries, is likely to sustain high levels of job satisfaction (Jordan, 2007). The following are reported average earnings for some of the most common IAR job titles (Indeed.com, 2009):

- SEO specialist: $49,000
- SEO strategist: $57,000
- Market research analyst: $61,000
- Data analyst: $63,000
- SEO manager: $82,000
- Search engineer: $92,000
- Data mining expert: $92,000
- Web Analytics Analyst: $96,000
- Natural language engineer/scientist: $110,000

Profiles—Perspectives of New Professionals

Derek J. Cooper, Systems Integration Specialist
Philips Healthcare
San Francisco, California

After completing an undergraduate program in computer science at the University of Michigan, I landed a position in a health center at a major university developing a Web-based radiology information system. While the primary focus was on Web development, the context of working in health care information technology (IT) sparked my interest in the field of informatics. I decided to attend a graduate program tailored to my interests of further developing my skill set in informatics and my knowledge of how it may be applied to health care. After I graduated from the University of Michigan School of Information, I moved into my current position at Philips Healthcare as Systems Integration Specialist.

My work is focused on three main areas: system implementation projects (40 percent), customer support (40 percent), and special projects (20 percent). As part of larger system implementation projects, I lead subprojects in which I analyze customer business goals, objectives, needs, and existing technical infrastructure to recommend and implement solutions for integrating Philips medical systems with other medical systems. I also provide top-tier technical support for issues discovered in the field. Special projects may include writing technical and procedural documentation, working with the Engineering division on new product development and/or testing, or sitting on task forces that are shaping organizational policies and strategies.

Hospitals are complex entities with a number of departments and functions. As such, they are comprised of a number of different information systems developed specifically for supporting these departments and functional areas. For instance, a typical hospital environment may consist of an electronic medical record (EMR) system providing a complete history of vital clinical information regarding any given patient; a laboratory information system (LIS) supporting the ability of running laboratory tests, receiving results, and providing the results to the necessary health care providers; and a medical billing system for soliciting payment for services from patients, insurance companies, Medicare/Medicaid, etc. Imagine someone who goes to the hospital with a bad infection. When this person arrives at the hospital, it may not be uncommon to have a complete blood count (CBC) done to evaluate the patient's blood cells. The patient's clinical history may already be stored in the EMR, his or her CBC test and results stored in the LIS, and the services paid for through the medical billing system. All of these systems need to know who the person is, when he or she was in the hospital, what procedures were performed, etc. The work I do ensures all of this information is communicated effectively and efficiently between these systems.

Furthermore, I work with hospitals to thoroughly understand the electronic transactions between the information systems and the workflows intended to be supported by them. I also make an effort to analyze business goals and objectives; for instance, accounting for time line, resource, or contractual constraints. In doing so, I help lead systems integration projects—designing, testing, and deploying electronic interfaces between systems.

In my job, I find solving new problems on a daily basis and developing customer relationships to be the most rewarding aspects of my work. No two customers are exactly the same, and the high level of complexity in the systems with which I work practically ensure that I never face a dull day—every day seems to bring a new set of problems to solve. As a result of the combination of my work being a customer-facing role and a relatively low-volume business, it's also nice to have an opportunity to develop quality personal relationships with customers over time. A perk of my job is that I work remotely, which allows me to work from home and maintain a flexible work schedule when necessary.

Within the organization itself, I work in a small group of highly specialized individuals. While we are really a small piece of the puzzle, we provide a critical service to the organization. Without our group, it would not be possible to implement Philips health care information systems in any sort of electronically integrated environment; all major hospitals are essentially comprised of a number of such systems, which all effectively need to communicate with one another. The impact outside of the organization may be where my group draws its greatest satisfaction. Our work effectively ensures that critical health care information is delivered correctly, to the right people, and in a timely fashion. In a sense, our work directly impacts the quality of health care patients may receive.

For those considering this field, I think that to be most effective in a health care IT position, an individual should have a solid technical background; however, something often overlooked is the importance of health care domain knowledge. As a result, I believe health care IT can be a difficult field to break into without some closely related experience. Because my role is fairly technical, my undergraduate training in computer science was critical in providing the foundation for the necessary technical skills to perform the essential duties. My graduate experience helped hone my soft skills to a point where I would be able to excel in my position. Critical analysis, problem solving, and communication (both written and verbal) are the three most essential skills that contribute to success in my job. A combination of technical abilities and thoroughly developed skills related to communication, analysis, and problem solving gained from internships or other entry-level experiences would suit any person well to set them up for a career in health care and/or IT domains.

Regarding the field overall, IT is still lagging behind in health care. As a result, a number of initiatives are currently being offered at a national level, even from the federal government, to help push the development and adoption of IT in health care. Therefore, it seems likely that health care will need a growing number of IT professionals in general (e.g., software developers, implementation specialists, systems analysts, project managers, etc.). This leads me to believe that the outlook for employment in health care IT is relatively solid. However, that being said, health care in general does have some things working against it as well. There are clear movements to bring down the cost of health care, and cuts to payments for health care services seem to be a frequent target. If revenue within the health care industry at large continues to decline, it may be difficult to sustain a continual effort to improve IT within health care as well.

Like many other positions, salary expectations seem to vary widely depending on a number of factors, but perhaps most important in health care is the type of organization. For instance, a nonprofit hospital may not necessarily pay as well as a medical device vendor. Even then, for a relatively highly specialized position, I would expect salaries to be very solid. For instance, in more expensive parts of the country, I would expect starting salaries of $80,000 per year; in less expensive parts of the country, a salary along the lines of $60,000 per year could be expected. (Cooper, 2009)

Fengfeng He, Search Engine Marketing Strategist/Campaign Operations Manager
Red Bricks Media
San Francisco, California

While I was in graduate school at the University of Michigan School of Information (SI), I participated in a summer internship at OneupWeb, one of the top 20 search engine marketing firms in America. As an intern at OneupWeb, I learned about the two major sections of search engine marketing: search engine optimization (SEO) and pay-per-click (PPC). The best way to understand them is to know that when one searches something in Google, the result page shows two columns. The left column shows organic result based on the search term, while the right column shows paid ranking result for the term. Organic ranking shows Web pages in an order based on Google's algorithm's decision of which is more relevant to the searched term, and the PPC result mainly reveals who is willing to pay more in order to rank higher for that term and how relevant the linked landing page is to the term. After I studied search engine marketing (SEM), I wrote a white paper about the prospect of search engine marketing on handheld and mobile devices for OneupWeb. It was presented at a national SEM conference and reported by major portals of the industry in 2005. This was how I stepped into the search engine marketing industry.

After graduate school, I took a position with Backbone Media as a search engine marketing analyst. In this position, my work related to SEO and PPC activities included conducting industry research, keyword research, and competitive analysis; performing technical and content evaluation of client Web sites for recommendations; setting up campaign goals; establishing content, linking, ad, bidding, and landing page strategies; managing implementation; and monitoring SEO and PPC campaign performance. I also conducted quantitative and qualitative analysis in relation to budget control and return on investment (ROI) tracking.

Now, as a Search Engine Marketing Strategist at Red Bricks Media, a full-service integrated marketing agency, my job entails working on PPC strategies and execution based on search engine data and other Web analytics analysis. PPC strategies include on which search engine or search network to carry out a campaign, what keywords and ad copy to use for it, any geotargeting or day parting necessities, etc. Web analytics include all Web log data one can obtain from a Web site or Web page's performance. Our analytics analysis is essential in measuring how successful a PPC campaign is considering the cost of each visit or the amount of people who sign up for newsletters, make purchases, or generate any other forms of conversions from the PPC links. My daily work routine requests knowledge and skills in computer science, economics, and statistics, which were heavily covered in SI's curricula.

Currently, our organization is working to drive down cost by increasing professionalism in operation practice and rolling out templatized operations. Being the solution provider and operation executer, my role is pivotal to the PPC team. In all of my positions, it has been integral to build close relationships with clients to be updated with their needs and concerns and to keep close watch on the latest SEM, e-marketing development, and business intelligence so that I am informed of what's cutting edge in this field.

I like my job because it is at the forefront of the future marketing scene, which relates to a large part of the future reality of how people live their lives and interact with the other people and the outside world. It is the cleanest marketing industry I could think of. Also, economically, it could be the most efficient for all B2B (business to business), B2C (business to consumer), or C2C (consumer to consumer) marketing criteria. What interests me less right now is the lack of professional mechanism design in the working environment, which is eventually translated to higher cost in operations.

My degrees from Nanjing International Studies Institute and SI were highly influential in my ability to attain this position. At SI, I specialized in information economics, management, and policy, a multifaceted specialization that provides me with a sound foundation to manage people and projects as well as analyze and distill information effectively. Every day I use my knowledge of statistics, economics, mechanism design, and communication skills to be effective. Also being culturally and technically savvy is very important.

For people who are considering this field, I suggest playing with your Web site or blogs to implement Web analytics tools (like Google analytics) to get a taste of it. Follow major search engine marketing portals (like Search Engine Land) to learn about the industry development. I think that social media sites such as Facebook and Twitter are going to be the hot areas for this field, as with time they will reveal more power in defining the future digital marketing. What's great about this is that the employment outlook for this field looks pretty good, especially compared with the general economic depression in the next couple of years.

The earning potential for this field is positive. For beginners it could start lower as general marketing personnel ($45,000–$50,000). But with a decent educational background, years of work experience, and strong research abilities, the salary expectation could look really good in the next five to ten years. (He, 2009)

Jessica Hullman, Doctoral Candidate
University of Michigan School of Information
formerly, Analytics Muse
Pure Visibility Inc.
Ann Arbor, Michigan

I have always enjoyed work that requires analytical thinking and have tended to be interested in innovative new areas of theory and development. At first, I had some trouble finding the right mix of disciplines to satisfy both my creative and analytical sides. My undergrad work was in comparative studies at The Ohio State University, followed by a master's degree in writing from Naropa University, which was motivated by the desire to hone my writing skills. While I loved theories of writing and communication as well, I found that my analytical side left me wanting more scientific theory.

I became interested in the role of the Internet as a mass communication device, first from the perspective of natural language processing, and it was this that led me to the University of Michigan School of Information (SI). A degree in information analysis and retrieval felt to me like the most direct way to meet the growing needs I saw for new ways of processing and retrieving information. After graduating I got a job at Pure Visibility, where I gained real-world experience in analysis and online search technologies. More recently, research in information visualization with a former professor from SI incited me to apply for the doctoral program, to study information visualization. I was accepted to the University of Michigan's program, and I plan to start in the fall.

Pure Visibility addresses the fact that you can sometimes have too much of a good thing, as in information online. They address this from the perspective of the companies that are drowning in data by helping them make sense of site usage and marketing data in order to address problems with their Web site as well as integrate new technologies into their online sales engine. The searchers on the other side of the search engine benefit as well, since search engine optimization helps connect them to the companies that they are really interested in.

As one of the only formally trained analysts at Pure Visibility, I get to do what I consider the fun stuff: visitor behavior analysis, or making sense of how people use a Web site using logfile analysis or Web analytics software like Google Analytics. I'll work on monthly reporting for a large client each month as well as on additional reports that various companies request, either to address problems with their Web sites or to figure out the best way to install analytics tracking on a complex system of sites. I did this for Kellogg's Company, which was fun—lots of cereal sites. Another type of analysis that I've done often is called a word market assessment. Keyword query statistics and search engine ranking results are combined to analyze which words will best optimize a Web site, given both online popularity and competition levels.

Pure Visibility helps businesses connect to their customers online, and gaining a better understanding of how users search for, find, and use a Web site is insight that can lead to dramatic changes in a company's online strategy. As a result of analytics, changes may be made to how the site is structured, presented, or advertised online, often meaning big increases in return on investment. I think that the company and my role as an analyst in particular are crucial toward helping companies gain this understanding. I like to think that my own contribution also has to do with helping others see how much fun it can be to analyze what happens online, how genuinely interesting it can be even to those who don't normally think about it.

I love being able to contribute new ideas to the company "toolbox" for types of analysis, or ways to present information to clients, or ways to streamline internal processes or deliverables. I designed a one-day class on Web analytics with Google Analytics, which I enjoy teaching because it helps me better understand how I can present Web analysis to those less familiar with it and hopefully get them excited about looking at data. When it comes to the analyst work I do, I also really like that I get to follow the information through its entire life cycle, from initial pattern-finding in the data set, to narrating the findings to others in the company, to communicating the insights to the clients, including thinking about the best way to visualize any complicated relationships.

As someone who likes to think deeply about problems, the parts I dislike most are the times when the hours allotted for a project just don't allow a "deep-dive" type of analysis. This can be frustrating. But the company is always busy, so even when it happens I know that another project will be coming my way soon.

My master's degree from SI was crucial for me to gain entrance to my current field because it gave me access to knowledge about information use at a high level in addition to specific analysis and presentation methods that I would've otherwise remained unaware of. My master's in writing was also important. Being able to write clearly, effectively, and quickly is really important in consulting. You need to be able to communicate what you learn from the data, after all. Usability analysis, Web analytics methodologies, statistical analysis, information visualization tools and guidelines, business writing, return on investment (ROI) and sales cycle analysis, requirements analysis, and client facing and interpersonal communication skills are also all very important in my job and will be in my future career and research pursuits.

If you are considering this field, you should figure out whether analytical thinking suits you and whether you like thinking analytically about the scenarios that play out online as people search for a service or product—what words they use, what sites they reference for help, etc. Also, you shouldn't be afraid of technical and math and statistics work; to be an analyst in information retrieval, you don't necessarily need to be a mathematician, but you may have to use concepts or methods on a regular basis.

Video search and devising ways to quantify what happens in social networking spaces online in terms of revenue or value to a company are a couple of trends in the online search industry. The effects on search engine and online behavior of attributes that have been less studied—culture, for example—are also being discussed more frequently. The field is definitely growing, as the number of people turning to the Internet to find and purchase services they used to find using phone books, word of mouth, or print advertising parallels an analogous increase in the number of companies taking online visibility and visitor behavior analysis more seriously. For work in the field of search engine optimization and Web analytics, I think that a $50k–$60k starting salary range is about average, assuming some experience or education, and depending on the part of the country. (Hullman, 2009)

Careers in Information Analysis and Retrieval: At a Glance

Your career in information analysis and retrieval can take many directions as you connect your interests and values to the type of functional area and type of organization that you pursue. Here are a few examples of real jobs representing some exciting "tracks" you can follow.

Health Informatics Track
Clinical Informatics Scientist/Engineer
Philips
Briarcliff Manor, New York

Participate in the expansion of the Clinical Decision Support Systems program for diagnostic, therapeutic, and real-time interventional guidance decision support research and applications investigations; lead in the development of the imaging informatics competency; participate in the prototype effort for imaging and natural language processing systems used in decision support applications; and participate in the application development that is underway in the areas of predictive modeling, simulation, outcome management, context-aware platforms, and evidence-based medicine. (LinkUp, "Philips Human Resources," accessed 2009)

Corporate Track
Natural Language QA Engineer
Apple
Tampa, Florida

Responsible for a wide range of natural-language processing and data, including managing corpus and lexical data for spellchecking, correction, and other technologies that incorporate natural-language information; develop and run tests in these areas, including both manual and automated test cases and associated tools; testing and quality assurance of checking, correction, other language-related features and the linguistic data they depend on, including testing of functionality, correctness, user experience, and performance. (LinkUp, "Apple Human Resources," accessed 2009)

Media/Entertainment Track
Senior Analyst, Business Analytics
DIRECTV
El Segundo, California

Support the analytical and reporting needs through data analytics development and support of engineering data-mart, including developing and maintaining

Cognos solutions leveraging Analysis Studio, Report Studio, Enterprise Planning, and other tools; construct data models and reports using IBM's Cognos 8 Business Intelligence application; optimize existing queries and troubleshoot database performance; complete data extraction using complex SQL statements; provide timely support for ad hoc report requests and for maintaining established Enterprise Business Portal reporting suites; interface with business users to define requirements and specifications, including scope and time estimation, to build Enterprise analytical solutions; verify integrity of data in Engineering data-mart and IT data warehouse. (DIRECTV Human Resources, accessed 2009)

Social Justice Track
Specialist, Web Performance Analyst
Save the Children
Westport, Connecticut

Apply best practices in analytics and measurement strategies to allow content and marketing decisions to be based on measurable business value; own the analytical data collection as well as process for converting data to actionable information by developing dashboards to help guide decision making; develop and maintain an ongoing qualitative and quantitative research and analytics foundation to support decision making processes related to the overall interactive experience, fund-raising and social networking; play a key role in developing and encouraging a fact-based decision making culture and help support the organization in driving an interactive strategy based on quantifiable Web metrics. (LinkUp, "Save the Children," accessed 2009)

Global Track
Software Development Engineer–Search Technology Center
Microsoft Research
Munich, Germany

Index every database in the world and build a rich user interface to expose this information in a structured, strongly typed fashion; code and architect solutions to difficult problems, with the ability to create, innovate, and define the next generation of search; code efficient implementations of challenging algorithms; produce production-quality services that compete directly with offerings from Yahoo!, Google, and others; work on many levels—from high level vision to design and implementations of both self-contained components and large, team-oriented code bases. (Microsoft Corporation, accessed 2009)

Resources for Further Information/Exploration

The following resources can help guide you in your career exploration within the field of information analysis and retrieval. Note that this is not a comprehensive list; there are numerous resources available related to the nuances of the field that are not included. The purpose of identifying key job posting sites and professional organizations is to make you aware of some of the main resources available and to also provide you with gateways to resources that will inform you of the types of careers available in the field.

Professional Organizations Relevant to Information Analysis and Retrieval

- ACM—Association for Computing Machinery
  www.acm.org
- ACM SIG—Information Retrieval
  www.sigir.org/index.html
- ACM SIG—Knowledge Discovery and Data Mining
  www.kdd.org
- ACM SIG—Electronic Commerce
  www.sigecom.org
- CRA—Computing Research Association
  www.cra.ogg
- WAA—Web Analytics Association
  www.webanalyticsassociation.org/index.asp
- ASIS&T—The American Society for Information Science and Technology
  www.asis.org
- ACL—Association for Computational Linguistics
  www.aclweb.org

Career Sites Relevant to Information Analysis and Retrieval

- SearchEngineWatch Job Board
  http://jobs.searchenginewatch.com/c/search_results.cfm?site_id=2660
- KDnuggets
  www.kdnuggets.com/jobs
- StartUpLy
  www.startuply.com

- Dice
  www.dice.com
- CRA Job Announcements
  www.cra.org/ads/
- Corp-Corp.com
  www.corp-corp.com
- International IT Jobs
  www.iitjobs.com
- TechCareers
  www.techcareers.com
- ComputerJobs.com
  www.computerjobs.com
- Intelligence Careers
  www.intelligencecareers.com
- VerticalMove
  www.verticalmove.com
- Network Engineer
  www.networkengineer.com
- Nonprofit Tech Jobs
  www.nten.org/jobs
- JustTechJobs
  www.justtechjobs.com
- Tech-Centric
  www.tech-centric.net
- TechJobsOnline
  www.techjobsonline.com
- WiredJobs
  http://jobs.wired.com
- DevBistro
  www.devbistro.com
- Krop
  www.krop.com
- Silicon.com Jobs
  www.silicon.com/jobs
- ACM SIG–Symbolic and Algebraic Manipulation Opportunities
  www.sigsam.org/opportunities.phtml

Education and Training

Information analysis and retrieval (IAR) is an interdisciplinary field and as such educational options cut across disciplines, including computer science, math, linguistics, information science, and statistics. Yet pursuing a bachelor's or master's degree in informatics or information will include coursework from these areas while providing a cohesive intellectual framework for professional work. Most informatics programs include a track or an overall focus that ties well to the field of information analysis and retrieval. A bachelor's degree will afford ready employment opportunity and with experience, advancement.

Those who are interested in deeper training and faster career advancement, or who are changing career directions having already obtained a bachelor's degree, will find graduate level education beneficial. Since at the graduate level programs tend to have more distinctive areas of focus depending on the faculty backgrounds and research interests, it is important to examine programs of interest to evaluate the course offerings, research opportunities, and career outcomes of graduates to determine if there is a sufficient emphasis in IAR.

Similarly, if one chooses to take an educational path such as computer science, statistics, or math, it will be helpful to know the interests of the faculty, and it may be useful to attend a university that has undergraduate and/or graduate programs in informatics, information science, or information in order to take some coursework that provides the broader perspective and integrated approaches these programs provide. For those interested in doctoral level education, there are ample research and funding opportunities, and the outlook is good for faculty and research positions.

While IAR tends to be a more technical branch of the information profession, not all positions require heavy technical skills, and students who gain a solid understanding and reasonable skill level with technologies used in IAR can parlay these skills into positions that focus more on strategic use of Web analytics tools, for example, rather than on the design and development of the Web analytics tool itself. Still, for many IAR positions, strong programming, quantitative, and statistical skills will be essential.

References

Boland, Michael. 2009. "Surrounded by Search Engines: A New Kind of Mobile Search." Search Engine Watch, August 7. Available: http://searchenginewatch.com/3634640 (accessed August 10, 2009).

Cooper, Derek J. 2009. Interview by Kelly Kowatch. December 16.

DIRECTV Human Resources. "DIRECTV Careers." Available: www.directv.com/DTVAPP/about/careers.jsp?footernavtype=5 (accessed August 10, 2009).

Enge, Eric. 2008. "Building a Data-Driven Organization." Search Engine Watch, October 22. Available: http://searchenginewatch.com/3631252 (accessed July 10, 2009).

Grossman, Robert L., Chandrika Kamath, Philip Kegelmeyer, Vipin Kumar, and Raju R. Namburu, eds. 2001. *Data Mining for Scientific and Engineering Applications.* Norwell, MA: Kluwer Academic Publishers.

Guruswamy, Mini. 2008. "Emerging Digital Trends Impacting Web Analytics." Web Analytics Association, September 8. Available: www.webanalyticsassociation.org/en/art/534 (accessed August 10, 2009).

He, Fengfeng. 2009. Interview by Kelly Kowatch. August 17.

Hullman, Jessica. 2009. Interview by Kelly Kowatch. August 3.

Indeed.com. 2009. "SEO Salaries." Available: www.indeed.com/salary?q1=Seo (accessed August 2009).

Jordan, Kalena. 2007. "11 Reasons Why You Should Consider a Job in Search Engine Marketing." Internet Search Engine Database, January 2. Available: www.isedb .com/d/Barticles/1582/1/11-Reasons-Why-You-Should-Consider-a-Job-in-Search -Engine-Marketing/Page1.html (accessed August 2009).

Landis, Grant. 2009. "Yebol Announces Launch of Revolutionary Knowledge-Based Search Engine." PR.com press release, July 29. Available: www.pr.com/press-release/168115 (accessed August 11, 2009).

LinkUp. "Apple Human Resources." Available: www.linkup.com/results.php#a:10:{s: 1:%22q%22;s:16:%22natural%20language%22;s:1:%22l%22;s:0:%22%22;s:1:%22m %22;s:6:%22normal%22;s:1:%22c%22;s:0:%22%22;s:4:%22list%22;s:0: (accessed August 10, 2009).

LinkUp. "Philips Human Resources." Available: www.linkup.com/results.php#a:26:{s: 1:%22q%22;s:21:%22Information%20retrieval%22;s:1:%22l%22;s:0:%22%22;s:1:% 22m%22;s:8:%22normal-d%22;s:1:%22d%22;s:2:%2225%22;s:1:%22c%22;s:0: (accessed August 11, 2009).

LinkUp. "Save the Children." Available: www.linkup.com/results.php#q=%22 Social%20network%22%20analyst&l=&c=&list=&d=25&m=normal&p=25&sort= r&tm=ALL&page=1&jobHash=df7cd8d68c0aa9ce6def1c874611f714 (accessed May 22, 2009).

Microsoft Corporation. "Microsoft Careers Global." Available: https://careers .microsoft.com/JobDetails.aspx?ss=&pg=0&so=&rw=10&jid=5356&jlang=EN (accessed August 1, 2009).

Newcomb, Kevin. 2008. "Where's Search Heading? Ask Yahoo's Chief Scientist." Search Engine Watch, March 20. Available: http://searchenginewatch.com/3628767 (accessed August 10, 2009).

Niznik, John S. 2009. "Web Analytics Jobs." About.com: Tech Careers. Available: http://jobsearchtech.about.com/od/internetjobs//Aweb_analytics.htm (accessed August 2009).

Smillie, Dirk. 2009. "A $65 Billion Advertising Shift?" Forbes.com, July 21. Available: www.forbes.com/2009/07/21/advertising-marketing-business-media-stratigos .html (accessed August 10, 2009).

University of Michigan School of Information. 2009. "Information Analysis and Retrieval (IAR) Specialization." Available: www.si.umich.edu/msi/iar.htm (accessed August 2009).

U.S. Department of Labor, Bureau of Labor Statistics. 2009. *Occupational Outlook Handbook*, 2008–2009 ed. Available: www.bls.gov/oco/ (accessed August 2009).

Additional Source

Wikipedia. 2009. "Search Results: Information Analysis and Retrieval." Available: http://en.wikipedia.org/w/index.php?title=Special%3ASearch&redirs=1&search= information+analysis+and+retrieval&fulltext=Search&ns0=1 (accessed April 2009).

Chapter 9

Planning for Your Career in Information

A Step-by-Step Guide to Career Fulfillment

Self-Assessment

The first step toward your career in information is self-assessment. Exploring your personal interests, values, skills, and environmental/cultural preferences can help ensure that you will make fulfilling career decisions now and in the future. There are many different opportunities across the information profession, but even if your career planning process takes you in a different direction, the most important thing is that you discover the path that is right for you.

This section will provide you with reflective questions to guide your exploration and will help you identify resources and strategies to build your awareness of potential career options. Consider your interests first and foremost. Your current hobbies may be a strong indicator of what it is that you like to do best, or you may have certain abilities that you enjoy using. What you wanted to do as a child may also be an indicator of some fundamental interest areas. Start by asking yourself the following questions to help determine what interests might lend well to shaping your career:

- As a child, what activities did I enjoy the most? What did I enjoy the least?
- In my youth, what did I see myself being when I grew up? Has that changed? If so, why?
- Who are the people I consider to be heroes or who I admire? What about them do I wish to emulate?
- What products or services do I use regularly? Which ones do I tell others about?

- In my work experiences, what work was interesting or exciting? What work did I find myself commonly putting off doing?

Considering your values is equally important in career exploration as interests, if not more so. Your personal emphasis on salary, lifestyle, and purpose can be critical in deciding what career area to pursue, as you may find yourself in a job function that you sincerely enjoy yet you still dread coming to work because your values are compromised. Ask yourself the following questions to help determine what is important to you in a career:

- Is it important for me that my work be dedicated toward making a contribution to society or helping others?
  - If it is important, is it good enough for me to work for an organization that has a positive societal mission, even though my work is not specifically in that area?
- Do I currently maintain or seek a lifestyle that will require a substantial salary?
- Does working at a prestigious organization matter to me?

Ability is also very important when considering your career choices. If you really aren't all that fond of calculus nor are you very talented at it, then a quantitative career is probably not for you. However, the possibilities for nonquantitative jobs are endless, and vice versa. Consider these questions to help you reflect on your skills and abilities.

- What do I think that I am good at?
- Are there things that I do that others commonly compliment me on?
- In past work or academic experiences, what work did I excel at or came much easier to me than it did other colleagues? (Consider both soft skills and hard skills.)
- In what areas have I been recognized with awards or for accomplishments?

Your preferred work culture is also a very important indicator of what sort of job is ideal for you. The following questions can provide direction for seeking a culture that is an ideal fit for your preferences:

- Do I prefer to work with people or alone?

- Do I work well under stress?
- Do I prefer to do things in a routine manner or do I prefer to be spontaneous?
- Would I prefer to work in an environment where I can exercise my artistic creativity?
- Do I seek an organization that promotes work–life balance or one that encourages a work-hard, play-hard culture?

As you read (or reread) *The New Information Professional,* keep these questions in mind and make notes on the career areas that seem to connect with your interests, skills, and values. Some of the positions and career tracks shared may match perfectly with your answers while others may be a good fit but the connection between your preferences and what's described will be less clear. Others may clearly not be a good fit for you.

There are many other reflective questions that you can ask yourself to help point you in the direction of an ideal career for you. Note that there is not one perfect job for everyone. For some, the career exploration process can be very exciting because they are able to distill information into a very realistic and appealing career option; others will be overwhelmed by choices that all sound very interesting or not at all.

This leads us to assessments. There are many very good assessments available that you can take that can provide you with great insight into your interests, values, skills, and cultural inclinations. The Strong Interest Inventory is one popular interest inventory. Another is the Self-Directed Search (SDS) by John Holland. You can contact a career counselor or utilize the Internet to administer these tests. A trained professional is suggested to guide you through the analysis to help you properly interpret the outcomes.

Last, consider talking with family, friends, classmates, colleagues, or mentors about these exploratory questions. Ask them what they perceive as a good fit for your interests, skills, and other preferences. Others' perception of yourself can be a very revealing and indicative perspective of what could be a good fit for you.

Researching Your Career Options
In this age of information overload, researching career options is not unlike any other area of information: there is an overwhelming amount of resources and options to consider. In fact, one of the main reasons that people find career dissatisfaction in their lives is because they did not thoroughly self-assess or do the proper research before they chose a career, often because there is too much information to

consider. Often we have a lot of information on one option and little on another. It is important to try to gather comparable information so that you can make an informed decision between a career that is already familiar to you and one that is new but has for some reason captured your interest.

Self-assessment should give some shape to what you foresee as your potential work environment, job function, and skill set to be developed or utilized. However, it is also important to weigh other factors such as job availability, economic trends, your geographic location, and educational requirements. Be sure to consider these questions as you explore the following resources:

- Does my field of interest have many jobs in my local area? If not, is it possible for me to move to an area that has more related careers?
- If I cannot move, are there companies in my area that offer both entry-level career options and career growth options for me in this field?
- Does the field that I am interested in require further education?
  - If so, does my current life situation allow me to pursue further education?
  - Is there a quality program in the area that will allow me to gain an accredited degree or the required training?
- Are there currently jobs in this area or is the field highly competitive?
- If I require further education or training for this career area, will there be positions when I am ready to secure a job?
- Beyond the entry-level position, are there many career opportunities, or is the field limited or lending itself to a flat organizational structure?

The following is a summary of various resources that you can utilize in your career exploration. You don't need to utilize all of these resources, but utilizing at least three is recommended.

Career Videos

Career videos are a relatively new way to gain some great information about potential career options. Companies like Google (www.youtube.com/lifeatgoogle) now have videos on YouTube or embedded in their Web site that show current employers talking about their work, the culture, and other relevant information to help you make a career choice. General career search Web sites such as CareerOneStop (www.acinet.org/videos_by_occupation.asp?id=&nodeid=28) have videos on a variety of different positions that you can view to gather information.

Career Guides or Books

By reading this guide, you are already utilizing this type of resource. Career guides provide an in-depth overview of certain fields and will provide you with a wide range of ideas and alternatives for careers that fit your ideal industry, skill set, or interests. Career guides come in a variety of types that include career fields (such as this one), industry types, trendy jobs, and jobs by skill sets, interests, and many other types. Your college career center and local public library are good sources for career resource books, or you can browse at your favorite bookstore.

Informational Interviews

Informational interviews are one of the best ways to explore careers. In an informational interview, you'll set up an appointment or phone call with current professionals and ask them questions about what it is that they do and how they got to where they are now. You can also ask for career advice and gain information on industry trends, organizations, and the outlook for the field. Informational interviews are also a great way to develop your network in your future career field, and you may be surprised at how eager people are to talk about their career with others and to share advice.

Company Web Sites

In this guide, a plethora of companies have been mentioned to consider for your future employment. Some you have probably heard of, some you probably have not. This is okay because this is a great place to start doing some research to learn about what jobs are out there, which ones fit your skills and interests, where they are located, and what they pay. Many of these sites have well-developed career pages that provide you with information on careers types, culture, and profiles of current employees. Furthermore, by simply visiting a company's careers Web site and doing a keyword search using any of the keywords or job titles that we've provided in the chapters before, you can generate a list of potential employment sites and gain an understanding of what is available. Note the pages that have interview hints and tips for later in your job search.

Online Job Boards

Hundreds of online job boards are available via the Internet; these are useful career exploration tools. By doing a quick search using keywords or job titles, you can gain timely information on available career types in your area and learn what companies are hiring, if your field of interest is available in your geographic area, and valuable salary information.

Career Exploration Web Sites

Myriad career exploration and career advice Web sites are available for you to use. One of the most authoritative career exploration Web sites available is O*Net On-line, which is sponsored by the United States Department of Labor. This Web site lists over 800 occupational areas and provides information on new and emerging occupations and what is in demand currently. You can also search for careers by skills, tools, and technology. Vault.com is also a leading career resource Web site. The Web site lists thousands of companies and hundreds of both professions and industries to explore. Furthermore, a job board, information on salaries and reviews, and a surplus of other resources to peruse can keep you swimming in information on potential careers. The employer reviews are a fantastic resource for gaining insider information on career possibilities within certain organizations.

College or University Resources

Your current educational institution has trained staff and resources that can help you shape your career decision making. Make an appointment with the career services office to take an assessment and to discuss potential career outcomes that are related to what you learned during your self-assessment. If you have narrowed your area of interest, you can also make an appointment with an admissions office of a program related to your potential field to learn about the career outcomes of graduates.

Job Shadowing

One of the best ways to quickly learn if a career is a good fit for you is to try it on for size. Job shadowing a current professional at a local organization is a great way to see what it's really like to do a certain job and see if the environment and activities are a good fit for your preferences. Although some industries are more open to job shadowing than others due to work associated with confidential information, many current professionals are flattered to be asked to be shadowed and will welcome the opportunity to share with you what their day is like.

Volunteering

If you are ready to make more of a commitment to a potential career outcome, volunteering is one of the best methods to learn if a career is a good fit for you. Many local organizations including public libraries, start-ups, historical societies, museums, and nonprofits are always seeking assistance in information management areas. Although you may not be given professional level responsibilities, the opportunity to meet people who work in your desired field and gain hands-on experience can be incredibly revealing of whether this career area is right for you. You can volunteer for a single project or commit to a certain amount of time; either way, the experience will look great on your resume.

Social Networking Sites

Last, but not least, don't forget the world of Web 2.0 resources. LinkedIn (www .linkedin.com) is an excellent resource to learn about companies that hire certain career titles, connect with current professionals, and identify common career paths from one position to the next. Facebook (www.facebook.com) also is a resource, although unintentionally, for career exploration. Many organizations have group pages or alumni groups. For example, the consulting firm Accenture has several Facebook groups, some of which are specifically focused on careers and recruitment, which allow users to explore and talk with recruiters about career opportunities. You can also connect with current employees to set up informational interviews. There are many other social and professional networking sites available that you can utilize for your career exploration.

Developing a Career Action Plan

Once you have evaluated your interests, skills, and values and have used these to evaluate the career options you have generated, the next step is to build a career action plan. If your decisions are still unclear or difficult to make, you can seek guidance from your college or university career center or from private career counselors, family members, or mentors. Remember that career decision making isn't a one shot deal. While the decisions you make today are important, there are many paths that can lead to success and happiness. You will continue to make career decisions over the course of your lifetime, and you will likely change jobs and directions many times along the way. Yet if you trust your instincts and thoroughly engage in the career planning process, you may well find that you are able to find an area of focus that will remain a part of your career trajectory for many years.

It may seem premature to start thinking in the long term about your career, especially if you're just getting started thinking about your career path. The best way to ensure success in your chosen field is to sketch a basic map of what you want to achieve throughout the course of your professional life—even if you haven't even picked a college, decided on a major, or landed your first professional job yet.

Career experts caution that by focusing exclusively on the here-and-now you may be shortchanging yourself and limiting your long term success. We're in the age of vision boards and self-reflection. Whether you are a person who cringes at the sound of these terms or if you are a person who embraces them, they are effective strategies for greater learning, increased self-awareness, and can ensure better odds for satisfaction and success in your future. Don't dread or skip this step in the process, as it is sure to be a liberating, fulfilling, and positive experience.

By this stage in your career planning process you've probably done a lot of self-exploration and self-reflection to assess your interests, skills, values, beliefs, likes, and dislikes, etc. You've researched career options and evaluated these against what you have come to understand about yourself. Now it's time to create your vision or career objective by designing a career action plan that will guide you to long-term career satisfaction and success.

A career action plan is a series of steps to help you attain a specific career objective. This objective is as individual as you are but could be about your dream occupation, your dream organization, or your dream salary level in ten years. The more specific a career action plan, the more effective it will be toward goal achievement. Although it should be specific, it should also allow for flexibility, as life has a funny way of throwing curveballs in the path of the best-laid plans. Life changes all the time, which is why your career action plan should be designed to allow for changes without completely throwing you off track in your progression to career fulfillment.

CREATING A CAREER ACTION PLAN

Step 1: Articulate Your Vision

Before you can articulate your vision or career objective, you must first assess where you are in the process today—your personal, educational and career pursuits. Start by asking yourself the following questions:

- Where am I today?
- What has it taken to make it to this point?
- Where would I like to be next year?
- What is it going to take to get to where I want to be in one year?
- What is it going to take to get where I want to be in five years?
- What will my dream job look like five years from now?

Step 2: Set Goals (short and long term)

It's important to set both short- and long-term goals for your career action plan. Short-term goals are ones that can be accomplished in one year or less. As the name implies, long-term goals will take longer to become a reality; generally speaking, you are looking at between three to five years for these to come to fruition.

Step 3: Define Concerns or Barriers

Be prepared for roadblocks along the way. It is important to identify and define concerns or potential barriers that may prevent you from reaching your goals. It's better to plan for these roadblocks ahead of time than to have them sneak up on you and prevent you from moving forward. Consider these statements to help you identify potential barriers:

- I have carefully reviewed and assessed my situation and where I am now in my personal, educational, and career pursuits, and the career pathway(s) I would like to explore further is . . .
- I am concerned about this career pathway because . . .
- The major facts that could become barriers to me pursuing this pathway are . . .

Step 4: Identify a Solution to Barriers

While some barriers might be harder to overcome than others, you can always seek and identify potential solutions to all barriers that may prevent you from reaching your goal. Even for substantial barriers that you think you could never overcome, while a direct solution might not always be apparent, you might surprise yourself with your know-how, creativity, and resourcefulness for facing each barrier head-on. Use these leading statements to help identify solutions to potential career barriers:

- The elements of my situation most amenable to change are . . .
- The elements of my situation least amenable to change are . . .
- I would use these indicators to consider my concerns to be satisfactorily resolved . . .
- The forces that I see as blocking my pursuits are . . .
- The solutions that I see to my concerns are . . .
- I see the time frame for my career action plan to be operative as follows . . .

Step 5: Set Time Lines

Set time lines to reach your stated goal. Allow for some flexibility in your timelines to allow for changes in circumstances. Give yourself a time range rather than a specific date to reach your goal.

Once you have completed steps one through five, it's now time to create your plan. Start by first developing your career objective, followed by charting out the specific steps to meet your objective.

Career Objective Examples

SHORT TERM

- To obtain an internship in the area of social networking for an advertising agency by next summer.
- To start a graduate program in the field of information that will lead me to the degree required for my chosen career field.

LONG TERM

- To obtain a full-time professional position as a social marketing specialist for a full-service interactive agency in New York City.
- To gain a master's degree in the field of information with a specialization in the areas of archives and electronic records management.

CAREER ACTION PLAN EXAMPLE 1

Career Objective: To obtain an internship in the area of digital archives for an advertising agency by next summer.

Goal #1	Action to be taken (short term)	Potential barriers	Solution to barriers	Deadline to reach goal
Complete required coursework.	Meet with academic advisor to identify the most relevant courses that will best prepare me for an internship.	Can't get into class. Class time conflicts with part-time job schedule.	Get on wait list and talk to faculty/instructor for permission to add class if another student drops. Talk with supervisor to discuss options for work schedule adjustments.	During preregistration time frame

Goal #2	Action to be taken (short term)	Potential barriers	Solution to barriers	Deadline to reach goal
Identify and develop necessary skills for internship.	Network with a professional in the field to determine the required skills. Research careers and job trends in the field through professional publications.	Don't have contacts with anyone in the field.	Talk to career counselor or alumni relations to identify contacts in the field. Use LinkedIn to identify professionals in the field.	By Thanksgiving break
	Action to be taken (ongoing/ long term)	**Potential barriers**	**Solution to barriers**	
	Volunteer at local organization to help build skills.	No free time!	Set up volunteer times during school breaks throughout the school year.	By summer

CAREER ACTION PLAN EXAMPLE 2

Career Objective: To obtain a full-time professional position as a social marketing specialist for a full-service interactive agency in New York City.

Goal #1	Action to be taken (short term)	Potential barriers	Solution to barriers	Deadline to reach goal
Complete degree requirements.	Meet with academic advisor to make sure I'm on track to graduate with the appropriate requirements.	Tuition	Meet with financial aid advisor to identify scholarships and other funding options.	Term prior to graduation

Goal #2	Action to be taken (ongoing/ long term)	Potential barriers	Solution to barriers	Deadline to reach goal
Participate in second internship in the same field but in different industry.	Start internship search by updating resume and identifying internship opportunities.	The cost of relocation Have a lease that extends through summer.	Apply for paid internships only. Sublet apartment for the summer.	Spring break

A customizable Career Action Plan Worksheet appears on page 226.

If you've followed all of the valuable tips and advice in this chapter, you should have an idea of whether you are in a position to pursue an active professional job search or pursue graduate programs that are in direct alignment with your career interests. Once you've reached the goals necessary to begin to implement your career plan—whether this is to pursue an advanced degree or to start your active job search—we've provided you with some basic steps for doing so effectively in the Career Planning Checklists on pages 227–228.

If you make career planning a regular part of your ongoing professional development, you are more likely to always have an awareness of where you want to go next in your career, and you will be comfortable with the steps you need to take and the resources available to help you reach that next professional goal as an information professional or in the field you find fits you best.

CAREER ACTION PLAN WORKSHEET				

Personal Career Action Plan
Career Objective: _____
_____
_____

Goal #1	Action to be taken (short term)	Potential barriers	Solution to barriers	Deadline to reach goal
	Action to be taken (ongoing/ long term)			
Goal #2	Action to be taken (short term)	Potential barriers	Solution to barriers	Deadline to reach goal
	Action to be taken (ongoing/ long term)			

CAREER PLANNING CHECKLISTS

Job Search Steps

- Set up an appointment with a career counselor/advisor in your college career center to discuss the most effective job search strategies and resources specific to your career objective.
- Create an effective resume and cover letter for your specific industry of choice. Have your resume reviewed by career counselor/advisor to ensure it is letter-perfect.
- Post your resume to online job posting boards such as Monster, Yahoo! Jobs, Careerbuilder, etc.
- Create an online portfolio to showcase your work or project samples. Online portfolios are not required or expected for all career fields. If your field of interest requires technical, Web, or design skills, it's likely that an online portfolio is required or preferred as part of the job application process (it's typically stated in the job description, but not always).
- Network with peers, faculty, past employers, family, friends—let everyone know you are job searching and what type of job you are seeking.
- Keep a record of your job applications.
- Follow up with all applications—if you have contact information.
- Prepare for interview.
- Receive job offer.
- Evaluate job offer and negotiate salary.
- Accept job—congratulations!

Graduate School Steps

- Further research and identify your graduate program(s) of choice.
- Meet with admissions counselor to identify criteria, requirements, and most effective application strategy.
- Apply to graduate school(s).
- Identify graduate school funding options.
- Once you have accepted an offer, set up an appointment with a career counselor to utilize all career resources available to you from day one in the program.

Annual Review

Review your career action plan every year. A lot can happen in a year. Most of us visit the doctor or dentist every year to review our health status, identify problems/concerns, and come up with solutions to avoid illness and to reach and maintain personal health goals. Why not make career planning an annual event to ensure the good health and positive status of your career goals?

(continued)

(continued)

- Map your path since your last career planning efforts.
- Reflect on your likes, dislikes, wants, and needs.
- Reflect on life circumstances or changes over the past year.
- Make note of your accomplishments over the past year.
- Identify new skills you have developed (don't forget about those very important transferrable skills).
- Review current career and job trends.
- Review career goals—Which goals have you accomplished? Which ones haven't been accomplished yet? Adjust goals, if needed.
- Identify potential barriers and solutions to barriers.
- Set deadlines—flexible ones—to reach your goal.

Listing of Relevant Academic Programs

iSchools

The iSchools are a set of 24 schools focused on the relationships among people, information, and technology. Visit www.ischools.com to learn more and to link to the following programs.

- University of California, Berkeley, School of Information
- University of California, Irvine, The Donald Bren School of Information and Computer Sciences
- University of California, Los Angeles, Graduate School of Education and Information Studies
- Carnegie Mellon University, School of Information Systems and Management, Heinz College
- Drexel University, College of Information Science and Technology
- Florida State University, College of Communication and Information
- Georgia Institute of Technology, College of Computing
- Humboldt-Universitat zu Berlin, Berlin School of Library and Information Science
- University of Illinois, Graduate School of Library and Information Science
- Indiana University, School of Informatics and Computing
- University of Maryland, College of Information Studies
- University of Maryland Baltimore County, Department of Information Systems
- University of Michigan, Ann Arbor, School of Information
- University of North Carolina, School of Information and Library Science
- University of North Texas, College of Information

- The Pennsylvania State University, College of Information Sciences and Technology
- University of Pittsburgh, School of Information Sciences
- Royal School of Library and Information Science, Denmark
- Rutgers, the State University of New Jersey, School of Communication and Information
- University of Sheffield, England, Information Studies
- Singapore Management University, School of Information Systems
- Syracuse University, School of Information Studies
- University of Texas, Austin, School of Information
- University of Toronto, Faculty of Information
- University of Washington, Information School
- Wuhan University, China, School of Information Management

American Library Association Accredited Programs

There are 62 programs in library and information studies accredited by the American Library Association (ALA), a number of which are also counted among iSchools, listed previously. For a database of ALA accredited programs searchable by location, distance or campus based, areas offered such as archival science or school library media, and more, visit www.ala.org/ala/educationcareers/education/accreditedprograms/index.cfm.

Human–Computer Interaction Programs

Human–computer interaction (HCI) programs may be found across the United States and abroad within computer science departments, within information schools, as stand-alone institutes, or in other schools or colleges such as design, engineering, or media arts and sciences. A listing of HCI programs is available online at www.hcibib.org/education/#PROGRAMS.

Archives and Records Management Programs

The Society of American Archivists maintains an online directory of archival (as well as preservation and records management) education (see www.archivists.org/prof-education) and has published guidelines and standards for degree programs. While there are a few master's programs that focus exclusively on archival studies (mostly in Canada), it is more common to find archival courses as part of an information or library and information science degree.

Additional Programs

For additional guidance and resources on educational opportunities in information, such as information policy, information analysis and retrieval, social computing, and information systems management, refer to the education section of each career information chapter in this guide. To explore a wide range of educational options at the undergraduate and graduate level, search by field of interest using online databases such as Petersons.com or GradSchools.com.

Index

Page numbers followed by the letter "f" indicate figures.

About the Authors

Judy Lawson is Director of Admissions and Student Affairs at the University of Michigan (UM) School of Information. She holds a Master of Arts degree in higher education and student affairs and a Bachelor of Arts degree in psychology from The Ohio State University. Judy is currently pursuing a PhD in higher education administration at the Center for the Study of Higher and Postsecondary Education at the University of Michigan. Since 2000 she has overseen the growth and development of the Master of Science in Information program at UM, including recruiting, admissions, student services, and career services. She has advised prospective and current students on their academic and career plans, reviews applications to the master's program, and serves on the undergraduate committee, which is developing undergraduate offerings at the school. Judy began her career at the University of Michigan Career Center in 1989, where she provided career counseling to hundreds of undergraduate and graduate students and presented workshops on self-assessment, resume writing, and job searching. She continued at the UM Career Center until 2000, serving as Assistant Director of Internship Services and then as Senior Assistant Director, Recruitment Services. Judy has been a member of the American College Personnel Association (ACPA) since 1989. She was a founding directorate member of the ACPA Commission for Graduate and Professional Student Affairs and has presented at the national conference. She was selected as the 2008 recipient of the University's Outstanding Leadership Award.

Joanna Kroll is Senior Associate Director, Career Development, at the University of Michigan School of Information. She holds a Master of Arts degree in counselor education with specialization in career counseling from Wayne State University and a Bachelor of Arts degree in psychology from Central Michigan University. Joanna has over 13 years experience providing career counseling to both undergraduate and graduate students. For the past nine years, she has managed career services for graduate students at the University of Michigan School of Information (SI). A major component of her job has been to provide professional career counseling and job search advice to students pursuing careers in the information field. She has developed and conducted countless career development and job search workshops focused on information careers. Joanna manages the internship program for the school as well. For the past eight years she has surveyed SI students on their job outcomes and has produced the annual employment report for the school. Joanna manages SI's on-campus recruiting activities and has established strong recruiting relationships with high profile companies in the information field. She is a member of the National Association of Colleges and Employers (NACE) and the American College Personnel Association (ACPA) and has presented at national conferences (NACE and ACPA) on the topic of career development and experiential learning.

Kelly Kowatch is Assistant Director, Career Development, at the University of Michigan (UM) School of Information. She holds a Master of Arts degree in higher education and student affairs from The Ohio State University and a Bachelor of Arts degree in policy and applied economics from Michigan State University. At UM, she counsels first year master's students on internship and job searching, develops and facilitates a wide range of career development workshops, and assists in the management of the internship program. Kelly also oversees the School of Information's Alternative Spring Program, which places students in service projects related to their studies at high-profile nonprofit organizations. Kelly is a member of the American College Personnel Association (ACPA), a Directorate member of the ACPA Commission for Graduate and Professional Student Affairs, and has presented at the national conference. She was a grant recipient of the 2009 U.S. Fulbright Commission's International Education Administrators Program.